# Too Close for Comfort

## Exploring the Risks of Intimacy

# Too Close for Comfort

## Exploring the Risks of Intimacy

Geraldine K. Piorkowski, Ph. D.

Foreword by
Samuel S. Cardone, Ph. D.

PERSEUS PUBLISHING

*Cambridge, Massachusetts*

Library of Congress Cataloging-in-Publication Data

Piorkowski, Geraldine K.
    Too close for comfort : exploring the risks of intimacy /
Geraldine K. Piorkowski ; foreword by Samuel S. Cardone.
        p.    cm.
    Includes bibliographical references and index.
    ISBN 0-306-44641-3
    1. Intimacy (Psychology)    I. Title.
    [DNLM: 1. Interpersonal Relations.  2. Fear.  3. Psychotherapy.
HM 132 P662t 1994]
BF575.I5P56   1994
158'.2--dc20
  DNLM/DLC
for Library of Congress                                          93-51487
                                                                     CIP

Perseus Publishing books are available at special discounts for bulk purchases in the U.S. by corporations, institutions, and other organizations. For more information, please contact the Special Markets Department at the Perseus Books Group, 11 Cambridge Center, Cambridge, MA 02142, or call (617) 252-5298.

10  9  8  7  6  5  4  3  2  1

All names and identifying characteristics of the individuals described in this book have been changed to protect their privacy.

Published by Perseus Publishing
A Member of the Perseus Books Group

Find us on the World Wide Web at
http://www.perseuspublishing.com/

Printed in the United States of America

To my son Mike,
who shares with intimacy seekers
the same kind of hope for a
brighter tomorrow that defies the odds

# Foreword

Intimacy is a concept that defines close relationships, and is most associated with a range of interactions. Beginning with mother and child, father and child, continuing with friendships and other pairings, and culminating in an adult romantic interaction with levels of sharing and commitment, this special sense of closeness can appear to be magical and pure, confusing and complex, or just plain hard work. Intimacy has been used as a theme in films, books, plays, and music. In fact, Dr. Piorkowski introduces the reader to *Too Close for Comfort* by citing from a song for the title of Chapter 1, namely, "What's It All About, Alfie?"

We begin our journey of examining romantic intimacy with Dr. Piorkowski in Chapter 1, which establishes some guidelines and benchmarks for the reader regarding intimacy. There are familiar terms such as "relationship styles," as well as challenging and provocative ideas, characterized by the presentation of "ambivalence as a two-headed dilemma." Dr. Piorkowski adeptly continues by orienting the reader to the fears and risks associated with intimacy, and presents a most comprehensive array of situations that elucidate the dangers, resulting in a selection of examples or illustrations that will surely touch everyone personally and/or professionally. From these risks it is apparent that romantic intimacy, while highly sought after, is not for everyone.

The flow of ideas, case illustrations, and information truly emerge in Chapters 4, 5, and 6, especially Dr. Piorkowski's examination of sex differences and attraction. It is in Chapter 6 that the reader begins to attain some insight into Dr. Piorkowski's style as psychotherapist and her ability to translate her theoretical knowledge into clinical practice.

The next two chapters, namely, "Intimacy and Alcohol Abuse" and "Intimacy and Violence," are extraordinarily timely. In addition to alcohol being the most abused drug in the United States, its involvement in pervasive dysfunction has been recognized and well documented. Dr. Piorkowski's sensitive treatment of this destructive force in relationships highlights, corroborates, and mirrors a current societal malady. Violence dominates the news in every medium; thus, it is only appropriate that it should be an integral factor in troubled relationships. Dr. Piorkowski's rendition of power and control provides insight into the nature of violence, and how it may be expressed between intimate partners.

The final chapters of *Too Close for Comfort* begin to identify ways and means of repairing those shortfalls, maladaptive behaviors, and areas of discontent that truly prevent individuals from engaging in the enjoyment of intimacy, beginning with identifying vulnerabilities, working toward conflict-free zones, and striving for the common ingredients of happy and healthy relationships. *Too Close for Comfort* provides a broad range of avenues in which to shift from problem-laden approaches to more communicative, trusting exchanges.

Throughout *Too Close for Comfort*, Dr. Piorkowski utilizes her own psychotherapeutic cases and those of her supervisees to elucidate and clarify specific aspects of intimacy. The cases are timely, authentic, and, at times, painfully realistic. This is especially cogent in the chapters focusing on the masks we wear and intimacy and alcohol abuse. The use of cases when dealing with a phenomenon such as intimacy can be problematic. Dr. Piorkowski handles this area with a firm, perceptive, honest flair that befits a skilled psychotherapist. There is a clarity of presentation of the issues, insight into each individual, and most important, a focus on the dynamic interaction that gives the reader a sense of the relationship. It is this talent of Dr. Piorkowski that adds a richness to the twelve chapters of *Too Close for Comfort*. As a clinical psychologist and psychotherapist, I can attest to the credibility of these case illustrations.

Dr. Piorkowski's organizational skills and mastery of the topic have produced an extraordinarily well-paced, most readable book. The content begins with basic information, setting the stage for many variations on the theme of intimacy. The flow of the material is captivating, making the absorption of the information appear effortless. There were times when it seemed as if I was reading a novel with a great deal of substance, yet intrigue. The reader may begin to read sections that appear to be somewhat similar to parts of a prior chapter. However, it becomes clear that it is new information imparting other relevant aspects of intimacy. This theme of continually adding to the complex concept of intimacy is a thread that provides the reader with a feeling of continuity.

*Too Close for Comfort* can be read at various levels of meaning and application. For example, the clinician and psychotherapist will discover new, unique ways of reflecting on intimacy and its many facets. The case examples may afford this group some insights into the interactions of a couple struggling with intimacy issues. Other health care providers will come away with a new understanding of relationships, communication patterns, and the variables that have a major impact on the outcome of relating to another individual. The educator will begin to view patterns of behavior that may be termed "intimate" or "destructive," but more generally, themes that are prevalent in human beings as they interact with each other. The average reader will observe familiar scenes through a unique lens and attain a new understanding of these actions and, it is hoped, alternative solutions.

Dr. Piorkowski has skillfully managed to translate the theoretical construct of intimacy into clearly identifiable behaviors. This has been accomplished by combining theoretical information, case studies, and an underlying personal viewpoint, gleaned from her professional and personal experiences. The integration of these means of expression has afforded the reader a window into a most familiar, yet foreign, strived-for experience, namely, intimacy. In *Too Close for Comfort*, the recognition of the risks and rewards of intimacy is presented in a style that is most compelling.

SAMUEL S. CARDONE, PH.D.
*Assistant Professor of Psychiatry and*
*Behavioral Sciences*
*Northwestern University Medical School*
*Chicago, Illinois*

# Acknowledgments

I want to express my deepest gratitude to the many people whose struggles about intimacy have taught me all that I know. Foremost, appreciation is due my immediate family, who provided me with an abundance of experiences—most of them positive—that enhanced my understanding of what intimacy is all about. Frank, my husband of thirty-five years and co-captain of our sailing adventures, has been a steadfast, loving, and loyal Rock of Gibraltar, accommodating my many professional activities without much complaint. My three children—Paul, Mike, and Julie—have shown me the durability, intensity, and permanence of the mother-child bond with moments of joy and pride beyond compare.

Friends have also been important. My relationship with my late friend and colleague, Joan Taylor, with whom I shared my deepest feelings in letters that spanned eighteen years, geographical moves, job changes, children's graduations, and the tragic death of her daughter, revealed the depth of friendship and the pleasure of mutual letter writing, now a dying art. Joan died unexpectedly in October 1991, leaving an emotional void that won't be filled.

As I wandered the uncharted territory of writing a first book, a friend and colleague, Jonathan Smith, a prolific writer, provided me with hope, encouragement, and example. Other friends—Sam and Ida Cardone, Danuta Ehrlich, Roberta Fireman, Ceil Lark,

Ann Schoonmacher, Felicia Svoboda—have contributed insights and much support.

I am especially grateful to my clients for sharing their personal stories about intimacy with courage and candor. Without them, this book would not have been possible.

Last, I thank Norma Fox, past Executive Editor of Insight Books, for her enthusiasm and direction. It was her comment on my initial draft—"But there are happy relationships"—that stimulated my producing a more balanced perspective in this book.

# Contents

xiii

*Chapter 3*

*Chapter 4*

*Chapter 5*

*Chapter 6*

*Chapter 7*

*Chapter 8*

*Chapter 9*

*Chapter 10*

*Chapter 11*

*Chapter 12*

HAPPY AND HEALTHY RELATIONSHIPS:
COMMON INGREDIENTS. . . . . . . . . . . . . . . . . . . . . . . . . . . . . 263

# Too Close for Comfort

## Exploring the Risks of Intimacy

# Introduction

Accompanying the proliferation of "how to" books on relationships is the implication that a perfect intimate relationship is just around the corner. If only we knew enough about how to communicate, be assertive, fight fair, or be better lovers, we could have the best of all possible worlds—a deep, enriching, intimate relationship with another human being.

What is misleading about the "how to" books is their refusal to acknowledge the perils inherent in intimate relationships. Intimacy is not only difficult to achieve but it is also treacherous in some fundamental ways. Because intimacy is so perilous, people panic when they attempt to make a commitment to another person. Because of the dangers involved, people erect elaborate barriers to shield themselves from closeness.

The closer we get to another person, the greater the risk. The risks of being hurt, exposed, and threatened are all enhanced by intimacy. In an intimate relationship, we are more vulnerable and defenseless than in any other kind of relationship. We are also more childish, more petulant, angrier, more emotionally unstable, and less intelligent than in any other situation. We can run a large corporation with leadership skill, sound judgment, and creativity but be immature, ultrasensitive, and needy at home. Intimacy is unnerving and baffling.

People are often disturbed by their own feelings and behavior in intimate relationships because they conflict so dramatically with their self-images. They cannot understand why they are hurt so easily or why they become enraged at the drop of a hat. One woman who could not recall being angry before marriage had to contend with her own angry tantrums when feeling slighted or misunderstood in her marriage. A man who prided himself on his sense of fair play at the office barked orders at his new bride, much to her dismay. This foreign behavior emerged in the alien land of intimacy, where all sorts of terrors abound and civilized rules of conduct are suspended.

The potential for emotional pain and upset in an intimate relationship is greater than in casual relationships because we are not cloaked in the protective garb of maturity. We are less defended. "What did he mean when he commented that Mary was attractive? Was he saying that I'm not?" a woman in love might worry. The subtleties of behavior become amplified and exaggerated in close relationships. Jealousy and feelings of inadequacy often surface.

One woman who came into therapy because of panic attacks associated with a marriage commitment became hypervigilant and anxious at social gatherings. She believed that her boyfriend found other women more attractive and screened the environment for confirmation of this suspicion. Social occasions suddenly became distasteful for her—in marked contrast to her sociable and gregarious behavior when she felt more casual about her relationships with men.

## Old Issues Resurface

Because intimate relationships reactivate earlier unresolved conflicts, intimacy has a built-in potential for regression. Those needs or wishes that were not fully satisfied in earlier relationships become aroused as we get closer to another person. If we did not feel loved enough, understood enough, special enough, or in control enough, the hope is that this time around it will be different. The hope is that this new intimacy will make up for earlier failures—an expectation that is often thwarted.

The expectation that this time around will be better fails because present-day lovers feel burdened by demands that have their roots in old relationships. When the "you never appreciate anything I do" comes from historical depths, the partner may feel that the complaint is out of proportion to the current situation. The intensity of the cry bespeaks its earlier origins, and sensing this, the partner has difficulty hearing the validity of the complaint and tunes out.

As the complaint continues to be ignored, a dysfunctional cycle is set up. The complainer gets louder in hopes that the sheer volume of the message will ensure that it gets heard. In response to the hysterical pitch of the message, however, the receiver withdraws even further. And so, as one partner gets louder and more out of control, the other utilizes stronger and stronger defenses— both as self-protection and as protection for the other. For the receiver's own rage is beginning to surface because he or she feels bombarded by intrusive and overwhelmingly unrealistic demands.

## Time to Tune Out

Thus, in response to the dangers involved in intimacy, numerous protective barriers are erected. Most frequently, withdrawal is the defense of choice. Tuning out, not hearing, and being preoccupied serve to keep a safe distance between people. The retreat into ourselves is often a way of licking our wounds, a way of regrouping before venturing out again. The withdrawal can function as a time-out, where we garner reinforcements for the next round.

The workaholic, who spends most of his or her free time in work-related activities, is a good example of withdrawal from intimacy that is viewed as "productive" in the eyes of the world. Work involvement often serves as a means of avoiding intimacy for the doctor or clergyman devoted to humanitarian goals, the business magnate zealous about pursuing the best business deal, or the physicist dedicated to uncovering scientific truth.

Withdrawal coupled with an air of superiority is another common defensive strategy. We attempt to distance ourselves from potential harm by critically looking down on the other, sending the message, "I am superior to you and in control of the situation, whereas you're not." In Transactional Analysis[1] terms, one partner becomes the "in charge, know-it-all" parent and the other a helpless, out-of-control child. The game of one-upmanship is won at the expense of intimacy.

The "mystery man" approach (saying very little about ourselves) and preoccupation with our health or hobbies are other ways of avoiding intimacy. Relating in an intellectualized rather than an emotional manner is another avoidance strategy. While it is clear that we as a species spend a great deal of time avoiding intimacy, the questions remain: How close can we get to another human being and for how long? In the best of all possible relationships, how much time is spent with the other and how much time alone? Can we get close to another and still be ourselves?

## In Hot Pursuit of the Perfect Relationship

Perhaps this current preoccupation with intimacy is unnatural, not in keeping with the physical and psychological natures of people. We may be asking too much of others—expecting them to serve too many roles and too many functions. We want our intimate others to be lovers, friends, playmates, companions, and parents to us. All possibilities rolled up into one person! This expectation, which has developed because of the personal isolation, family disintegration, and TV romanticism of our culture, may be unrealistic. Sociologist Philip Slater wrote that contemporary spouses are being asked to play a multiplicity of roles from lover to best friend and that with these increased demands, the marriage bond is "likely to fall short" and be dissolved.[2]

According to Clifford Sager and Bernice Hunt, authors of *Intimate Partners*, the main problem with today's marriages is that couples want marriages that fulfill their emotional needs rather than economic, parental, or familial responsibilities. "It is this shift in our expectation of marriage, the new priority of fulfilling emotional needs rather than external ones, that is creating chaos."[3]

## How Close Is Too Close?

Another unresolved question has to do with the amount of closeness that people can tolerate. If we spent every waking moment enmeshed in an intimate contact of one kind or another, what would happen to the self and its capacity for creativity and productivity? How much time alone is necessary to replenish psychological resources is unknown. However, it is apparent that people from time immemorial have spent part of each waking day engaged in extrarelationship pursuits. Some of these pursuits are related to survival (hunting, fishing, or holding down a white-collar job), while other activities have as their main function the maintenance or enhancement of the self. Self-maintenance or self-enhancement activities are times alone when we rehash the problems of the day, express ourselves (paint, sew, play the piano, fix the lawn mower), or simply relax. These times alone appear to meet the important psychological function of solidifying the boundaries of the self. The often-heard phrase "I need more space" is a popular expression of the need for distance in intimate relationships.

Human nature may dictate that intimate relationships have to be cyclical; that is, periods of closeness have to be followed by periods of distance. The intimacy dance seems to consist of two steps forward followed by one step backward. When I asked a male friend how intimate people can get, he said, with his usual penchant for offbeat humor, "Within an inch or so and for as long as the deodorant lasts." While this friend uses humor to keep distance, his comment illustrates the awareness that there are limitations to intimacy.

Individual and sex differences clearly affect the parameters of closeness. Women, as a general rule, crave more intimate contact than men, and the kind of contact preferred is different. For women, the preferred contact is likely to be intimate conversation, while for men the preferred form of intimacy is sexual contact.[4] Women are more apt to experience sex and emotional intimacy as a total package, while for men sex and emotional intimacy are viewed as separate dimensions. Whether these differences are biological in nature or a function of different child-rearing environments is not clear.

## Violence Rears Its Ugly Head

What *is* clear is that for both sexes, the potential danger in intimate relationships is great. Every eighteen seconds in the United States, a woman is beaten by her husband or lover.[5] Almost 10,000 homicides a year occur among family members; the victims of lesser forms of family violence are estimated to number several million a year.[6] Homicides, suicides, and physical assaults occur in response to relationship breakdowns, not in response to isolation, boredom, or loneliness. People kill themselves or others because they feel slighted, misunderstood, unloved, or rejected. On their own, people may feel depressed and inadequate and crave contact with others, but the extent of their pain and agitation is much less severe than the pain that can be experienced in the context of a relationship.

In a newspaper article in the *Chicago Tribune* entitled "Many Singles Joining the 'I Quit' Brigade," columnists Cheryl Lavin and Laura Kavesh talk about the "No More Dating Syndrome" that is picking up steam among today's singles. "We're talking about reasonably healthy, more or less well-adjusted single men and women who have simply stopped dating. They've stopped accepting fix-ups and blind dates, stopped obsessively checking out every gathering for unattached members of the opposite sex, stopped instinctively staring at the ring fingers on left hands. Sometimes it happens suddenly, the result of a devastating break-up. Other times it sneaks up more slowly."[7] In the article, they describe Joe's string of broken love affairs after which he decides not to have anything to do with women again. Lavin and Kavesh write, "He prefers aloneness to heartbreak and really doesn't believe there's anything in between."[8] The dangers involved in intimate relationships have hit today's singles hard.

This book explores the nature of intimacy, the fears and risks involved in relationships, the needs and wishes that get aroused in intimacy, defensive maneuvers people use to protect themselves from intimacy, sex differences and sexual attraction, intimacy and violence, as well as the role of alcohol abuse in intimacy. In addition, guidelines for minimizing the risks, avoiding the pitfalls, and improving troubled relationships are presented. Finally, an examination of happy relationships identifies the common ingredients in contented unions.

The theoretical material in this book is a distillation of psychodynamic and family systems thinking, along with original contributions based on clinical work. The case examples in Chapters 1–11 are drawn from my psychotherapy experiences along with those of my supervisees. In a different vein, Chapter 12 is a review of the current literature on couple or marital satisfaction, with the examples based on interviews with "happy couples," so designated by friends and neighbors.

## Chapter 1

# What's It All About, Alfie?[1]

It was the best of times, it was the worst of times, it was the age of wisdom, it was the age of foolishness—it was the Season of Light, it was the Season of Darkness, it was the spring of hope, it was the winter of despair.
—CHARLES DICKENS, *A Tale of Two Cities*[2]

While Dickens was referring to London and Paris in 1775, he could just as easily have been writing about intimacy. For intimacy provides us with the best moments of our lives along with the worst, times of ecstasy along with despair. Intimacy takes us to the heights of joyful passion one moment, and to the depths of despondency the next. Intimacy runs the gamut of emotions, taking us on an enlightening journey into the deepest recesses of ourselves in the process. What is this enchanted state—with its potential for emotional highs and lows—all about?

## The Nature of Intimacy

Intimacy is one of those terms frequently bandied about in conversation and in the popular literature but little understood. Experientially, we know what it feels like to be emotionally intimate with another person, but we would be hard-pressed to put that experience into words. Feeling "close" or "connected" are the

9

terms that most readily come to mind, but beyond that, the experience of intimacy seems too elusive to capture in language.

In general, we are well aware of the passionate, sexual side of intimacy in contrast to its quieter, companionable component. The literature on love and intimacy clearly supports this distinction by differentiating romantic from conjugal love and, similarly, passionate from companionate love. In passionate or romantic love, intense, sometimes turbulent, emotional and sexual feelings are involved, whereas in conjugal or companionate love, trust, reliability, and friendship are the calmer ingredients.

Passionate feelings, where there is total absorption in an idealized other, jealousy, daydreaming, and mystical beliefs in true, eternal, destined love,[3] are found most intensely at the start of a love affair. Whether the passion will remain as infatuation or be transformed into romantic love will depend on whether emotional intimacy is added to the sexual component. Typically, infatuation ("love at first sight," or limerence[4]) is sexually intense, strongly motivated by unconscious impulses and associations, and short-lived.

In contrast to the red-hot excitement of passionate or romantic love, conjugal or companionate relationships are mellow and steady. Typically found in long-standing friendships or among settled married couples, conjugal love is like the glowing ember that remains after the flames of passion have died down. It is warm, comfortable, dependable, predictable, secure, and emotionally close.

## Defining Intimacy

In a recent attempt to delineate more precisely the concepts of love and intimacy, Robert Sternberg, a Yale University psychologist and researcher, described intimacy as one component of love, the other two ingredients being passion and commitment. He refers specifically to intimacy as "those feelings in a relationship that provide closeness, bondedness, and connectedness,"[5] including, among other things, a desire to promote the welfare of, high regard for, sharing of one's self with, and mutual understanding of the loved one. For Sternberg, intimacy is an important dimension in romantic love, companionate love, and filial love. In fact, he sees intimacy at the core of all loving relationships.

Other writers on the topic of intimacy have stressed self-disclosure as an important component of or as a vital vehicle in the development of intimacy. Psychoanalyst Douglas Ingram's poetic definition of intimacy as the experience where one most feels like oneself conjures up images of meaningful self-disclosure and dialogue.[6] Social-penetration theory, which elaborates how different layers of the personality are permeated by messages varying in depth, more explicitly views self-disclosure as important to the development of intimacy.[7] In research stemming from this theory, intimacy is measured by the breadth and depth of self-disclosure (how many topics are talked about and how central these issues are to the person). According to this theory, intimacy is enhanced by sharing values and feelings from the deepest levels of the personality.

While the manner in which love and intimacy are defined varies from writer to writer, all definitions of intimacy tend to emphasize feelings of closeness. Besides closeness, Sharon Brehm, a researcher in intimacy and author of *Intimate Relationships*, includes behavioral interdependence and need fulfillment as criteria for intimate relationships.[8] Others, like Stephanie Covington and Liann Beckett, authors of *Leaving the Enchanted Forest*, have an idealistic view of what intimacy is all about, defining it as "the open sharing of feelings in an atmosphere of trust, acceptance, mutuality and reciprocal empathy between equals."[9] Similarly, Harriet Lerner, author of the best-selling book *The Dance of Intimacy*, emphasizes being who we are in intimacy and allowing the other person to do the same. For her, "an intimate relationship is one in which neither party silences, sacrifices or betrays the self and each party expresses strength and vulnerability, weakness and competence in a balanced way."[10]

Still other writers distinguish between three kinds of intimacy—physical (sex, hugging, and touching), affective (feeling close), and verbal (self-disclosure)—and point out that they are not perfectly correlated with one another. Interestingly, all three kinds of intimacy are highly related to marital satisfaction, with physical intimacy being the least important.[11]

While the definitions and distinctions are sometimes confusing and contradictory, it is clear that no one definition of intimacy encompasses all that intimacy connotes. What is important, however, is clarity about what any specific discussion of intimacy is all about. In this book, the focus is on adult relationships in which both emotional closeness and sexual feelings are involved. Romantic love, in all of its myriad shapes and colors, is examined from a variety of perspectives.

## The Journey into the Private Self

In intimacy, the deepest and most vulnerable parts of our personality become exposed. Our personalities appear to be organized as a series of layers with the innermost core, our Private Self, being the earliest and most primitive aspect of our being. Basic emotional needs, such as the need to be loved, taken care of, and protected, are concentrated at this level. In infancy and early childhood, the groundwork for this level is laid down with modification possible throughout life, provided that the boundaries between personality levels are permeable rather than rigid. With some regularity, however, the contents of this early level become walled off from awareness and later experience, only to be jolted into existence by the stirrings of intimacy. Early self-esteem damage, caused by critical, insensitive, or neglectful caretakers, affects both the quantity and quality of the basic emotional needs that have their foundation in our innermost core.

The Private, or Intimate, Self consists of emotionally laden fantasies, daydreams, memories, night dreams, and semiforbidden thoughts. Our most personal longings, deepest feelings, and most tender vulnerabilities are part and parcel of this area. The child within us, with all its spontaneity, creativity, and playfulness, is also a resident of this personality level.

As with Freud's impulse-driven id[12] and Berne's child ego-state (Eric Berne is the author of *Games People Play*[13]), anxiety is attached to some of the contents of the Private Self. Fantasies, daydreams, and thoughts remain private because of fears that exposure will lead to dangerous consequences. If found out, we are afraid that we will be attacked, betrayed, rejected, or made to feel guilty in some way. And so, we hide our Private Selves under one or more bushel baskets of self-protection. It is only with emotional closeness that we begin to risk exposing the private, most tender parts of ourselves to another person.

## The Emergence of the Social Self

Most typically, it is the socialized or Social Self that is manifest to others. Comprising the middle layer of personality, the Social Self is the interpersonal style that we show to our family and friends. Developed primarily during the preschool and latency years, the Social, or Public, Self typically consists of the acceptable parts of our personality. Mr. Nice Guy, the Good Girl, the Clown, the Athlete, and Mr. Sociability are universally positive roles, which can be displayed with abandon because they endear themselves to parents and friends alike. Other generally acceptable qualities, like shyness, smartness, and generosity, also top the list of traits that can be paraded unabashedly before others. While it is obvious that not all Social Selves are positive—witness the Troublemaker or the Crybaby—the Social Self is generally the best option available and clearly preferable to the Private Self in the eyes of the individual. Even in the case of negative interpersonal styles, what is hidden seems even worse.

## The Development of the Work Self

The outermost layer of our onionlike personality structure consists of our professional and work-related selves. Formed last developmentally in response to school and work demands, the Work Self is the part of us that functions objectively, logically, and realistically most of the time. Whether we are accountants, actresses, or bricklayers, our Work Selves know the techniques of our craft and how to utilize these professional skills in our work environment. Begun in our grade-school days, the Work Self concerns itself primarily with the acquisition of new cognitive information, mastery of skills, and problem-solving. The adult, rational side of our personality with its emphasis on achievement tends to be the dominating force in our work or professional identities. Like Freud's ego-state,[14] our Work Selves operate according to the dictates of reality and reason.

## Distinct or Overlapping Selves

If these three aspects of our personality, the Private Self, the Social Self, and the Work Self, were to function as three distinct and nonoverlapping parts, we would be a different person in each of the three spheres. The Private, or Intimate, Self that needs love, reassurance, and protection would seem very infantile to the adult Work Self or to the superaccommodating Social Self where the needs of others come first. Ordinarily, however, these three basic levels have semipermeable boundaries allowing some overlap between regions. The integrating of qualities from all levels into specific roles is actually the ideal. For example, a parent who can be both rational and playful, serious and funny, task-oriented and spontaneous earns both love and respect. Likewise, the boss who can be fair, reasonable, decisive, and yet "human" (which usually means sharing some aspect of his or her personal life with others) is loved and admired. The most significant problems in intimacy arise for those individuals who have split off significant aspects of their private inner world from their social and work identities. Because the schism occurred in the early years in response to a nonsupportive and sometimes dangerous environment, these individuals often are not in touch with the nature of the emotional needs that lie buried in their innermost cores or, if aware of these inner longings through their manifestation in daydreams or night dreams, regard these wishes as too infantile to talk about to anyone.

## Defenses Crumble with Intimacy

However, as we begin to get close to another person, and the intensity of our emotional and sexual feelings overrides our defenses, the walls of self-protection start to crumble. With increasing closeness, we move from outer personality zones to deeper levels. As we become more intimate, our conversation shifts from cocktail party chatter (politics, vacations, movies) to the public facets of our personal lives (birthplace, school experience, job) before gradually settling into our most private self-revelations—those hopes and dreams that we have never breathed to another soul.

The headlong rush into intimate territory is often exhilarating, like a dangerous and exciting roller coaster ride. For most of us, the early or courtship phase of a relationship tends to have all the thrills with few of the dangers as we bask in blissful moments of sharing. The excitement of getting to know another person, of meeting new people (our lover's friends and relatives), and of experiencing new sights is stimulating. Ordinarily, it is only after living together, when the star-struck moments of our first meeting begin to fade, that we encounter the dangers of intimacy.

Continued existence in the private or intimate zone of our personalities resurrects buried emotional needs. The daily intimate encounters gradually erode the last vestiges of self-defense, and we are left face-to-face with our basic emotional longings. Wanting to be loved unconditionally, known perfectly, comforted, reassured, taken care of, protected, and viewed as highly special are among the most powerful of our emotional yearnings. Which of these needs is the most salient and emotionally charged for a particular individual will depend on the frustrations and deprivations of his or her earlier years. For example, when the desire for protection is the dominant emotional need, strong feelings about being unprotected in childhood are usually at the core. If the desire to be special is the strongest longing that becomes aroused in intimacy, unresolved issues around competition with a sibling can usually be found. The unmet emotional needs from childhood tend to be those that are resurrected with the most intensity in adult intimacy.

## The Dangers of Closeness

Along with the vulnerability and shamefulness of having our basic emotional needs exposed in intimacy are other dangers. We may be afraid of losing control or losing autonomy, that is, independence and selfhood. We may be fearful of being attacked, disappointed, betrayed, or rejected. Then, too, we may be fearful about feeling overly responsible and guilty for all the relationship's problems. As with the basic emotional needs, the particular fears that an individual experiences and their intensity are determined by both past and current relationships. For example, when the fear of being attacked is the major intimacy anxiety, the fear may derive from childhood experiences of being criticized or assaulted and/or from similar experiences in adult intimacy. The woman who is battered repeatedly by her spouse will fear attack in intimacy even if she was never criticized or beaten as a child. Similarly, the woman whose history of abuse goes back to childhood will express some degree of fearfulness regarding potential assault with her adult intimate partner, at least initially, even if he has never struck her.

At times, the fears of intimacy prevent us from even attempting to get close to another. Anxieties may be so intense that they restrict our relationships to casual ones where we can maneuver safely in the social or public arena. As adults, we may never risk sharing our secret thoughts, hopes, and feelings with another person because the early damage was so severe. At other times, the fears of intimacy limit our vulnerability by calling into play one or more defensive strategies.

## The Masks of Intimacy

For self-protection, we may tune out whenever we get frightened or bury ourselves in a hobby, addiction, or other pastime. We can adopt a disarming, superior stance when feeling vulnerable or hide behind a mysterious "Mona Lisa" smile. We can play the Comic, shifting to humor whenever closeness becomes anxiety-arousing, or, like Don Juan, change lovers frequently to avoid intimacy. Or, by adopting a superindependent stance, we can pretend that we need no one.

The tender, childlike core of our personality with its emotional longings is protected from total exposure by fears of intimacy and the defenses we erect. Ensconced within these layers of protection, the Private Self is often invisible to the objective eye and can remain hidden through all casual encounters. However, with the demands of emotional and sexual intimacy, the shape and content of the Private Self become manifest to our intimate partners and sometimes, shockingly, for the first time to ourselves as well.

## Developmental Stages and Intimacy

The kind of loss or trauma we experienced in our childhoods affects the degree to which we can become intimate. The nature of the damage and its timing also affect the kinds of unmet emotional needs and the specific fears of intimacy that we carry with us. Besides environmental neglect or cruelty, genetic and constitutional vulnerabilities may affect our insecurities about intimacy. For example, our ability to feel love may be a function of our biological receptivity to tactile sensations or of other physical factors.

If the environmental deprivation or genetic vulnerability was manifest primarily during the first two years of life, when the core of our selves was being formed and our basic attitude of trust toward the world was being developed, the effect on our capacity for intimacy could be profound. Severe psychopathology, even when there is a strong genetic predisposition, can trace some of its symptomatology to disturbed functioning during those early years. For example, the schizophrenic with a fragile sense of self and profound distrust of others manifests disturbance at an early developmental level. A young schizophrenic woman's description "of being dismembered at age two by the Mafia and put back together with egg white" conveys in powerful imagery both her fragmented sense of self and her belief that the world is a dangerous place. Because she, like many others who are similarly disturbed, can barely keep her self together, her ability to relate to others in an intimate manner is virtually nonexistent.

While not all of those who experienced emotional deprivation in infancy wind up with severe mental illness, the severe frustration of emotional needs early in life results in intense fears of intimacy, at the very least. The child who has been criticized frequently will fear attack in intimacy. Likewise, the childhood experience of being intruded upon will result in fears of loss of autonomy in adulthood. Similarly, when disappointed early on, the fear of being disappointed anew renders adult intimacy treacherous. While the need for closeness, that is, the wish for love, nurturance, and protection, may override the fears, the search for intimacy when there is early deprivation is often desperate with poor partner choice and frequent disappointments. In *Looking for Mr. Goodbar*, a popular book and movie of the same title, Terry Dunn's behavior exemplifies the indiscriminate search for love that is clouded by impulsivity and poor judgment.[15] Terry's dangerous quest ends when she is savagely murdered by one of the partners she picks up at a local bar.

### Erikson's Contributions

In determining which fears arise at which time, Erik Erikson's developmental model is especially useful.[16] The author of the classic text *Childhood and Society*, Erikson is a psychoanalyst whose developmental stages integrate both biological and cultural factors. His first stage of Basic Trust vs. Distrust is the setting for the development of the most severe fears of intimacy. As mentioned earlier, fears of annihilation through merger, attack, or abandonment are the primitive fears derived from this early stage. Also, fear of intense disappointment and the potential for depression have their origins during these early years, according to psychoanalytic thinking.

The second stage of Autonomy vs. Shame and Doubt has the potential for the development of two additional fears: fear of exposure and loss of control. According to Erikson, the toddler at this stage either develops a healthy sense of self as autonomous and separate from others or, at the other extreme, becomes a doubt-ridden person troubled by feelings of inadequacy and fearful of ridicule. The fear of being exposed as defective in some way is accompanied by a sense of shame, a self-consciousness about being seen as imperfect. This fear can lie dormant throughout childhood until it is resurrected in adolescence or early adulthood with the dawning of intimacy. Often acting as a deterrent to the development of further closeness, the fear of exposure can limit relationships to the most superficial contacts.

Part of the development of healthy autonomy during Erikson's second stage is the achievement of self-control. Our first feats of self-control occur with bowel and urinary control and later extend into the areas of aggression and sexual-impulse control. With self-control, we achieve some sense of mastery over our minds and bodies. In this way, we ward off feelings of helplessness, that is, the sense of being at the mercy of outside forces.

Fears of loss of control in intimacy relate both to self-control and the control of the relationship. Because emotional and sexual longings are so powerful in combination, the danger of being overwhelmed by our own feelings appears to be a real possibility. Then, too, we have little control of our intimate partners, who are also caught up in the throes of strong emotion. Thus, concerns about loss of control, which derive from Erikson's second stage, are common in romantic relationships.

The developmental stage of Initiative vs. Guilt occurring in the preschool years may sow the seeds of two additional intimacy fears: guilt and betrayal. Concerns about being "bad" and subsequent punishment, which are pervasive in the four- to six-year-old age group, relate to guilt about sins and other crimes. As little children, our most common misdemeanors were typically in the area of aggression. Having hit our brothers or sisters or taken their toys, we were fearful about being punished for our bad behavior. The childhood moments of waiting in agony for our crimes to be discovered are among the longest and most anxiety-ridden times many of us can recall.

If punishment and guilt were dominant parts of our early years, we are afraid that in adult intimacy we will be blamed and made to feel guilty for anything that goes wrong in our relationships. When our partner feels hurt and upset, it will be our fault. Any cruel remark or angry outburst on our part will be a significant trigger for breast-beating just as it was in our early days. No matter what happens, the adult who was blamed unjustly as a child for family problems fears that in the new intimate situation, the same scenario will prevail.

Fear of betrayal, which is basically a serious breach of trust or a violation of a contract between two people, has its major developmental thrust during Erikson's third stage. The Oedipal/Electra triangle, a major motivational theme of this period, has the seeds of betrayal within its conflictual outlines. Failing to win the competition with the same-sex parent for the opposite-sex parent feels like betrayal to the young child.

Apart from families where the Oedipal drama occupied center stage, fear of betrayal is a significant concern in homes where marital infidelity played a major role. Dad's or Mom's extramarital affairs, especially when the spouse was unhappy about these trysts, tend to be viewed as the primary cause of family disharmony by the children. As adults, then, these grown-up children fear betrayal in one form or another (being tricked, lied to, manipulated, or taken advantage of) from their intimate partners.

Several of the fears that had their origin in an earlier developmental phase have a more mature version in Erikson's third stage. Anxieties about losing the self in intimacy may be psychotic in nature, as in severe fear of merger, or more neurotic, as in fear of loss of autonomy. Likewise, the fear of attack, when experienced as a fear of total destruction or annihilation, is more primitive than castration concerns, which are more circumscribed and less lethal in nature. The fear of abandonment also varies in intensity and severity across developmental stages, ranging from fear for survival at the most primitive level to fear of loneliness at the healthier end of the spectrum.

During Erikson's remaining childhood and adolescent stages, the focus tends to be on the enhancement or diminution of self-esteem (the stage of Industry vs. Inferiority) and the development or fragmentation of an adult identity (Ego Identity vs. Role Diffusion). In addition, learning how to relate to peers in both a co-operative and competitive manner is the major interpersonal task of the latency or school-age years.

## Modification of Fears and Needs

While our capacity for intimacy and our fears about closeness can be modified at any time along the developmental cycle, there are relatively few opportunities prior to adolescence for the alteration of the intimacy expectations we learned in our nuclear family. Because so few people are allowed into our intimate spheres until sex hormones start raging and romantic fantasies dominate awareness, our parents tend to be the primary intimacy transmitters for most of us. In extended families where grandparents, aunts, uncles, and cousins lived in the same house or on the same block, there was greater opportunity for these relatives to exert a profound impact upon the child's developing intimacy attitudes than is true in modern, nuclear households.

Ordinarily, our parents, siblings, a grandparent or two, a special teacher, best friends, and lovers are the primary players in our intimacy drama. In each of these relationships, our degree of trust, our emotional needs, and our fears of intimacy are modified to one degree or another. If we felt betrayed by our parents and every other significant person in our lives, then the expectation of betrayal will be a part of each new relationship. Conversely, if our past intimate relationships have been satisfying for the most part, then we will come to expect a fulfilling experience this new time around.

It is as if we ask ourselves the following questions subliminally at the dawn of each new relationship: Can I trust the other? Will this person disappoint me? Will the other be distant or intrusive? Will I ultimately be loved or rejected? These and other emotionally laden questions arise as each new intimate relationship begins. The answers, unfortunately, are often determined more by our past experiences than by the current reality.

## Ambivalence: A Two-Headed Dilemma

Ambivalence is a common psychological phenomenon in intimacy that poses problems for both partners. For the possessor, ambivalence feels like an unnatural and disturbed state much like schizophrenia. However, rather than facing a split personality, in ambivalence we are faced with divided and contrasting feelings. One moment we love our intimate partners, and the next moment we are filled with hatred. One moment we want to be close, and the next moment we want to move as far away from the other as we can possibly get. During the positive moments, our partners are seen as lovely, godlike creatures who can do no wrong, while during the negative times, they are the epitomes of evil cloaked in nothing but sin. The rapid shifts in feeling-tone occur because positive feelings are anxiety-arousing (e.g., we worry that if we love someone, they will not reciprocate or that once we get involved, we will be sitting ducks for criticism).

Ambivalence causes us to feel confused by our mood changes. Intensely longing for our lovers one moment and then detesting them the next feels emotionally unstable. We would rather be certain of what we feel and use that knowledge to make decisions. However, with ambivalence, there is little clarity and certitude because of the frequent changes in feelings. The question "Should I stay or go?" cannot be answered with any degree of permanence when the responses vary from moment to moment.

Our shifting perceptions, like the changing colors and patterns of a kaleidoscope, have more to do with us than with the chameleonlike behavior of our partners. While our partners change their colors in response to environmental factors and internal mood states, we have primary access to the dials governing our perceptions. Our own moods and interpretations are the primary factors affecting our feelings about others. If we are in a good mood and our partner appears on our doorstep dressed in a disheveled manner, our first response might be light-hearted amusement or genuine concern. If, however, we have had the worst day of our lives, our partner's hobolike appearance would probably be more a source of irritation than anything else.

While ambivalence is a natural phenomenon occurring to some degree in all of us, ambivalence is basically a failure in integration. We fail to put together all of the feelings and perceptions about our partner into a whole composite. The hurts and disappointments are not interwoven into the fabric of the relationship in a manner that tones down the intensity of the positive feelings. Rather, in extreme ambivalence, all of the positive feelings appear grouped on one side of a stone wall and the negative on the other. The positive image of the other is not affected by negative experiences and vice versa. We can suffer cruel and repeated physical abuse at the hands of an intimate partner and still wind up saying, "But I love him." It is as if one set of feelings has no impact on the other.

The splitting of feelings into good-bad or black-white dichotomies is manifest dramatically with young children who alternatively love and hate their parents with equal intensity. Over time, this extreme ambivalence tends to be resolved in most of us by a more realistic picture of our parents and more moderation in our feelings. With our intimate partners, however, the ambivalence often persists, causing confusion in both partners.

## The Impact of Ambivalence on Partners

Ambivalence breeds insecurity in partners because of our unpredictability. One moment we seem warm and loving and the next we are cold and distant. Because of shifts in feeling-tone, our partners are unsure of where they stand. The question "How can she love me when she gets so moody?" becomes a source of anguish. It is difficult to feel secure about another's love when there is little constancy.

Ambivalence in which there is approach-avoidance behavior is particularly difficult to handle. Typically, this sort of ambivalent lover approaches his or her partner only when the partner is distant, because loving/sexual feelings are experienced most intimately when the beloved is afar. Because the distant, unattainable object is viewed as an exciting challenge, the mating dance is intensified at those moments. When the partner starts to respond to the passionate pleas of undying love, however, ambivalent partners start to retreat emotionally because feelings of anxiety begin to surface. Now that they have won what they most wanted, ambivalent lovers become aware of their panic and start to notice their partner's imperfections. Overwhelmed by the closeness and disappointed by their partner's failings, the impulse to run away into a safe corner becomes intense.

In approach-avoidance conflicts of this kind, there is both positive attraction and intimacy anxiety, with the desire to get close being stronger than the fear experienced at a distance. In close proximity, the anxiety feelings are decidedly more intense than the attraction. Usually, however, the ambivalent person with approach-avoidance behavior can tolerate brief periods of closeness before backing off. It is the long stretches of intimacy, especially when initiated by the partner, that produce the panic.

## Playing Hard to Get and Other Games

For the persons caught up in the approach-avoidance behavior of their partners, intimate life is frustrating. On the one hand, attempts to achieve intimate contact are likely to be rebuffed; distancing behaviors, on the other hand, are apt to result in pursuit. While playing "hard to get" may be the smartest strategy in obtaining some romance, inauthentic games do not result in much emotional connection. Then, too, the resentment created by unmet needs can undermine the relationship.

Ken, a forty-five-year-old architect, could only tolerate three days of a vacation with his girlfriend before becoming tense and distant. The son of an abusive, alcoholic father, Ken was an outgoing, energetic, witty, and ambitious professional. He and Myra, his thirty-eight-year-old, single friend, had met fifteen years earlier, shortly after the death of her mother. At the time, Ken was a married man with three young children. For ten years while he was married, they maintained their relationship by seeing each other two hours a week. Even with such limited amounts of intimacy, however, Ken would periodically bolt from the relationship—ostensibly because he was overwhelmed by guilt. He would also report that his girlfriend's emotional demands were suffocating to him. When they were close for any length of time, he became critical of her shortcomings—her neediness in particular. At those times, she reminded him of his daughter and he felt asexual toward her.

Their movements toward and away from intimacy were like the two-step, back and forth without any progression. Soon after his divorce, they broke up. Then, they got back together and continued an on-again, off-again cycle of togetherness, interrupted by months of distance for five more years. While his problems with intimacy were the most obvious, Myra also had difficulties with closeness. Intimate contact for her stimulated intense childhood longings for nurturance along with fears of abandonment.

A passive and dependent woman in intimate relationships, which was in marked contrast to her autonomous professional self, Myra had experienced four major losses by the age of twenty-five through the deaths of both her parents, her grandmother, and her first boyfriend. The extent of her dependency longings would have frightened even a less ambivalent partner because her emotional neediness was excessive. In intimacy, she essentially gave over her autonomy and the responsibility for her happiness to her partner—a situation that is burdensome by most people's standards. (An exception would be the die-hard nurturer whose self-esteem resides exclusively in taking care of others.) At this time, the man in the fifteen-year ambivalent dance appears to be moving away from the relationship in a more determined manner than previously, while the woman is desperately hanging on as if the relationship were her only salvation, the sole antidote against a bitter and lonely old age.

## Creating Distance by Criticism

In other cases, ambivalence about intimacy is manifest by the criticality of one partner toward the other. After moments of intense closeness, one partner may begin to complain about the other. An injury or misunderstanding from the past is dredged up just as intimacy starts to feel frightening. The moment of emotional contact between the two may be interrupted by a flashback to an earlier quarrel, and the spell is broken. For example, just as they get close, she may remember how he mistreated her last year when he was drinking heavily. The distance and bitterness toward him that grew out of years of heavy drinking and neglect now interfere with their closeness. The fact that he has been sober for a year and has been making every effort to repair their relationship may be hard for her to see; her ambivalence toward him renders it difficult to live in the present moment. The baggage from their marital past weighs too heavily on their present relationship.

Past negative feelings and perceptions are not easily modified by current realities. One woman reported becoming very fearful of her boyfriend when they were drinking together in a bar because in this situation in the past he would become angry and shout at her. In spite of the reality (and they both agreed) that this had not occurred in over a year, she described these events as vividly as if they had happened yesterday. Or in another situation, a husband may continue to feel distrustful toward his wife because she was unfaithful ten years earlier. Ambivalence, born of our past experiences, unnecessarily restricts the amount of positive contact that we can enjoy in the present.

The emotional baggage coloring the present moment can arrive not only from a specific relationship's past but from the history of all previous relationships. Past disappointments and rejections clearly take their toll and affect the degree of ambivalence we bring to each new relationship. From our first contact with our parents, our perceptions and expectations of others are built with each new experience adding to the collective whole.

## A Blurred Vision

A forty-five-year-old social worker who prided herself on being an intelligent, perceptive human being was jolted by her therapist's comment that she did not see her husband very clearly. At the time the comment was made, she had no idea what was meant and left the session feeling confused. She believed that her perceptions of her husband as childlike, dependent, and irresponsible were unbiased and objective. Unbeknownst to her, part of her viewing filter was constructed from the disappointing experiences she had had with important people earlier in her life. As the oldest daughter of two alcoholic parents, she often felt superresponsible and totally alone with no one to count on. Understandably, significant others were seen as irresponsible and childish—a perception that was gradually superimposed on her husband, who was, by most standards, a fairly responsible and mature individual.

The blurring of our current vision because of past conflicts is commonplace in intimacy. Even before a relationship is established, the past affects our sexual choices and the degree of attraction we feel. The past also has an impact on the expectations, perceptions, and feelings we have about our current partners. Because we do not approach adult intimacy with a tabula rasa (or blank screen) but rather with a complicated pattern of earlier experiences, the past is present in today's moment.

## Distance and Closeness Boundaries

In every intimate relationship, the distance and closeness boundaries need to be calibrated and then readjusted as needed. By distance and closeness boundaries is meant the degrees of distance and closeness two people can tolerate in the relationship. In a healthy relationship, the boundaries operate to keep the relationship from becoming "too distant" or "too close." "Too distant" means feeling lonely, empty, or disconnected, while "too close" has a smothering, intruded upon, or enmeshed connotation. Like a thermostat regulating the household temperature, the distance and closeness boundaries keep a relationship from going too far off course. To function like regulators, however, boundary signals need to be heeded and adjustments made. The feeling of becoming distant from the other is ordinarily a signal that more quality time needs to be spent together. The opposite warning—anxiety related to feeling "too close"—requires separate time and space.

These distance and closeness boundaries vary with each couple and change developmentally as a relationship progresses. One couple might have no difficulty in tolerating long periods of silence during an evening out together, separate vacations, working in different cities, or sex once a month or less. For another couple, any of the above would sound the death knell for the relationship. One man complained bitterly that his wife and he did not have any "together time" in the evenings after work and that theirs was "a great weekend relationship only." For him, emotional contact on a daily basis was important, while for her, great weekends were emotionally satisfying enough. One woman found her husband's after-work silence and retreat to the TV set annoying and distance-creating, while for him, spending the evening together, even though watching TV, felt close. For one partner, talking may be the only way of maintaining emotional contact, while for the other, being in the other's presence may be sufficient to feel connected. For still others, sex and physical contact are essential to maintain the emotional bond. It is clear that there are many roads to "relationship heaven," and no one way is guaranteed to be the golden path.

## Different Requirements Create Conflict

Problems arise in a relationship when a couple cannot agree on the boundaries. After intense closeness following sex, she may want to hang on to the intimacy by staying intertwined in his arms; he may be feeling smothered and want to roll over and fall asleep. On the one hand, the kind of closeness she wants may feel clinging and stultifying to him. On the other hand, sex on a daily basis may feel like a demand to her, while for him, it may feel like a requirement for his emotional well-being. Her need to talk intimately with her husband every evening may feel draining to him because all he wants to do is collapse when he gets home from work. He may have been sitting on the train exhausted from hundreds of office hassles, looking forward to a football evening on TV. Her questions about his day the minute he walks in the door may feel like an intrusion into the protective cocoon he has retreated into once the workday was over. But for her, their distance during the day has felt "too far," and she wants to reestablish the emotional connection as soon as he appears on the doorstep.

With very different intimacy requirements, the stage is set for battle. He accuses her of being self-centered and demanding, while she complains that he is cold and insensitive. Or he is regarded as dominating and she is viewed as an emotional baby—constantly seeking attention. Because emotional needs are not being met, resentment creeps in and colors every interaction. Resentment also affects each partner's perception of the other—transforming the love of one's life into a thoughtless, inconsiderate clod. Unless the distance and closeness boundaries can be negotiated and recalibrated, the ongoing conflicts will rob the relationship of any vitality and lead to a permanent "cold war" or the dissolution of the relationship.

## Relationship Styles

Gradually, most intimate relationships lose their spontaneity and settle down into a series of fixed interactions. Because habits get formed easily, we can develop a specific interactional style with our partners that displays only a limited sample of our interactional repertoire. We may be demure and deferential to our intimate partners while being talkative and assertive with our friends. Conversely, we may be dominating and controlling with our partners and egalitarian with everyone else.

The side of our personalities that is characteristic of our intimate interpersonal style in a particular relationship is a function of several factors, chief of which is the mutually developed system that the couple creates. For example, if he is very dominating, she might be more submissive than she ordinarily would be in order to avoid conflict. Conversely, if he is needy and dependent, she might become stronger than she might have been to balance the relationship. Or if he is moody, she might be cheerful to alleviate the gloom in the household. In a similar vein, shyness may be compensated for by talkativeness, and vice versa. We attempt to fill the voids or take on complementary roles to make the relationship work. Whether the accommodation is ultimately adaptive will depend on the degree of self-sacrifice involved and how rewarding the relationship is for each partner.

### The Interactive Loop

Basically, the interactional system the couple establishes acts as a mutually reinforcing feedback loop. His behavior affects her behavior, which, in turn, affects his actions, and the circularity goes on. We respond not only to our internal feelings and motives, but to the other person's cues. On the one hand, if we feel like having sex and our partner is distant and preoccupied, we might quickly be turned off. On the other hand, if we feel anxious and worried and our partner is amorous, the seductiveness might shift our gears. In a relationship, we exist in an emotional atmosphere that is charged by both parties. Thus, not only are the moment-to-moment interactions affected by the other's behavior but the overall relationship style is also influenced by the other. Just as "it takes two to tango" so does it take both partners to create a particular interactional pattern. Among the relationship styles that couples establish are complementary, symmetrical,[17] and antagonistic patterns.

## Complementary Pairs

In a complementary pattern where opposite roles are taken, the different roles are exaggerated by the need to accommodate the others's style.

**Distancer-Pursuer Pattern.** For example, in the distancer-pursuer pattern, where one partner regularly seeks closeness and the other routinely pulls away, the couple's system of relating keeps each partner fixated at an opposite pole. The more intently one partner chases the other, the more frantically the other tries to escape. On the one hand, the intensity of the pursuit frightens the distancer, who can only tolerate limited amounts of intimacy. The pursuer, on the other hand, becomes anxious when there is distance in the relationship and intensifies the chase whenever withdrawal is more pronounced than usual.

Kimberly, a pursuer, felt lost and anxious whenever Scott, her distancing partner, seemed preoccupied. At those times, she was convinced that he was having second thoughts about their relationship when, in fact, he was thinking about his work situation. Whenever Kim would snuggle up to him as a way of seeking reassurance and to ask him if he loved her, Scott became annoyed at her intrusion into his reverie. His abrupt "Of course, I love you" lacked conviction, and Kim became even more insistent that he prove his devotion. Her increasing persistence, however, was anxiety-arousing to him and he would withdraw even further. It was only when he felt less bombarded by her demands that he would seek closeness. Their complementary roles in effect maintained their relationship style.

**Competent-Inadequate Unions.** In a similar fashion, overadequate-underadequate pairings tend to magnify a couple's differences and solidify their roles. Alcoholic marriages are good examples of this type of relationship style. As the alcoholic becomes less and less capable of handling family duties with the progression of the addiction, the nonalcoholic gradually takes on increasing responsibility for work and family obligations. Thus, over time, the nonalcoholic assumes the role of the superadequate member of the family and the alcoholic takes on a more childlike, inadequate role. While this kind of complementarity can last for years, eventually the nonalcoholic spouse becomes burned out by the superresponsible role and seeks help or leaves. Or the physical and psychological deterioration of the alcoholic precipitates a crisis that necessitates change. Typically, this kind of overadequate-underadequate merger is maladaptive for both partners.

At times, however, the overadequate partner comes to enjoy the power of the position and does not want to relinquish some of the responsibilities even when the partner can reassume them. One alcoholic man returned home from a three-week hospital rehabilitation program to discover that his wife enjoyed running the family business. Even after he was sober for six months, she was reluctant to relinquish any business duties, thereby contributing to his increasing sense of uselessness and inadequacy. Fortunately, marital counseling was helpful to them in establishing a more equitable distribution of power in their relationship.

**The Barter System.** The pawnbrokers represent another complementary style. Basically, this relationship style is a trade-off in which each partner gains a valued quality or commodity from the other. One partner may achieve money and status, while the other reaps the benefits of youth and beauty. The wealthy, aging entrepreneur married to the beauty queen twenty years his junior, "the wise old owl" professor having an affair with his adoring student, and the irresponsible, fun-loving womanizer attracted to a nurturant, stable "older woman" are all examples of the quid pro quo, or barter, factor in relationships. In exchange for a valued commodity or quality (money, beauty, sex appeal, status, intelligence, emotional stability, power, adoration, youth, liveliness, wisdom, and nurturance are among the most common), a person is willing to provide an equally valued asset or characteristic of a different order. While this kind of arrangement seems fair enough and would appear to have staying power or durability, what often happens is that one partner's needs and values change over time and the relationship loses its appeal. Beauty fades, power corrupts, and even stability has its boring, dark side.

## Symmetrical Pairs

In symmetrical relationships, on the other hand, there is similarity rather than oppositeness. At times, the partners seem to be "cut from the same cloth," sharing identical values and interests. Both may be shy, introverted souls content to spend hours sitting in the same room engrossed in their own reading. Or they may be easy-going, nondemanding individuals who are content both within and outside the relationship. When together, they look like good friends enjoying intellectual and emotional camaraderie with deep attachment but little apparent passion. They may share a love of nature, music, theater, farming, church, or their family. Whatever the attachment, it is the commonality of their interests and values that functions as glue to cement the relationship.

**United-Front Couple.** A negative variation of the symmetrical relationship is the "united-front" couple, who agree not to disagree. Married for twenty-five years, Pat and Ralph had similar opinions on almost every subject. Childhood sweethearts, they grew up in the same town and attended the same schools. Sharing the same hobbies, politics, and religious philosophy, they seemed to be ideally suited to one another. Often, each would nod in agreement at the other's remarks or open a conversation with, "As Pat (or Ralph) said. . . . " While their partnership (or rather twin-ship) appeared destined to last forever, their only daughter's ano-rexia in early adolescence provided the only hint to the observer that something was amiss in their household.

While a united-front couple may have shared values and/or interests, the most salient aspect of their union is their inability to tolerate differences and resolve conflict. Usually rigid, black-and-white thinkers who believe there is only one valid political view, only one true religion, and only one worthwhile lifestyle, the united-front couple cannot tolerate the ambiguity of anything less than certainty. With each other, their philosophy is basically, "If you're not with me, you're against me." In addition to their rig-idity, each partner in this sort of union is very dependent upon the other. Thus, the combination of rigidity and dependency makes it difficult for them to accept an alternative point of view from the other without feeling threatened and abandoned.

Early in their relationship, the united-front couple may have gone through a phase of overt conflict. However, because the angry interchanges were too anxiety-arousing, someplace along the way they made a silent pact not to disagree. No matter how difficult "biting one's tongue" was, it was preferable to open war-fare or passive-aggressive withdrawal. Over time, one or both partners became facile at submerging their own idiosyncratic per-ceptions and ideas into a collective whole. They learned how to think alike and became adept at finishing each other's sentences. While a merged union of this sort may appear to be a heavenly twinship, the children of such unions have problems in identifying with parents and in acquiring conflict resolution skills.

Identification with a parent who is a shadowy figure rather than a whole person is difficult. Since both partners are a blended unity, the blurred and indistinct boundaries between them make it difficult to discern where one leaves off and the other begins. In contrast, identifying with a beloved and/or powerful parent who is a unique character is a more substantive task. We want to become like the heroic or virtuous characters in our lives rather than merged, undifferentiated blobs.

In addition, there is no opportunity to learn how to resolve conflict in the united-front family. Since conflict tends to be swept under the rug rather than faced squarely, children in these families become adept at denial and avoidance. They do not learn how to negotiate, compromise, or take turns, but rather develop a talent for comic relief and other distraction maneuvers. Projection of undesirable qualities onto the partner and blaming are other common defensive strategies.

## Chronic Battlers

In contrast to symmetrical and complementary styles, the antagonists or chronically conflicted couples are obviously in trouble. Like the warring couple in *Who's Afraid of Virginia Woolf?*,[18] the perpetual wranglers appear to be engaged in a vicious and competitive contest of destruction and survival. As in mortal combat, every attack is met with an increasingly destructive counterattack until exhaustion overtakes them or police arrive on the scene. Even when physical violence is not part of the picture, the verbal onslaught is hard to witness because of its unrelenting cruelty.

Less destructive but similarly antagonistic interactional styles are evident in couples who constantly contradict each other and bicker. "No, it was not my mother but my aunt who said that," or "It happened on Tuesday, not Monday," or "We walked south on Main Street, not east." Every step of the anecdote is met with opposition as if precision of detail were the hallmark of both a good story and a virtuous character.

In the antagonistic style, each partner wants to be supremely right and victorious over the other. Because "being wrong" in relation to one's partner is synonymous with feeling inadequate or "less than," much energy is expended to prove one's own correctness. Grace and Sam, whose relationship was a prototype of the antagonistic style, argued incessantly about most aspects of their married life from child-rearing and in-laws to politics. Both stubborn, opinionated but insecure people, they could not acknowledge the other's point of view without feeling inferior or controlled by the other. If Grace said, "Children need to be given the opportunity of making their own mistakes," Sam would say, "But all children need guidance." Grace would then elaborate on her position, to which Sam would counter with a variation of his thesis that discipline is important to children. The exquisitely programmed bout of jab and counterpunch would continue until an all-out fight broke out, after which both partners wound up feeling unsupported and misunderstood. Even seemingly innocent remarks, such as "This has been an unusually cold winter," would be countered, so that neutral interchanges became few and far-between. Their power struggle was the bid by each partner for control or domination of the other in order not to feel inferior.

While hostile competitiveness is the most overt characteristic of this style, a less apparent feature is the high degree of dependency the partners have on each other. More important than the desire to be better is the need to be approved of and, thereby, validated by the other. However, because the need for approval is excessive in these couples, they are repeatedly hurt and frustrated by their partner's failure to be unconditionally positive. The hurt and frustration generated by less-than-perfect acceptance serve to fuel the angry competitiveness. The message seems to be, "If you can't regularly tell me how wonderful I am, I'll show you how much better I am than you are."

The verbal feuding serves not only as a means of regulating emotional closeness, that is, keeping distance and yet, paradoxically, maintaining contact, but as a way of validating the self. The intense emotional confrontations, even though negatively charged, are often the only sort of emotional connection the couple experiences. Then, too, the fighting brings excitement and liveliness into a relationship that feels dead. Thus, in spite of the negative appearance, some psychological benefits are being accrued.

All relationship styles, whether complementary, symmetrical, or antagonistic, fall short of the ideal to one degree or another. Even when adaptive, intimacy roles limit behaviors and result in fixed patterns of relating rather than a wide range of flexible interactions. In any relationship, we are less than we could be because of the constraints imposed by the other and the need to accommodate. Over time, however, there is the potential for changing many of the parameters of intimacy: the needs that get aroused, the fears, defenses, distance-closeness boundaries, and relationship styles. If both partners are emotionally healthy and change in response to their own developmental strivings and the needs of the other, more adaptive resolutions can occur over time than were possible at the beginning of the relationship. Unfortunately, most people get locked into habitual responding, thereby limiting the relationship's possibilities.

# Chapter 2

# Fears and Risks

Love without pain is a contradiction in terms! We may go for months or years without a hurt feeling but as surely as night follows day, there will be suffering somewhere along love's pathway. "You always hurt the one you love, the one you shouldn't hurt at all," sang the Mills Brothers long ago. They further intoned, "So if I broke your heart last night, it's because I love you most of all."[1]

While the realization that love and pain go together is unsettling, it is clear that people are vulnerable and likely to get hurt in intimate relationships. A poignant example of this truth can be found in the interaction between a young boy and his father in Erich Segal's best-selling novel, *The Class.*[2] The young boy, upon seeing his father in tears, asks gently, "Why are you crying Father—is it for Mama?" "Yes boy. To love someone is terrible. It brings such pain." "But, Father, I love you." "Then, you're a little fool. Go out and let me be." Are we all fools for rushing into intimacy without careful scrutiny? Is our eternal quest for love blind stupidity, masochism, or a biological imperative? Having been disappointed repeatedly, should we not have learned our lesson?

Hope *does* spring eternal in the human heart. However, because we have been hurt in earlier relationships, we are afraid of being too hopeful. Sometimes, the intensity of our fears prevents us from even attempting another relationship. At other times, the earlier hurts leave us gun-shy as we start to get involved.

Besides the basic fear of being hurt in intimacy, there are other related sources of danger. We are afraid of having our weaknesses exposed, losing control, giving up autonomy, being attacked, being disappointed and/or betrayed, feeling guilty for the relationship's shortcomings, and most importantly, we are fearful about being rejected and abandoned. Feldman's five intimacy anxieties (fear of merger, fear of exposure, fear of attack, fear of abandonment, and fear of one's own destructive impulses)[3] are similar to these categories but more limited and psychoanalytic in nature (Larry Feldman is a psychiatrist who specializes in family therapy).

Because we are often unaware of what we are afraid of, we have a hard time assessing how realistic these fears are in a particular situation. "Should I be apprehensive about an involvement with John?" becomes an impossible question to answer if we are not sure what exactly we are afraid of. Besides that, unknown dangers are particularly threatening. Thus, to reduce the threat and improve our ability to assess the dangers, it is important to examine these fears in detail.

## Fear of Exposure

Picture a small, naked child huddled against a building trying to shield herself from the cold, biting wind, or an old, partially clothed man with wrinkled and pockmarked skin coming out of his hut into the blinding sunlight—his blemishes visible for all the world to see.

Like the small child or the wrinkled old man, in intimacy we feel naked, defenseless, unprotected, and exposed to the light of day with all of our imperfections showing. We feel like a raw, exposed nerve with the protective sheath stripped away. The person whom we have admitted into our intimate zone has an inside track on the weakest part of us, the part we are most ashamed of or feel guiltiest about. With all our vulnerabilities and weaknesses exposed, we fear that our intimate partner will be in a better position to hurt, humiliate, control, or reject us.

## The Unveiling of Our Achilles' Heels

What are we afraid of exposing? If a random sample of today's adults were asked that question, the answers would vary from real or imagined physical defects to emotional and personality inadequacies. In the physical realm, inadequacy concerns typically focus on genital and secondary sexual characteristics or other bodily parts. We are either too fat or too thin; our thighs, arms, or buttocks are too flabby; our muscle tone is poor; our breasts are too small, too large, the wrong shape, or they hang too low; our penises are too small; we have too much or too little hair on our bodies; we have too many blemishes, freckles, or other skin problems; our stomachs protrude; we have bad breath or a disgustingly offensive body odor; and the list goes on. The imperfection is a source of shame, and we are fearful of exposing that imperfection to broad daylight.

In fear of exposure, the emotional and personality concerns are equally varied. The inadequacy concerns revolve around the fear that something vital and necessary to a relationship is lacking in ourselves. There is a "missing piece." The missing piece may be viewed as deep and central: "The core of me is empty"; "I'm incapable of love"; "I'm just basically unlovable"; "She'll find out that underneath all of that tinsel is more tinsel—I'm a phony." Or we may fear that we lack some important quality, like conversational skill, assertiveness, or creativity, as noted in the complaint "I'm just too ordinary—there's nothing exciting about me."

## Being Shamed

The fear is that we will be exposed and found wanting or lacking in some way; we will be shamed. Erik Erikson wrote:

Shame supposes that one is completely exposed and conscious of being looked at: in one word, self-conscious. One is visible and not ready to be visible, which is why we dream of shame as a situation in which we are stared at in a condition of incomplete dress, in night attire, with one's pants down.[4]

Shame is early expressed in an impulse to bury one's face, or the desire to sink right then and there into the ground. In intimacy, we are fearful of being found deficient in some way. And once found defective, the resultant fear is that we will be shamed and rejected outright.

The sense of shame is manifested in night dreams of sitting on a toilet and being looked at through the half-open door. Or of being small and insignificant in the midst of a group of tall figures and of being humiliated in some way. One woman who had some concerns about her teaching abilities related a dream in which she was surrounded by a group of giants who were chanting, "No, stupid, CAT is spelled C-A-T, not K-A-T," as she was struggling to write the correct spelling on the blackboard. In this dream, she was exposed as small, inadequate, and stupid.

Dream images of wearing dirty, soiled, or tattered clothes or of being seen as fumbling, bumbling, or inept all relate to the fear of being exposed as lacking a fundamental quality, whether intelligence, goodness, common sense, grace, moral fiber, or depth. Just like the scarecrow, tin man, and lion in *The Wizard of Oz*, we wish that we possessed sufficient brain, heart, or courage to make it in the land of close interpersonal relationships.

## Exposing Badness

Another aspect of the fear of exposure is the fear of being discovered to be "bad" in some way. Our partners will find out that we are selfish, mean, cruel, or ungrateful. Of all the negative vices that we might possess, selfishness is clearly at the top of the heap. In our culture, kids are called "selfish" for anything from not cleaning up their rooms to being inattentive or insensitive to parental needs. Selfishness is viewed as a significant character flaw that interferes with our ability to form interpersonal relationships. If we are selfish, then we cannot relate to, tune into, or love another human being. Selfishness is the ultimate indictment against our humanity. We cannot be deep, caring, loving human beings if we are *selfish*. Like Narcissus, we may have fallen in love with our own images, making us unable to care about other people. In intimate relationships, this concern about our selfishness is heightened.

## We Are Too Much

We can also be afraid of exposing other kinds of "badness." We may fear that we are *too much* of something—too angry, seductive, dominating, manipulative, intrusive, or greedy. We may want too much, complain too much, drink too much, or ask too many questions.

In wanting "too much," whether marital possessions, adoration, power, fame, or stature, we believe we are overstepping our boundaries. Like Icarus, we are flying too close to the sun and we will get our wings singed and come tumbling down. If we want too much, fly too high, or strive for too much, our fear is that we will fall down and, like Humpty Dumpty following his great fall, we will not be put back together again. We will be punished by God, fate, or our fellow human beings, who, consumed with envy and rage at our excesses, will feel justified in shooting us down. In contrast to feelings of inadequacy with the resultant fear of being exposed and humiliated, being exposed as bad is related to the fear of retaliation and punishment.

In intimacy, then, the fear is that our partner will discover our hidden inadequacies and/or excesses and, ultimately, walk away.

## Too Demanding

Being discovered to be "too needy and greedy" is related both to concerns about adequacy and to the fear of being excessively demanding. A shy, forty-year-old accountant whose romantic relationships with women were marked by intense passion (on his part) and frequent rejections related: "I go into a relationship whole hog—I grab on and I don't want to let go. It's like I'm strangling her, not giving her enough freedom." He recounted his obsession with a "new love"—how he would spend every free moment thinking about her, wondering what she was doing, and whether she was thinking about him. His need to call her frequently to hear the sound of her voice and his desire to spend every available moment with her seemed frantic and desperate. His new love reacted by feeling suffocated and wanting more time apart. In "The Emotionally Draining Man," Annie Gottlieb, a writer for *McCalls*, wrote about the man who is so endlessly demanding of attention that the woman winds up feeling drained and depressed.[5] The situation is identical to that of emotionally draining and dependent women who demand more attention and reassurance than their partners can provide.

The fear of exposure is illustrated vividly in Betty's case. A thirty-three-year-old, professional woman with a Ph.D. in the humanities, Betty came into therapy because she was lonely and depressed. In addition, she was about thirty pounds overweight, a problem she had been struggling with since adolescence. She had moved into town from the East Coast about a year earlier and was experiencing an intensified version of the isolation that frequently accompanies a move to a new region. Betty had a few women friends in town but no male dating relationships. Even though she had avoided the dating scene with fervor since her only romantic relationship had ended years earlier, she was disappointed that there was no romance in her life at the present time. Essentially, she avoided the dating scene because she was fearful of exposing psychological and physical traits that she felt would inevitably lead to rejection.

Betty's only love affair was a brief romantic and sexual interlude that had ended suddenly eight years earlier. The rejection by this man left her reeling and sent her into a severe depression. Even worse, this rejection also validated her basic belief that she was unlovable in several fundamental ways. She commented poignantly but with certainty, "When someone gets to know me, they'll find there is nothing to love." She believed that no one could love her because she was "harsh and abrasive with a devastating talent for sticking to the truth." She also believed her father's criticism that she was "too self-centered and insensitive." In addition, she said, "No one could love me because I'm too needy and too arrogant." She viewed her neediness as "overwhelmingly gross and lacking in subtlety"; her arrogance was seen as obnoxious and likely to lead to resentful attacks. Besides these personality qualities that she was embarrassed about, she was ashamed of her body, which she viewed as ugly. The ugliness, in her own mind, derived from obesity, bodily hair, and sagging breasts. By avoiding intimacy, she was determined not to expose these physical and psychological flaws.

Her fears of exposure were apparent in several phobiclike behaviors and in her night dreams. Even though she loved to perform in the theater, she had severe anxiety about auditioning. There she was fearful that her flaws would become glaringly apparent. This fear of being exposed as defective even extended into the privacy of her home, where she avoided mirrors because they reflected back to her all of her perceived flaws. While she was able to avoid mirrors and the theater, there was no opportunity to hide in her recurrent nightmares. There she was seen by all, sitting completely naked on a potty. The sense of shame that accompanied this dream clearly reflected the discomfort she felt at being exposed.

Betty, who was the middle child of three girls, saw herself as the least loved by her father of all the women in her family. She was viewed as the one most capable of taking care of herself in contrast to an older, disturbed sister and the younger "baby of the family." As a result, she was convinced that she was intellectually and professionally competent but equally certain that she lacked those qualities that constitute lovability. She valued her intellect but was basically contemptuous of her emotional needs. For example, she described her reactions watching a home video of herself as a little girl hamming it up in front of the camera. She was horrified (rather than amused) at seeing "such an obnoxious child constantly seeking attention." Thus, not only did she perceive herself to be unlovable in the eyes of the world but she donned these same critical, uncaring glasses in viewing herself.

## Fear of Loss of Control

We are falling faster and faster down a deep, black hole, but just before hitting the ground we wake up in terror. In another dream, the car we are driving is skidding on the ice, veering off the highway in the direction of a 100-foot drop. Again, just as we are about to plunge through the guardrail and over the cliff, we wake up trembling. In these dreams, the fear of losing control is quite apparent.

What kind of control are we afraid of losing? In intimacy, the fear is that there will be no way out—we will be trapped and helpless. We will be unable to stop the clock or the merry-go-round and get off. In the courtship phase of a relationship, a frequent complaint is "It's moving too fast." The relationship is changing at a rate that is uncomfortable and anxiety-arousing. The old doubts and the newly acquired ones are as yet unresolved, while the commitment seems to be deepening. "I'm not ready for this whirlwind, breakneck speed—I want to slow down to a pace I can control" is what the complainant seems to be saying.

Carol, a forty-seven-year-old lesbian, had been depressed for five years following the breakup of an intense, emotional relationship that included strong passionate and sexual longings. She had been involved with a nun who had served as her spiritual mentor. They had met at a time when Carol was seriously considering becoming a nun herself. Following the breakup, she isolated herself in her apartment after work each day and cried off and on about the loss of the woman who rejected her. Starving herself emotionally, she obtained only occasional sustenance from her elderly landlady, who was housebound in the apartment below.

When Carol gradually began to emerge from her depression following the initiation of therapy, she found herself attracted to a childlike and confused, bisexual, married woman. After a five-year hiatus, her joy, excitement, and sexual attraction started to escalate to such an intensity that her feelings overwhelmed both herself and her potential partner. "It's like I have no emotional brakes with which to slow my feelings down once I'm involved," she said. For Carol, it seemed like withdrawal or being overwhelmed were the only possibilities. And for her, along with most of us, being flooded with feelings is clearly a much more frightening, out-of-control state than withdrawal and isolation.

## Out-of-Control Obsessions and Ambivalence

The preoccupation with the other that frequently accompanies passionate love in its beginning stage is experienced by many as loss of control. "I can't get him out of my mind" is a frequently heard complaint at the beginning of a love relationship. The thoughts and fantasies that bombard our consciousness are not only daydreams of unending romance but also worries about possible catastrophes. Will he call again, will she continue to find me attractive, does he have another girlfriend, and so forth. This state of turbulence and uncertainty feels irrational to most of us.

Also, ambivalent swings that are so characteristic of love relationships feel unnerving and out of control. One minute we feel positive, euphoric, or joyful, and the next we are worried and depressed about the negative aspects of the relationship. One moment he is handsome and charming, and the next second he is viewed as crude and overweight. Experiencing a variety of perceptions and feelings in short periods of time feels like a threat to our sanity. These rapid shifts result in a sense of confusion. The old, popular song "Smoke Gets in Your Eyes" is a poignant portrayal of the fuzziness, blurred vision, and lack of clarity in love relationships.

When we are involved with a highly ambivalent person, our partner's movements toward and away from intimacy feel chaotic. As we attempt to get close, our partner retreats. It is only when we walk away psychologically that our ambivalent partner comes-a-running. Because we are getting the opposite of what is desired, there is little sense of being in control.

One woman who had been in two long-term relationships with highly ambivalent men was extremely hesitant to make another commitment for fear that this new man would walk away the minute she said yes. Sitting on the fence with him felt much safer. From her earlier relationships, she had learned that the only way to maintain any sense of control with an ambivalent partner was to act the opposite of how she felt. She commented about her ex-husband: "If I wanted something from him, the only way to get it was to pretend that it didn't matter to me. If I wanted him to go to a party with me, acting like it didn't matter one way or the other was the only way of having him come along." While this ploy was effective in getting some of her needs met, the resentment brought about by her husband's insensitivity to her needs was the major factor in their divorce.

### Fatal Attraction

Another way in which a relationship can feel out of control is when the partner's behavior becomes irrational and disturbed in some way. Like the hero of *Fatal Attraction*, the popular movie in which a casual affair becomes transformed into a nightmare, we may find ourselves in deep water because the person we got involved with is emotionally unstable. One woman reported that she experienced months of daily harassment following her attempt to end a college romance. The young man kept following her around the campus and called her every evening to plead his case. It was only after she made a formal complaint to the dean of the college that his behavior stopped. Currently, beginning a relationship feels like falling into quicksand for her. She has no control over the other's behavior and also no control over the speed at which the relationship will proceed from a casual one to friendship to sex and/or love. The idea that she has some control over the speed and final destination of the relationship and that she can stop at any point along the relationship's developmental path is a novel one for her. In her past experiences with the important people in her life, intimacy was unpredictable and out of control.

## Am I Going Mad?

Another kind of anxiety about "loss of control" is the fear of falling apart or behaving in a primitive and uncontrolled manner. Because feelings are more intensely aroused in intimacy than in other kinds of relationships, we fear that we will be overwhelmed or overpowered by our feelings. We may be afraid of "going mad," that is, losing our minds or destroying someone. We may be afraid that our self-control will be unable to keep us from screaming at the top of our lungs, beating someone up, or punching our fists through a window. In a less dramatic vein, we may worry that we will start crying and never stop.

Of all the impulses that we are afraid of, anger is by far the most common and the most destructive. The surge of adrenaline accompanying anger, the rapid heartbeat and flushed face, may be signals of danger to us. These aspects of the "flight-or-fight" reaction are dangerous to us if we have never learned how to handle angry feelings constructively. We may have learned to withdraw and become depressed whenever we were frustrated. At the other extreme, we may have screamed, thrown things, or hit other people when we were angered. Or our vocal expressions of anger may have earned us a bloody lip or a vicious beating by an irate father. In any event, anger is associated with potential danger for many of us.

Those individuals who have seldom expressed negative emotion in the past may find themselves especially threatened by the intensity with which anger gets stirred up in intimacy. These overcontrolled types value highly the rational, reasonable side of their own personalities and are unprepared for the intensity of their angry feelings. They are not aware that the regular threats to self-esteem that occur in intimacy make it difficult to deal with anger in a cool, calm, and reasonable manner.

The overcontrolled, reasonable person, when discussing fears about losing control, will often cite an example from childhood to illustrate the destructive nature of anger. One young man related that he kicked in a steel door once when highly enraged (a factually implausible memory, given his small stature). Another remembered that he started the "Third World War" by shouting at his mother. What he meant by his comment was that the fighting among family members that his shouting set off felt as chaotic and destructive as a world war.

The chaotic and destructive aspects of losing control are often symbolized in dreams of natural and man-made disasters, such as hurricanes, floods, tornadoes, raging fires, and speeding trains on the verge of derailment. The sense of urgency and imminent danger in such dreams communicates the high degree of anxiety we experience about losing control. Other loss-of-control dream symbols, such as falling down stairs or losing control of bodily functions—as in uncontrolled vomiting, diarrhea, or incontinence—speak more to our sense of embarrassment than to the destructive potential of losing control. In either case, whether it is fear of destruction or embarrassment, the risks of losing control appear catastrophic.

### "Take Charge" Types

For people who have a strong need to be "in control," the fear of loss of control is especially intense. In a relationship, we have little control over whether the other person will have affairs, stay or go, live or die. We cannot control all of the happenings in a relationship because some of the responsibility for what occurs belongs to the other person. Some of the responsibility also belongs to fate, luck, or chance. While it is obvious that the responsibility for a relationship's success or failure is shared between several factors, the person who needs to be in control has difficulty accepting this aspect of human reality. He or she suffers when the other person is out of sight or out of character (behaving in an unusual or atypical manner). The person with a high need for control worries about possible catastrophes—what if the other falls in love with someone else, what if the partner is run over by a car, and other negative "what ifs?" By anticipating catastrophes, the take-charge person hopes to be better prepared and thus more in control.

For Sally, the fear of losing control was pervasive both in and out of relationships. A charming, interpersonally sensitive, and pretty twenty-three-year-old with blonde curls, Sally looked like a porcelain doll with a fixed smile. The fact that she was unhappy with all aspects of her life—her low-paying job, the lack of a social life, her weight, and her general appearance—was not evident on her face when she walked into the office. Talking rapidly, she immediately launched into an analysis of her problems. She felt that she was not keeping up with her college peers who had moved into professional jobs and dating relationships right after graduation. Instead, she was living at home and working at a local hospital as a psychiatric aide.

Growing up in a family with many rules (e.g., don't rock the boat, don't expose family secrets), Sally was afraid that she could not maintain this expected control and that "things would come spilling out." The family secrets that she was afraid of revealing centered around her father's alcoholism and abuse. She was also fearful about becoming out of control with respect to eating. In high school, she had been 110 pounds overweight, which left her feeling isolated and inadequate in comparison to her peers. At the time she came into therapy, she had lost most of that weight except for twenty pounds that she was still struggling with.

Sally was also concerned about losing control of anger, which was based more on her father's behavior than her own. Her father's drinking days were characterized by episodic violence and sexual provocation. Her anxiety filled nightmares about being attacked by snakes or pursued by tornadoes represented the terror that she experienced in her relationship with him.

While Sally decried the lack of men in her life, she was distrustful of men and believed that "all men are scum." Like many other women, however, she also felt admiration and envy toward men, whom she perceived as "more substantial or meatier" than women. They were also seen as having more freedom, respect, and power. Her ambivalence toward men and her poor self-image (she believed that guys viewed her "as a pig") kept her from the dating scene until she began to gain some self-confidence.

When Sally began to date, however, she started to feel dangerously out of control. Sexual feelings, in particular, were upsetting to her. She also found her romantic daydreams disturbing because they would intrude upon her waking moments at inconvenient times. The speed at which her own feelings developed once she got involved felt reckless. In addition, the uncertainty (e.g., wondering whether a new man was going to call or not) and ambiguity of a new dating relationship left her feeling that she was at the mercy of forces beyond her control. Fortunately, in Sally's case, therapy was successful in reducing her own need to be in control and her terror of relationships.

### Fear of Losing Autonomy

The image of being intertwined body and soul with another person is appealing to most of us. Being so close, so fused with another that we become one breathing, heart-beating soul feels like utopia at some romantic, mythical level. At the opposite end of this positive vision of blissful union is the image of being so close to another human being that we are suffocating in the process, literally choking for air, because there is no breathing room. Fears of being sucked dry, crowded upon, or smothered restrict the state of perfect unity to momentary, fleeting moments.

Fear of losing ourself, either totally or partially through loss of an important quality like independence, is common in intimacy. In the most extreme variation of this fear—fear of merging—we are fearful that the boundaries between self and other will become blurred, leading to confusion about where a feeling or idea is coming from. One woman, an identical twin with strong and paradoxical fears about both abandonment and suffocation in intimacy, emerged from a state of panic about "too much closeness with her husband," saying that "things were distant but healthier between the two of them—they were less entangled" (see detailed description of Dorothy in "Fear of Abandonment" section in Chapter 3). While fears of total loss of self are rare and occur primarily in psychotic and borderline states, milder, garden-variety variations of this fear, such as concerns about losing autonomy, occupy center stage in intimate relationships.

## Gasping for Air

What does the phrase "I need more space" really mean? Basically, when we are making that request, what we are saying is that the psychological and emotional needs of the other person are overwhelming to us. They want too much of our time, our energy, and our resources. As a result, we feel drained and burdened by them. We may want to escape into the TV or read a good book, while our partner wants to talk. Or the other may want to be held or have sex when all we want to do is hit the pillow and fall sound asleep. Or we may want to be alone to think about our lives or our problems when the other person needs or wants company.

The need for space (time alone and/or less intense contact with the other) is a requirement for the maintenance of our sense of self that varies considerably across individuals. Time to reflect upon and make sense of the day's events, time to think through problematic situations, time to feel autonomous by making solitary decisions, or simply time for minimal sensory stimulation when we are feeling overloaded are important psychologically. Solitude serves the psychological functions of restoring, consolidating, and integrating our sense of self.

## Outgoing Party Types and Solitary Bookworms

As for individual differences, it is clear that introverts, for example, require more time alone than extroverts. Being more comfortable with the inner world of ideas and feelings than with the external world, introverts are more relaxed when they are by themselves. For the introvert, relating to others, even to an especially cherished family member or friend, often feels like "work." Tuning into the other is often a total activity performed at the expense of the self, rather than an easy give-and-take. With other people, the introvert is more likely to be listening than talking— listening being, in general, an activity that is more emotionally draining than talking. For this reason, time alone is essential in order to replenish emotional reserves.

The extrovert, who often becomes stimulated and energized in the company of others, also needs space, but to a lesser degree than the introvert. He or she also needs time to reflect upon the meaning of the day's happenings, to sort through troubling feelings, and to assess progress being made toward life goals. We all need "examination of conscience" times on a regular basis.

## Is Compromise the Name of the Game?

In intimacy, however, we are afraid that we will not have enough psychological space for ourselves and that we will have to give up what is important to us. Our concern is that we will have to compromise or accommodate the other's needs or wishes too much of the time. One woman who was reevaluating her relatively isolated stance said, "I fear that being with people will mean a constant inner struggle. A lot of the time I don't have a preference, so I'll follow along. When I have a preference, though, I feel great pain in having it crossed. It makes me feel like a pressure cooker to play by someone else's rules."

The fear that we will be manipulated or controlled by the other into feeling or doing things that we are not prepared for is fairly common. We fear that we will be made to feel guilty for disagreeing, that we will have to go places that we do not want to go, or do things that are foreign or uncomfortable to us. Because it is clear that even soulmates have different vacation needs, movie preferences, political opinions, or child-rearing beliefs, compromise or accommodation is an integral part of intimacy.

Accommodating the other, however, is often experienced as a "giving up" of some aspect of the self, especially when the yielding occurs around important issues. As Lerner wrote in *The Dance of Intimacy*, "Being a self means ... we do not participate in relationships at the expense of the I."[6] Otherwise, she implies, there is the risk of loss of autonomy or selfhood. This loss of autonomy can be experienced in hundreds of different ways from the trivial to the significant: giving up our solitary morning coffee and paper-reading time because the other wants to talk; going out to the theatre for an anniversary outing when we would rather be at a sporting event; decorating the house in Early American when we love the Modern Scandinavian look. If we like the windows open when sleeping and our spouse does not, we may be giving up a wish, need, or preference that is important. Where to set the thermostat in the house, how to spend a particular holiday, where to go on joint vacations, how often to visit the in-laws, and how to deal with Johnny's school problems all require compromise. On the one hand, if we do not give in enough, we feel guilty. If we yield too frequently, on the other hand, we feel manipulated or controlled. Too many accommodations create a situation of unequal parity that results in resentment.

## Sacrificing Everything

One isolated young man, a twenty-five-year-old history major with strong philosophical and religious interests, felt that close relationships were "deadly." He saw them as so time-consuming, so involving, that he would have no time for himself. In an earlier love relationship, he had spent all of his time thinking and worrying about the relationship. Another client, a young woman in her midtwenties who was lonely and depressed a good deal of the time, said that she did not like "being in love" because she neglected herself in the process.

Megan Marshall, author of *The Cost of Loving*, wrote about how pervasive the fear of loss of autonomy has been for professional women who arrived at adulthood in the seventies and eighties. For them, love seems like "the first step to a life of gradual self-annihilation in marriage and motherhood."[7] Enjoying the power and autonomy of professional careers, they viewed intimate heterosexual relationships as regressive vehicles to their mothers' nurturing but empty lives. She wrote about one woman who said, "For me, it's beyond conflict—it's all or nothing. I hate the way I lose my independence when I'm with a man. I start giving up my reading time, my women friends, my overtime at the office. Intimacy swallows me up."[8]

Why do we give up so much for the sake of intimacy? It seems absurd that intelligent women (and men) would give up their reading time, their same-sex friendships, and their careers for the sake of another. And yet, somehow we (women in particular) have come to believe that if we do not sacrifice everything for the sake of an intimate relationship, we will never have one. We believe that the very nature of love demands self-sacrifice and self-denial to the nth degree.

### Women's Acquiescent Styles

Where do these beliefs come from? In part, they come from the romanticized aspects of our culture—the songs, novels, poems, and TV shows, but, more importantly, these beliefs arise from our experiences, which (for most of us) are devoid of role models of two self-actualized and autonomous, intimate partners happily in love. We have for the most part witnessed couples that include a less than autonomous mother-wife. So we women conclude that if an intimate relationship is to be truly wonderful, we must sacrifice all. And it is this concept of total self-sacrifice that intensifies the fear of loss of autonomy in intimacy.

The fear of losing her autonomy was part of the marital conflict that brought Rosemary, a successful, thirty-four-year-old real estate developer, into therapy. Rosemary had been having marital problems almost from the beginning of her ten-year marriage. Her husband's strong ambivalence about getting married in the first place and his refusal to have a wedding celebration or wear a wedding ring started their marriage off on the wrong foot for her. Her husband, a strong-willed, dominating man, would vacillate between being highly critical and withdrawing. He was, nevertheless, highly invested in their marriage and wanted to work out their problems in counseling at the time Rosemary came into therapy. The problem was that she had become romantically involved with a male colleague two years earlier and felt that she had to make a choice between recommitting to her marriage or ending it.

In an exploration of her marital problems, several issues became apparent. Rosemary's typical style of dealing with her husband was submissiveness and accommodation. However, this acquiescent style was interrupted by intensely angry fights during which Rosemary would loudly demand her rights. What appeared to be power struggles around dominance and control were literally battles for psychological survival because Rosemary often felt engulfed by the intensity of her husband's demands. His emotional power, that is, his forcefulness, confidence, and criticality, were overwhelming to her. In order to be heard, she felt that she had to scream at the top of her lungs.

In Rosemary's case, the fear of losing herself was evident in her feeling of being smothered, the sensation of gasping for air whenever her husband tried to get "too close." "I couldn't breathe—it felt like I would die of suffocation," she once said. "Too close" meant too demanding, too insistent, or too ever-present (being around the house all day). Over time, his sexual demands also felt "too close" and became anxiety-arousing. What had been intense sexual attraction at the beginning of their relationship gradually turned into revulsion at physical intimacy on her part.

For Rosemary, part of her identity as a person came from her relationships with the important men in her life. With her husband, being "his wife" was a significant aspect of how she saw herself. From the start of their relationship, she had idealized him and viewed him as the be-all and end-all of her life. "He was everything to me; I worshipped the ground he walked on," she related. He had appeared in her life at a time when she was recovering from several major losses—the death of her father, painful rejection by a lover, and the dramatic death of her favorite brother in a car accident. Because the loss of several important men left her feeling needy and vulnerable, she was ripe for the development of an intense emotional bond with a man when she met her husband.

Basing her identity on a significant man in her life was a process that had a long history in Rosemary's case. Prior to her husband, Rosemary had idealized her older brother, who had been a popular high school rock star. Being known around the school as "Bob's sister" was a significant source of pride and accomplishment for her. When Bob died suddenly at age twenty, Rosemary lost not only a very important person but a significant part of herself in the process.

As in Rosemary's situation, it may be that fears of smothering in intimacy are more likely to occur when there is strong identification with our partners. This identification can lead to a fusion or a blurring of the boundaries between self and other, a condition that may be the breeding ground in which fears of loss of autonomy can develop. At any rate, the need for distance, whether related to the fear of psychological death or loss of personal freedom, plays a significant role in intimate relationships.

## Chapter 3

# Additional Perils

Just as Dorothy walked cautiously in the Land of Oz worrying about lions, tigers, and bears, so we tread lightly when approaching intimacy. Not sure from where the dangers will spring, we look warily in all directions. Will we be attacked, disappointed, betrayed, guilt-ridden, or rejected the moment we set foot on intimate soil? Because of these concerns, we feel unsafe until we are ensconced in a comfortable relationship or alone again.

### Fear of Attack

Fear of attack is another basic anxiety that relates to survival concerns in intimacy. We are afraid that once we get close to another person, he or she will have free rein to assault us by shouting at, criticizing, ridiculing, or physically abusing us in some way.

Criticism is perhaps the most common form of attack that we fear. The angry critical remark "you're a jerk" or "you're stupid" is basically an assault upon our self-esteem or self-worth. It is hard to feel good about ourselves when an important person views us as an idiot, a failure, or a mean person. It is not true, as we used to pretend in our grade-school days, that "sticks and stones will break my bones but names will never hurt me." Names and criticisms do in fact hurt. In addition, chronic emotional abuse in the form of constant criticism undermines self-confidence. As one woman who was feeling particularly anxious and insecure upon returning to college said, "If you're constantly being told that you can't do anything right, you come to believe it."

## We Become What We Are Called

Being told repeatedly that we are "lazy" or "stupid" or "cruel" by a significant person gradually becomes a part of our own self-concept. Over time, we incorporate these labels into our own views of self. We begin to see ourselves as others have seen us and act in ways that are consistent with that internalized view. For example, if we have been called "lazy" repeatedly, laziness begins to be seen as an integral part of our own personality. We gradually begin to believe that we *are* lazy and that's that. Our own lazy behavior becomes ego-syntonic (compatible with our own view of self) and, therefore, less amenable to change. While parents tend to call their children critical names to shame them into good behavior, the result is more likely to be the opposite; namely, the child becomes the very characteristic he or she is being criticized for—a variation of the self-fulfilling prophecy. Thus, in addition to the pain and sense of rejection caused by constant criticism, permanent damage to our self-concepts can result from chronic verbal abuse.

Besides the hurtful nature of critical words, being shouted at by parental figures strengthens the impact of the criticism and adds further intensity to the attack. Being called "a stupid idiot," for example, in a loud, booming voice (rather than a whisper) conveys a powerful emotional message that is destructive. Furthermore, getting screamed at often feels like our own doing. It is not just that we possess some reprehensible trait that we deserve to be punished for, but we should also feel guilty for upsetting our caretakers. One woman who was both physically and verbally abused as a child recalls having to apologize to her father repeatedly for angering him. On one occasion, he became so enraged when she slammed the door upon arriving home that he kicked her violently. According to her mother, she was to blame for such incidents because her behavior severely upset her father. Thus, not only was the abuse damaging to her self-esteem, but the guilt she experienced about the abuse left her feeling unduly responsible for the behavior of those around her.

## The Tyranny of Abuse

In both verbally and physically abusive households, the fear of being attacked is often a constant terror. Claudia Black, in *It Will Never Happen to Me*,[1] describes the ongoing fear among family members that permeates alcoholic households. Children and spouses are afraid to say much of anything for fear of triggering an abusive attack. Figuratively, they walk around on eggs, slowly and deliberately, lest they become the next victims of an assault. In these households, a great deal of vigilance and accommodation to the demands or whims of the abusive parent are required to survive. Because survival is the dominant concern, the emotional growth of household members is almost totally ignored. In these households, familial intimacy is synonymous with terror, vigilance, accommodation to the tyranny of the abusive parent, neglect, and violence. As an adult, then, the person who grew up in such a household fears that intimate relationships will contain these same ingredients. Having experienced angry outbursts and physical abuse as an integral part of intimacy, they expect their own adult intimate relationships to be tinged with violence. While violence may not beget violence, at the very least it begets the fear of violence.

## Punishment for Badness

In intimacy, the fear of attack may relate directly to past experiences with familial abuse or it may relate to guilt and fears of punishment. We fear attack when we have been criticized repeatedly, physically assaulted, or made to feel guilty for our behavior time and time again. In children, especially between the ages of four and six, fears of attack are manifest directly in their nightmares and in their anxieties about monsters. Children at that age are afraid of sinister, Dracula-type men, witches, and other evil characters along with man-eating animals, such as lions, tigers, and bears. Their fears appear to be manifestations of their concern about being punished for being "bad" in some way, for example, for hitting a sibling, talking back to a parent, or taking another child's toy. Typically, badness has to do with feelings and/or acts of anger, jealousy, or greed. Failure to be considerate, cooperative, or generous also qualifies as bad behavior in our culture.

When we are feeling guilty for whatever reason, we fear that the punishment will be so severe that we will be destroyed. Not only will we be physically and emotionally hurt but our very selves will be annihilated. Thus, fears of attack, when aroused in intimacy, relate more to concerns about self-survival than physical pain. The physical wounds heal but the emotional injuries often persist for a lifetime.

Joan's concerns about intimacy related directly to the fear of being attacked. She was a married, thirty-five-year-old counselor who grew up in a physically abusive, alcoholic home. She came into treatment for depression and emotional alienation from her husband. In her childhood, besides having been physically punished for all sorts of "bad" behavior (slamming doors, not coming instantly when called, not eating all the food on her plate), saying what she thought or felt also had had dire consequences. In these latter instances, she was either beaten with a belt or subjected to an angry stream of verbal abuse, in which she was called names. Joan was also ridiculed repeatedly for being "clumsy," that is, for dropping things, getting dirty, or falling down. Joan's father was the abusive parent mentioned earlier, who had kicked his daughter in the head after knocking her down for slamming a door. For Joan, the safest course of action in her family was to say nothing and be obedient.

When Joan got married, she married a passive, easy-going engineer who appeared to be the antithesis of her father. He was very devoted to Joan but also dependent upon her for approval, nurturance, their social life, and household management. While he seemed to be mild-mannered and eager to please, appearance was deceiving. Her husband, who had also grown up with a strict, dominating, and physically abusive father, had a violent temper. In contrast to his typical manner of dealing with conflict, which was withdrawal, he would erupt occasionally and throw objects across the room or choke Joan, while she was shouting at him. During these short-lived but intense periods of rage, he would terrify Joan, who felt guilty for provoking these rageful attacks by a critical comment. For Joan, intimacy was not an arena where you could speak or move freely, because the consequences were likely to be far too dangerous. Walking on eggs and withdrawal were safer. Fortunately, in the course of couples therapy, Joan and her husband worked out a more adaptive solution to their problems and remain married.

## Fear of Disappointment and Betrayal

Disappointment and betrayal are other painful possibilities in intimacy. While the two are similar, there is an element of deceit in betrayal, whereas in disappointment, there is no attempt at subterfuge. In disappointment, we come to discover certain aspects of the other person that we do not like, or the negatives that we have been aware of take on greater importance over time. For example, we may discover that the person we have chosen has "feet of clay." He or she may not be as strong or as decisive as we had hoped. Our partner may have difficulty taking a stand on any issue and instead may yield passively to whatever prevailing wind is being encountered.

We may be disappointed that the soft, warm young woman we married has a sharp, biting tongue and turns into a shrew at a moment's notice. Or that the strong, rugged he-man is insecure and withdrawn, preferring the company of the TV set to the neighbors. Whenever an intimate partner does not meet our expectations, whether these are realistic or not, there is disappointment. We may be looking for someone to take care of us, be successful for us, or be the life of the party for us. Or we may have hoped to find companionship, only to find that the other is a workaholic who is never at home. Or we may have dreamt of sharing life's responsibilities with someone, only to find that our partner is a "slob" who hates household chores and never hangs up his clothes. If our intimate partners cannot quite meet our requirements, we feel let down and disappointed.

### Garden-Variety Letdowns

Besides the major disappointments in an intimate relationship, there are the humdrum, ordinary kind. She is a sloppy housekeeper, he is a poor conversationalist, he is inept at household repairs, she has no sense of humor, and the list goes on. Very often, the very quality that we are disappointed about is the attribute that we were attracted to in the first place. He may have admired her no-nonsense, solid character but is now bored by her lack of joviality and playfulness. She may have been dazzled by the fact that he was no ordinary, lackluster neighborhood boy, but rather a dreamer with all sorts of exciting plans for their future. Now she complains that he does not have his feet on the ground and does not support her or the kids in the style she had hoped for.

### Disappointment around Every Corner

Because not one of us is perfect, disappointment is an integral part of all intimate relationships. Somewhere along the developmental life of a relationship, we become disenchanted to one degree or another. Whether the disappointments are absorbed and accepted in the light of reality or fester underground, where they may undermine the relationship, is a function of many factors. Among these are the extent and depth of the positive features in the relationship and the importance of the characteristics that we are disappointed about.

For example, if we highly value a particular quality, such as intelligence, good looks, or moral integrity, and our partner is lacking in that feature, the degree of disappointment would be high. Conversely, if the lacking characteristic is viewed as having minor significance, the disappointment would be mitigated by an appreciation of the other's sterling attributes.

Individual differences in values play an enormous role in determining which characteristics in the other person are important. For some people, the intimate partner must possess "strength of character" because that quality is viewed as the very foundation of a relationship. When this is the case, any behavior that suggests character weakness, such as smoking, excessive drinking, or not paying bills on time, would be reacted to with strong negative feelings, including disappointment. For a person for whom strength of character is an insignificant issue, that same behavior might be viewed as "humanness" or seen in some other neutral light. Others who value playfulness and good humor in intimacy would be disappointed by stodginess or unremitting seriousness. Still others who regard kindness and nurturance as the sustaining attributes would find cruelty and/or self-centeredness as significant sources of disappointment. Clearly, the extent of disappointment is a function of our values.

## How Realistic Are We?

The extent of disappointment is also a function of how realistic our expectations are. If we had expected our partner to be eternally patient, loving, or always understanding, then we are doomed to be highly disappointed. For it is obvious that no one can be so highly tuned to our needs that they are always there for us. At times, they are preoccupied with their own problems and want to be left alone. At other times, they misread our signals and react in ways opposite to what we had hoped.

The extent to which unrealistically based disappointment can undermine a relationship is illustrated dramatically by Bill's case. His disappointment with his second wife began almost from the first day of his marriage when he showed his wife a copy of the divorce proceedings from his first marriage. Bill had hoped that his wife would be supportive of him and critical of his ex-wife. Instead, she was silent and thought to herself, "When is he going to forget all that bitterness?" Interpreting her silence as rejection, he became very disappointed and withdrew. Three months later when depression and insomnia began to overwhelm him, he and his wife came into couples therapy.

For Bill, disappointment in his second wife was a bitter pill that he felt he had to swallow. He was disappointed that his wife was sometimes "prickly" (irritable) and not available on a twenty-four-hour basis (she traveled frequently as part of her job). Underlying his disappointment was the expectation that his second wife be the loving, giving, and nonangry woman that he remembered his mother being when he was a small boy.

While his mother may have been the perfect woman for a period in his life, she was the original source of disappointment. Having had an unusually close relationship with Bill for his first seven years, she sided with her husband against him when her husband returned from the war. Her husband (Bill's father) had been stationed in another country during the first years of Bill's life. Upon his return home, he developed an antagonistic and hostile relationship with his only son, ending forever Bill's idyllic relationship with his mother. The memory of a perfectly available and loving woman (prior to the reappearance of his father) formed the basis of Bill's adult expectations of women.

The more our expectations are constructed to make up for childhood disappointments, the more unrealistic they tend to be. If our childhood disappointments were severe, we may have said to ourselves, "I'll never marry anyone like him (or her)." The determination to find an intimate partner with a personality opposite to that of the disappointing parent results in the construction of an ideal image against which our all-too-human partners are compared. Since the yardstick is an idealized person, all earthly applicants will fail to measure up. For example, if a parent was angry and abusive, we may be determined to marry someone who is always patient and kind. The problem arises when the easygoing and gentle partner becomes angry (which is bound to occur in all relationships). At these times, the sense of disappointment can be profound.

The extent to which the image of the "ideal partner" can be unrealistic and cause disappointment in intimate relationships is illustrated in Roberta's case. Roberta, a university faculty member in her midforties, came into therapy because of a drinking problem and marital unhappiness. She complained bitterly about her husband's lack of ambition, intellectual mediocrity, social ineptitude, and passivity. According to Roberta, her husband was miles away from an ideal partner. In her fantasies, her ideal soulmate, who was "nothing like her abusive father," was a combination of her own valued qualities—superior intelligence, ambition, and interpersonal sensitivity—plus several characteristics that were admired in the favorite men from her early life. For example, both her favorite grandfather and uncle were jovial men with quick wit and a teasing style of humor. Also, in her family, blond hair and blue eyes were viewed as desirable physical traits.

Not surprisingly, then, the love of her life turned out to be a blond, blue-eyed man of intelligence, ambition, and interpersonal sensitivity who teased her regularly. She had met him in her early twenties when they were both married. While the intensity of her emotional and sexual attraction toward him suggested that this was a merger made in heaven, it was only after they attempted a real relationship (after he was divorced from his first wife and she briefly separated from her husband) that she discovered his duplicity. While they were seeing each other, he continued to pursue secretly a relationship with another woman. Also, he tended to be more attracted to younger women who had strong feelings of inadequacy—relationships where he could be superior. Thus, she discovered that her "ideal man" had feet of clay in areas that overshadowed all of his sterling attributes.

## Second Time Around

For those people whose first marriages have failed, the fear of being disappointed the second time around can be acute and can act as a deterrent to a second commitment. The fear of making the same mistake—picking another ambivalent man, another alcoholic or unfaithful wife—can be immobilizing. Howard, a highly successful advertising executive in his midthirties, sought counseling because of the panic he experienced in a new love relationship that had marriage potential. An extroverted and ambitious man, he was unprepared for the anxiety he was experiencing about a woman he adored.

Howard had been divorced for five years from a chronically unhappy woman who did not want the divorce and who continued to blame him for her depression. The sense of disappointment in his first wife was experienced as a gradual, eroding process as he found himself less and less eager to return home from business trips. In contrast to his business associates, he found her dull and intellectually limited. His fear of being disappointed again was the major factor in his reluctance to tie the knot once more.

## The Kiss of Judas

Can I trust my partner? Will I be lied to, tricked, taken advantage of, deserted in a moment of need, seduced, or used in some way? In short, will I be betrayed? While the term "betrayal" denotes a serious act (the first definition of betrayal in the dictionary is "to deliver to an enemy by treachery or fraud"), interpersonal violations are commonplace. The "little white lie" used to cover up a momentary indiscretion, reneging on a promise, or poking fun at our partner are also forms of betrayal. Whether deadly or small, all acts of betrayal are basically breaches of trust, violations of an implicit or explicit contract. Something important that was needed, promised, or expected did not get delivered, not because of benign neglect, but because of blatant insensitivity and deceit.

Perhaps we had hoped to be loved and cherished. Instead, we found ourselves duped, seduced, or led along some other garden path. As children, we may have hoped (and reasonably expected) to be protected by a parent who instead used us to gratify sexual whims. Or, as adults, we counted on fidelity to be an integral part of the marriage contract, only to be betrayed and lied to.

There are still other kinds of betrayal. We may confide our worst failings or our darkest secrets and have the information used against us in some way. The possibility exists that we will be laughed at or ridiculed, or that others will be told about our weaknesses. We will be the laughingstock of our neighborhoods, churches, companies, or towns. In a moment of anger or indiscretion, our confidential disclosures may be thrown back in our faces—"You *are* afraid of your own shadow." The angry words are echoes of our own disclosure of days or months gone by. And we are left with a sense of betrayal.

One woman with intense fears about intimacy believed that if she loved too much (went out of her way to please another), the other would take advantage of her. This "being taken advantage of" could be anything from letting her carry all the burdens in the relationship (do all the cleaning, cooking, or disciplining of children) or having extramarital affairs. In her own childhood, her father abandoned the family when she was six years old and ran off with another woman. Her mother was seen as "loving too much," with the painful and damaging consequence of being deserted as the outcome of her devotion.

## Infidelity and Incest as Betrayal

Infidelity results in its own particular pain and damage to self-esteem. What seems to be hardest hit in infidelity is sexual identity and sexual worth. The partner's infidelity is typically interpreted as a sign of our own sexual failure. The betrayed partner feels that he or she is missing a vital sexual ingredient—innate sex appeal, sufficient sex drive, or finely honed bedroom skills. The rejected partner often feels that he or she does not have what it takes to keep a partner faithful—"I'm just not sexy enough" is a lament frequently heard. The blow to sexual self-worth is often devastating.

What is difficult for the rejected partner to grasp is that the sexual betrayal may be entirely (or in part) a reflection of the unfaithful partner's own insecurities and instability, not a measure of the betrayed's sexual adequacy. Because infidelity has many causes, the determination of those factors operating in a given instance is an arduous and often time-consuming task.

Incest is another form of betrayal that is particularly damaging, especially when it occurs between parents and their young children, according to Christine Courtois, author of *Healing the Incest Wound*.[2] In an incestuous relationship, the abusing parent fails to protect the child from harm and thus betrays the child's trust. In addition, the abusing parent creates a situation that fosters confusion, helplessness, and guilt in the child. As a result, the child often has difficulty in distinguishing between affection, aggression, and sex. Frequently, the child becomes alienated from his or her own emotions and bodily sensations. Overstimulated emotionally and unable to make sense of the incest experience, the child is left feeling damaged, used, and unloved. One incest survivor saw herself as a "broken porcelain doll"—the image reflecting both her views of self as an object and the damage inflicted upon her.

Fear of betrayal was a dominant concern of Kay, a lobbyist who had avoided a committed relationship for most of her thirty-seven years. Compared to Kay's competent professional and interpersonal level of functioning, her long-term, intimate relationships were with socially and emotionally inappropriate men, who were either married, serious drug users, or marginally employed. She was an intelligent, outgoing, and self-reliant woman in the political arena who had not been interested in marriage until she met Bob.

Love at first sight for both of them led to a whirlwind romantic courtship that appeared to be headed for the altar almost from the beginning. However, three weeks before the wedding was to take place, a prenuptial agreement, in which Kay was to renounce her right to Bob's estate in the event of his death, arrived unexpectedly on her doorstep. A prenuptial agreement had never been discussed up to that point in time. Because they could not agree on terms, the wedding was called off.

In the months following the wedding date, they tried to resume their relationship. However, each time they got close, Bob would lie about his whereabouts or refuse to take Kay along to a social event that he had been invited to. What had been a romantic and caring union became a stormy and unpredictable contest of wills as Bob's fear of intimacy surfaced. Bob's distancing maneuvers (the white lies and his insistence on going alone to certain social events) were met by frantic despair on Kay's part. She was shocked by these violations of their closeness and viewed these transgressions as acts of betrayal.

In Kay's own family of origin, her father's ongoing infidelity was the main source of family conflict and instability. The hurt and outrage her mother experienced when she discovered anew her husband's betrayals were similar to the intense feelings Kay experienced when disappointed by Bob. Sensitized to betrayal on the part of men in her childhood, this particular issue was the raw nerve, the vulnerable Achilles' heel, that she had tried to protect in the past by avoiding heterosexual intimacy. As long as she pursued inappropriate and unavailable men, she was safe. It was only with Bob, who appeared on the surface to be emotionally available and socially appropriate, that her concern about betrayal emerged.

## Fear of Guilt

The breast-beating "forgive me for it's all my fault" stance that becomes manifest in some people when they are involved in intimacy is a grueling, humiliating posture. Because begging for forgiveness is demeaning when it occurs regularly, guilt and relationships tend to be avoided like the plague. Guilt may be regarded as a sense of distress (or sense of badness) that occurs when we overstep or abuse our power in some way. In contrast to shame, which is typically experienced in response to real or imagined inadequacies, guilt implies an attitude or action that is excessive—too angry, too intrusive, too demanding, or too self-centered. In guilt, we have gone "too far" rather than not far enough.

We can feel guilty about our angry outbursts, our single-minded pursuit of our career, our lack of commitment to a relationship, or about almost anything. As one fifty-five-year-old man said about his relationships, "When I get too close and something goes wrong, I'm always blaming myself no matter whose fault it is." One of the dangers in intimacy for him is taking on all of the responsibility for the success or failure of the relationship. His intrapunitive style (blaming oneself rather than the other) makes it difficult for him to share the responsibility for the relationship's problems.

Others experience guilt when they withdraw from a "loving partner" (someone who appears on the surface to be caring, responsible, and trustworthy). When they reject the other, they believe that there must be something wrong with them if they cannot appreciate the other's fine qualities. One woman who came in for counseling about depression and weight gain said that her husband "didn't deserve a skinny wife" because he was indecisive and passive. She also said that she did not deserve to be thin because she could not accept him with his limitations. In this and countless other ways, guilt rears its ugly head.

### Need to Love Those Who Love Us

When we do not love someone as much as they seem to love us, we may feel guilty and compelled to love back in some way. The guilt is often related to our belief that we are too self-centered and incapable of loving another. In essence, we may believe that we are defective in our capacity to love. Our belief about our limited ability to return love further adds to our sense of inadequacy. And so, we redouble our efforts to love back. Our sense of duty, justice, and religion decrees that we should love those who love us. Not reciprocating love feels callous and indifferent. At some level, we believe that anyone who rejects the positive things in life, such as love, is destined to lose what he or she has. Thus, the compulsion to return love is born, transforming any natural stirring of affection into a guilt-ridden force.

When we are feeling distant or unhappy with someone who looks good on the surface, guilt can prevent any kind of action from taking place. A fifty-year-old woman described years of marital unhappiness with a man who was intelligent, faithful, and hard-working but emotionally distant and stingy. A good provider financially, he was nonetheless emotionally withdrawn and unresponsive to her needs. For years his only apparent reaction to her many complaints about his emotional unavailability was stony silence. However, she could not leave him because "he had many virtues and loved her." It was only after he became enraged about her complaints on one occasion (after years of swallowing his resentment) and broke her ribs that she felt justified in leaving him. The broken ribs were a tangible manifestation of his limitations—one that could not easily be refuted by well-meaning friends and relatives, who would regularly intone, "But he's loyal and dependable."

## Confused Motives

Getting involved in a relationship when we are unclear about our motives frequently leads to guilt. We may have gotten involved because of loneliness, sexual need, depression, insecurity, or the need to prove our desirability, only to find that the other is very much "in love" or dependent upon us. We may have wanted a one-night stand or simply someone to talk to, when suddenly we are in over our heads. The other person wants or needs much more than we are willing to give. An inner voice chides us with the familiar words "You should have known better." We feel guilty for leading the other person on, for misleading the other into thinking that more things were possible in the relationship than are true. Guilt, the burden borne out of our imperfections, lies heavily on our shoulders and casts a pall on intimacy.

The role of guilt in intimacy is illustrated in Ann's case. Ann was an energetic, twenty-seven-year-old career woman in the marketing field who came into therapy because of high levels of stress. The high degree of tension began to concern her when it started to interfere with her sleep, her concentration, and her work productivity. An ambitious, conscientious woman with a strong need to be perfect, she was also highly self-critical. As her anxiety level rose, so did her self-criticality, which made it even more difficult for her to cope.

While Ann's anxiety seemed related to work pressures (she was in a highly demanding job situation), her panic began the day after a particularly disappointing date. The man whom she had been dating for six months or so had behaved in an ambivalent manner the previous evening, which left her feeling confused about his intentions. While this one disappointment would have been easy enough to absorb at another time in her life, coming as it did on top of other dating frustrations, it left her reeling.

Since high school, Ann's dating relationships were marked by feelings of either rejection or guilt. It appeared as if there were only two possible scripts in her dating life. Either she was rejected in favor of a competitor or she was doing the rejecting. When rejected, she was left feeling inadequate in relation to other women. When rejecting, she also felt "not good enough."

In the latter instance, however, the "not good enough" was a moral indictment. She believed that she was not sufficiently loving, kind, or generous whenever she ended any relationship, even the most disturbed. She firmly believed that her task as a Christian woman was to "love the least of my brethren," even if that meant sacrificing her own mental health in the process. Thus, ending a romantic relationship with a high school sweetheart who became a heavy drug user left her racked with endless self-recrimination. Because the two choices in intimacy—risking rejection or guilt—

were both negative, intimacy began to feel like an aversive experience. Fortunately, over the course of her therapy, she came to envision intimacy as a land of many more possibilities.

## Fear of Rejection and Abandonment

Underlying all of the other risks in intimacy is the most basic of intimacy fears, namely, fear of rejection and abandonment. While there are a few people who are able to withstand rejection without much discomfort, being rejected is a painful experience for the vast majority of us. Rejection is usually interpreted as a sign that something is wrong with us—we are not pretty enough, sexy enough, masculine enough, interesting enough, and so on. Because rejection is a fundamental threat to our sense of self-worth, we live in fear of that injury. Attention and approval validate us; inattention, disapproval, and rejection have the opposite effect. The degree of invalidation, however, is directly related to our degree of self-esteem. The more secure we are, the less intense will be the pain associated with any rejection, even rejection by the most important people in our lives. The degree of pain is also related to the nature of rejection itself. Rejection can take many forms and can range in intensity from withdrawal of attention (being ignored) to actual physical desertion or abandonment.

### Attention as Lifeblood

The most common form of rejection is the absence of attention, that is, being ignored. We may be in emotional turmoil, physical pain, or simply in need of conversation only to find our partner absent in some way. Whether the other is preoccupied with his or her own thoughts, a project, or another person is immaterial, for what matters is that the other person is not there for us. Something else (TV, computer, alcohol, the family dog) has been chosen in preference to us and we are left alone with our needs.

"He never even notices me—I might as well be part of the woodwork for all the attention I get" communicates poignantly the pain of being ignored repeatedly. With chronic inattention, we begin to question our worth. If we cannot elicit basic attentiveness, we wonder whether we have any value at all.

Rejection of our needs, desires, and feelings also hurts. Being told that we have no right to feel something, that we are too sensitive or insecure, is a source of pain. "You shouldn't feel angry at your brother—that's not nice!" or "You shouldn't cry!" or "You're a big baby!" are common examples of parental rejection familiar to all of us.

## One-Sided Relationships

Being talked at without our opinions being asked, being seduced without regard for our own sexual needs, or otherwise being treated as a nonperson without ideas, feelings, and beliefs of our own are forms of inattention and rejection. In all one-sided relationships, one partner winds up feeling unknown and, as a consequence, uncared about. "How can she love me if she doesn't know who I am?" is a valid question. For in order to feel cared about, we must first of all feel known. If we are not known, the love someone is showering on us feels like it belongs to someone else or is ours only under certain restricted conditions, such as when we are being good, clever, or pretty. Being known is a precondition for feeling loved, and conversely, being unknown in a relationship is synonymous with rejection.

One woman worked for a man who talked to her for hours on end about his weekend activities, his children, and the books he was reading. Never in the course of the monologue did he ask her about her weekend or about any other aspect of her life. When she finally mustered up the courage to throw some minor aspects of her life into the "conversation," he totally ignored them. Her comments about the movie she saw or the cousin who was visiting were met with a brief silence followed by a further elaboration of his activities. Not only did she feel unknown and rejected but her own irritation at his insensitivity made it difficult for her to attend to his ramblings.

## Losing the Battle to Alcohol

Adults who grew up in alcoholic homes have special difficulties with relationships because they were ignored repeatedly in favor of the bottle. Not understanding the nature of addiction, the children of alcoholics cannot fathom why a parent would prefer alcohol to them. The only explanation that makes sense is that there is something fundamentally wrong with the children themselves (not with their parents, because parents are viewed as wiser, more knowledgeable, better, and kinder than they are). That perceived failing may be badness, selfishness, or stupidity, but whatever it is, it helps to explain the alcoholic parent's lack of attentiveness. Claudia Black, who has written extensively about adult children of alcoholics, describes in detail the excessive guilt and self-blame of these children.[3] The child of an alcoholic parent not only fears rejection for its own sake but also the painful self-blaming and self-deprecating state the rejection elicits. In other words, where there is rejection, not far behind are guilt and worthlessness.

## Alone Again

While all the fears and risks involved in intimacy are painful, the ultimate rejection, of course, is being deserted. With all of the other fears and risks, there is some hope of healing and recovery for the relationship. If we are hurt, betrayed, or disappointed, we can get over it. However, if we are abandoned, a death knell is ordinarily sounded for the relationship. It is over and we are alone again.

People stay in all sorts of destructive relationships because of their fears related to being abandoned and alone. The battered wife and alcoholic spouse put up with years of emotional abuse before finally leaving the marital bed (and some are never able to do so). The fear of being unable to survive alone, either financially or emotionally, is widespread. One woman, in talking about life without her husband, asked incredulously, "How am I going to get up in the morning without him?" While her husband actually woke her up for work every morning, she was not asking the literal question but rather wondering how she was going to structure her life without him. She was concerned about how she was going to deal with the emptiness in her life, the painful aloneness.

## Can We Survive?

The fear of abandonment relates to anxieties about survival in childhood. When we were little children, our very lives depended upon our caretakers; we were unable to take care of ourselves without them. In intimate adult relationships, particularly those that are highly dependent, the fear of abandonment is reactivated whenever the partner becomes distant. In these instances, we worry about our emotional survival should our partner abandon us. For those adults whose childhoods were marked by traumatic separation or desertion, the fear of abandonment is especially intense.

Dorothy, whose fears of intimacy revolved around abandonment, smothering, loss of control, and betrayal, came to psychotherapy because of panic attacks that reemerged after her second wedding. During the first session, she reported that she felt generally unsafe and that this feeling had increased in severity after her father died several weeks earlier. She had said to her husband the day before that she "shouldn't have married him because he knew her too well," implying that his knowledge of her made her too vulnerable. Most of her concern was that he would find someone more attractive and leave, just as her father had done when she was six years old. Dorothy, her identical twin sister, an infant sister, and her mother were all deserted when her father ran off with a "beautiful woman."

Dorothy's panic attacks began the day after she became engaged to her first husband and continued throughout her first seven-year marriage. Her fears in that marriage were identical to those she was currently experiencing. When she was single or divorced, she was outgoing, confident, and free of debilitating anxiety. Thus, it was clear that her vulnerability and insecurity became aroused only when she made a marriage commitment.

Dorothy's panic attacks were most likely to occur at or in anticipation of social gatherings (parties and conferences) where other women were around. These occasions, which ordinarily were pleasurable to her, became dangerous settings where the possibility of betrayal lurked around every corner. She feared that she could not compete with other women and that her husband did not have the willpower to successfully withstand seduction attempts. Thus, men were seen as weak and untrustworthy and women were perceived as seductive and strongly competitive. In this kind of sexual competition, Dorothy feared that she was not good enough, unique enough, or pretty enough to win out. Her fear that she was, in fact, replaceable seemed to derive directly from being an identical twin, whom most people easily confused with her sister. Her father's promiscuity also contributed significantly to her belief that people were interchangeable.

Dorothy early was given the role of "the older, responsible mother's helper" by her mother, who was overwhelmed by being left with three small children. As a result, Dorothy saw herself as smarter and more responsible than her twin sister (she was, in fact, the older by a few minutes). As to which twin was more attractive, Dorothy was conflicted about that. Apparently, her twin sister was more seductive and popular with the boys during adolescence. However, Dorothy was "Daddy's favorite." This bittersweet victory resulted in her father being more important to Dorothy than to her sisters, with the consequence that his loss (both at age six and again at his death) was more painful to her than to them.

While distrustful of men and fearful that they would "take advantage" in some way, Dorothy was also envious of them. She was envious of their greater freedom, power, and advantages. An ardent feminist, she was hypersensitive to chauvinistic attitudes on every front. In her relationship with her second husband, she was overtly competitive and envious of his role as "the good guy" with their kids (he was more uncomfortable with conflict and enjoyed a more easygoing role than she did).

In an intimate relationship, Dorothy believed there was no way of being happy, because disasters (betrayal and abandonment) were potentially everywhere. She also believed that she did not deserve happiness because she was "bad" in some way (for her, badness was synonymous with anger). While believing that danger was inevitable, she also felt paradoxically that she was responsible for warding it off. Her hypervigilance at social gatherings with her husband (constant checking of the environment to see who was noticing whom) was both a means of confirming her worst fears and an attempt to control her fate by preventing danger. She also believed that interpersonal failures, especially angry outbursts, led to disastrous consequences and so tried to pursue a very cautious and repressed road in intimate relationships.

Dorothy illustrates the dramatic differences in attitude, feeling, and behavior that can occur between a Social Self and an Intimate Self. Ordinarily, Dorothy was a spontaneous, witty, outgoing, sensitive, highly intelligent, and motivated woman who enjoyed intellectual pursuits. A competent professional woman, she had many interests, enjoyed talking with people, and also found solitude restorative. The frightened, suspicious, and insecure little girl was nowhere in evidence in her daily life as she pursued her mothering role (she had a fifteen-year-old son from her first marriage), her professional life, and her friendships with energy and vigor. It was only when she was involved in a committed sexual and emotional relationship with a man that her fears and vulnerabilities surfaced. Fortunately, she was able to resolve her fears in the course of treatment and maintain a healthy, mutually beneficial second marriage.

The basic fear in intimacy is that we will be dropped, rejected, or abandoned and that it will *hurt*. As one woman said, "I invest everything (it's all or nothing for me); then when it's over, it's very painful. Once I cried for a solid two weeks." Another woman commented, "I will get strongly attached and the affection won't be reciprocated—it will be wasted and I'll feel foolish and hurt." The emotional pain of rejection and consequent damage to our self-esteem are difficult for most of us to handle. Unless we are very secure, rejection leaves us with some serious doubts about how lovable or worthwhile we really are. While most of us eventually recover from the trauma of rejection, the self-esteem damage can last a lifetime for some individuals.

*Chapter 4*

# Reaching for the Stars

---

In *The Unbearable Lightness of Being*, Milan Kundera contrasts the love of the central female character (Tereza) for her dog (Karenin) with the love adult human beings typically have for each other:

> It is a completely selfless love. Tereza did not want anything of Karenin; she did not ever ask him to love her back. Nor had she ever asked herself the questions that plague human couples: Does he love me? Does he love anyone more than me? Does he love me more than I love him? Perhaps all the questions we ask of love, to measure, test, probe, and save it, have the additional effect of cutting it short. Perhaps the reason we are unable to love is that we yearn to be loved, that is, we demand something (love) from our partner instead of delivering ourselves up to him demand-free and asking for nothing but his company.[1]

In short, Kundera sees the problem with human love as stemming from our constant questioning and evaluation of the love that is being offered us; from our loving with demand, that is, wanting something back; from our attempts to make over our lovers in our own images; and from the fact that we often feel compelled to love. Why are we so insecure about the love we get? And why do we expect so much in return for the love we give?

## Insecurities about Love

In looking at the familial roots of our insecurities, it is obvious that even in the best of families, we were loved imperfectly. We were not loved all of the time. Some of the time, our parents were angry with us. Some of the time, they ignored us. Typically, their lives did not revolve around us. They had their own jobs, their own friends, and their own problems. If we were lucky, we wound up feeling special and worthwhile. Not superhuman or perfect or "the center of the universe," but special. One woman whose parents got married late in life and who were ecstatic when she arrived on the scene described herself as a "precious bundle." She felt special because she was precious to the first people in her life.

A lot of us, however, wound up not feeling special enough. We did not feel unique in any way. We felt conditionally loved; that is, we were loved only if we behaved in certain ways. If we were good, cheerful, or smart, then we merited affection. However, if we were disobedient, angry, or stupid, then we were not worth loving. Out of her own irritation, one mother said to her daughter, "Nobody is going to love you if you're so angry." The message was clear—only if she was cheerful was she worth loving. So gradually she, like most of us, learned that we are lovable only under certain conditions. And if someone appears to love us totally, we doubt the sincerity of the love or discredit the wisdom of the lover.

### *The Social Self: A Safe and Limited Arena*

Accompanying the knowledge of our conditional lovability is the creation of a social or public personality, which consists of rather limited and rigid interpersonal patterns. Rather than displaying the richness and variety of our perceptions, thoughts, and feelings with others, we restrict our manner of being to a few safe interpersonal styles—those that were approved of by parents and consist of our sterling qualities, such as generosity, altruism, or optimism. The unsafe or discarded parts of the self are those attributes that were disapproved of by parental figures. We reason, if our family could not accept the unlovable parts of us, how can we expect our friends to do so?

While our public personality is created for the benefit of others, this social facade can become, unfortunately, the self we identify with. In other words, we can grow to see ourselves as possessing only those qualities that were designed for public consumption. For example, if kindness was rewarded and angry behavior punished, we could see ourselves as having only loving thoughts and feelings toward others. The negative aspects of ourselves, or angry feelings in this case, would then be disowned and either buried or projected onto others. This lack of self-knowledge can have all sorts of damaging consequences, both for ourselves and others. Paranoid behavior, eating disorders, and psychosomatic symptoms are among the many pathological results of minimal or distorted self-knowledge.

## Hiding the Unacceptable

Others, while not identifying with their public personalities, feel that they cannot show the negative sides of themselves to anyone, not even their closest friends. They cannot be crabby, cynical, or depressed because they believe no one could accept them with their emotional blemishes. "Who wants to be around someone who's unhappy?" is a frequently asked question by those who live by the "put on a happy face" philosophy of interpersonal relationships. Because of their own histories, they are convinced that their lovability is contingent upon their behaving in certain ways. And when they do not feel like behaving in those ways, they isolate themselves. Ashamed of feeling depressed or lonely, they hide away like lepers in self-imposed exile. They would rather be by themselves than reach out to friends and relatives. For them, loneliness and depression are not fit for public scrutiny.

## Wish for Unconditional Love

As a result of our being loved conditionally and then creating inauthentic social roles with which to relate to most people, we are left with a powerful need to be loved unconditionally. Fundamentally, we wish to be loved and accepted no matter what we do. To be understood when angry, cherished when lonely, and comforted when disappointed are the ingredients of interpersonal Nirvana for most of us.

Carl Rogers, the father of client-centered therapy, viewed unconditional positive regard as one of the facilitating conditions for therapeutic change.[2] He defined unconditional positive acceptance as a warm regard for another person, a valuing of the other no matter what his or her condition, behavior, or feelings. It is essentially a nonjudgmental, noncritical, nonblaming, and loving stance. The fact that this attitude is effective in counseling suggests that it resonates with an important longing in all of us. John Welwood, in an article about the potency of love, wrote "Unconditional love has tremendous power, activating a larger energy which connects us with the vastness and profundity of what it is to be human."[3] He saw unconditional love as touching and flowing from the most tender and vulnerable parts of our personalities.

Powerful and primitive, the wish to be loved unconditionally appears to be a basic human need. Typically, however, this need lies dormant. The rational, reasonable side of our personality is in control as we move through our daily lives. Rationally, we have come to accept other people's limitations insofar as their ability to love us is concerned. We know that they cannot understand what we need unless we tell them. We have learned that they cannot be accepting of us if what we do is a source of conflict for them. We realize that they cannot pay attention if they are preoccupied with something else. We have learned these interpersonal lessons well. And yet, in spite of these realistic considerations, the wish to be loved unconditionally remains. To be loved for oneself, warts and all, remains a poignant and powerful yearning.

## The Intimate Zone

The double standard—knowing what is reasonable to expect, and yet expecting the unreasonable—operates in all of us to one degree or another. We are reasonable with our friends and acquaintances, but with our intimate partners we want it all. Once a person has crossed over the line into our intimate zone, he or she becomes the object of our more basic emotional needs. "Didn't you know that I was tired and wanted to be left alone today?" "How could you even think that I wanted them over tonight?" "Didn't you know that I would never have said that to her?" "Couldn't you have taken the kids outside when I told you how harassed I was all day?" We want to be perfectly known and perfectly loved.

These dysfunctional patterns of communication stem from the dual wishes of wanting to be known and loved perfectly. The vague communicator, the overgeneralizer, and the mind-reading seeker all expect to be understood perfectly, even though their messages are garbled and unclear. The person who says, "You know what I mean," while omitting significant details of the story, expects the intimate partner to fill in the gaps. The overgeneralizer, who says, "You *never* pay attention to me," or "*All* men are insensitive," expects that her partner will understand the depths of frustration and the range of upsetting experiences that led to those sweeping conclusions. The mind-reading seeker, whose favorite utterance is, "You should have known what I wanted," hopes that his needs will be understood to such a degree that he will not have to utter a word.

## Need for Nurturance

The wish to be understood and loved perfectly is often accompanied by a related desire, that is, the wish to be taken care of. At times we want to be comforted, reassured, and/or relieved of adult responsibilities. At its most basic level, however, being taken care of has to do with physical and psychological nourishment. In intimacy, we want to be fed, both literally and symbolically. Not only do we need food for our bodies, but we need praise and recognition for our efforts. We want to be appreciated for all the effort we expend and the struggles we experience as we go through our daily lives.

The connection between love and nourishment is a deep and powerfully forged bond that was established in the earliest days of our infancy. Our mothers fed us, held us, and comforted us when we were in pain. As adults, we are reminded of the love-food connection by many images and references, among them family gatherings replete with food-laden tables, romantic dinners for two, and phrases such as "The way to a man's heart is through his stomach." The Christian Communion wafer is a visible manifestation of the love-food connection in that the wafer is believed to be the Body of Christ given out of love as food for the world. Intrinsic to love, then, is nourishment, which we have come to expect from our closest relationships.

## Wanting to Be Held

Another component of being taken care of is physical contact. Being held, stroked, petted, or touched are all pleasurable and soothing acts. The importance of tactile gratification in infancy on adult development was demonstrated by Harry Harlow's work with monkeys. The monkeys who were deprived of physical contact with their mothers manifested disturbed behavior as adults, including mating difficulty.[4] Likewise, children who experienced early maternal deprivation manifest depression and other emotional ills throughout their lives.

In adulthood, physical contact and comforting, reminiscent of our infancy days when cuddling was synonymous with need gratification and love, continue to be sources of pleasure and stress reduction for all of us. Whenever we are feeling vulnerable or overwhelmed by the cares of the world, nothing is quite as soothing as being held. One woman who was overwhelmed by the daylong care of her colicky infant daughter simply wanted to be held by her husband when he came home from work each evening. Unfortunately, he was more interested in holding his daughter than his wife at that time and could not relate to his wife's exhaustion and need for physical contact.

In intense grief and physical or emotional pain, words are pale substitutes for physical contact in providing comfort. Because physical holding and caressing have their roots in our early sense of security, physical contact is decidedly more soothing than verbal reassurance. Likewise, a warm bear hug in greeting provides more of an emotional connection than even the warmest of words.

## Wish for Constancy

Another aspect of the wish for nurturance is constancy. We want our intimate partners to be nurturant in a predictable, dependable manner. Our partner's ongoing emotional availability is important to our psychological well-being. The frequent complaints "He's never there for me" or "He can't find time for me" speak to the frustration experienced when our intimate partners are not regularly available. Being able to count on someone to meet our daily and often mundane needs is intrinsic to the development of trust and stability in a relationship.

## Longing to Be Passive

The longing to be taken care of often lies buried in the deepest and earliest levels of our personalities. Surfacing in some people only when they are physically ill or highly stressed, this yearning to be passive and nurtured is often experienced as a childlike and regressive wish—the antithesis of maturity. And yet, being a responsible adult 100 percent of the time is impossible work that requires occasional respites.

The wish to be taken care of is regularly manifest in the symptomatic behaviors that characterize certain psychiatric classifications. The hypochondriac with multifaceted ills, the alcoholic with alcohol-induced passivity, and the depressed person with a low energy level all wear their passive longings on their sleeves, so to speak. Crying out for nurturance, the symptomatic person seeks out soup kitchens, psychiatric hospitals, and other sympathetic listeners to help provide care.

What about the rest of us? How do our wishes to be cared for get attended to? In the years before the Women's Liberation Movement, men were cared for by their traditional wives, who cooked, cleaned, and ironed shirts for them. In those days, women got taken care of by their strong, dominating husbands, who paid bills, drove the car, and handled the outside world for them. A kind of quid pro quo contract was established where each person's dependency needs were handled by the traditional sex-role behavior of the partner.

In today's age with its blurred sex roles and with each sex aspiring to be all things to all people, the wish to be taken care of gets buried, only to be gratified erratically when we collapse into illness. Influenza, allergies, "the common cold," mental health days, and vacations allow us, in a culturally acceptable way, to gratify our passive longings.

Another way to be passive in today's society is in front of the TV set. During hours of nightly TV watching, we do not have to move a muscle or activate many brain cells. The state of half-hearted attention required by most TV shows does not necessitate the expenditure of much physical or emotional energy. While TV does not provide much nurturance or protection, it does allow us to function as passive creatures. In essence, it allows us to rest— to suspend adult functions for a period of time—and feel gratified.

## Wish for Protection

The wish to be protected is another longing that gets stirred up in intimacy. We want to be protected from danger, assault, intrusion, or exposure. We want someone to act as a shield between us and all those aspects of the world that are unpleasant or dangerous. We also want someone to set limits for us, to protect us from our own unbridled and dangerous impulses, such as gambling, drinking too much, or otherwise acting in a self-destructive manner.

In our infancy and toddler days, we needed our parents to protect us from a whole host of dangerous possibilities, such as falling from heights, being hit by cars, eating poisonous food, or putting our fingers in electrical outlets. As adults, our needs for protection are often less physical in nature, but more complicated psychologically than they were in our infancy. For example, the psychological danger of verbal assault or criticism is a daily possibility as we spend most of our days on the front line in the world of work. Failure, rejection, and stimulus overload are other commonplace dangers that we encounter daily. While these daily perils are often unapparent in our conscious thoughts, these dangers abound in our nighttime dreams where we are scratched by cats, stung by bees, or bitten by dogs.

## Keeping the World at Bay

What kind of protection from these dangers do we yearn for? Mostly, we want to be freed from additional demands when drained so that we can replenish our own resources. When we need peace and quiet, we want our intimate partners to keep the world at bay, to act as intermediaries between us and the world's intrusions (e.g., "Tell them I can't come to the phone right now, dear!"). When we are distraught and vulnerable, we want our intimate partner to function like a good secretary in screening the outside world and permitting only important callers and correspondence to have access to us.

One woman in therapy reported that she only felt protected as a child when her father was home. An imaginative child who grew up in a chaotic, alcoholic household, she needed protection from the monsters that filled her nighttime hours. Her father's large imposing presence in the house felt like her only salvation against these night terrors. Her mother's smaller size and less commanding manner seemed inadequate in coping with gigantic creatures from another world. Like many women today, this woman felt protected only with a man around the house. Without a man, her life felt empty and unsafe in some fundamental manner.

## Desire to Be Special

In addition to being understood, totally accepted, cared about, and protected, we want to be special to our intimate partners. In fact, for many of us, "special" means the most important person or thing in our partner's life, more important than work, parents, or children. Second best will not do, especially if second or third best were painful positions in our families of origin.

Whenever a sibling or parent was the family superstar on a regular basis, we were left feeling inferior. The contrast between our rival's exalted status and the attention we received typically resulted in a resentful sense of inadequacy about our own worth. Siblings or parents who are very talented, good-looking, or brilliant are tough acts to follow because of the high standards for self-comparison that result. In some ways, it is much easier to live in a household with few shining lights where the competition for glory is less intense than in a family with many radiant stars. The Kennedy and Rockefeller families with all of their wealth and talent appear to have been settings where the competition for "special status" was especially intense.

### Family Roles

In many families, roles are assigned or developed that result in some sort of family status, not necessarily a positive one. Some children are the "bright ones"; others are "the pretty ones"; and still others, the "sick" or the "bad ones." While these family roles provide some special status, they unnecessarily restrict the self-concept and corresponding behavior. These family roles put people into pigeonholes, out of which the climb is often steep and difficult. One bright, professional woman who saw her sister as "the pretty, charming one" had trouble seeing herself as lovable, a condition she associated with good looks and an extroverted manner. Conversely, her pretty sister saw herself as lacking intelligence and competence, two characteristics she ascribed to the older, more studious sister. In both cases, their self-concepts were distorted by their roles because both of them were good-looking and intelligent.

In an alcoholic family of social and economic prominence, each of the four children had special family role assignments that stifled each child's growth and development. All of the children required professional treatment for moderate to severe psychiatric problems at some time in their lives. The only son was the heir apparent, the competent and intelligent child who was expected to succeed in the professional world. While exhibiting prolonged emotional turmoil in adolescence, he left the family at the age of nineteen to marry and appears to have few problems as a young adult.

In this same family, the oldest daughter was regarded as the highly imaginative and intellectually incompetent "good girl," a role which found her imprisoned in 300 pounds of obesity as an adolescent. The second daughter, in spite of severe temper tantrums, was regarded as the "normal child," a role which made it difficult for her to express normal emotional upset (e.g., feelings of sadness and fear) in the family. The third and youngest daughter was "the baby," a role which left her socially isolated and suicidal in adolescence. In dysfunctional families such as this, roles are very rigid and confining, thus preventing the emergence of new and more adaptive behavioral patterns at critical points in development.

Regardless of the role we played in our families of origin, we all wanted to be special to our parents. We wanted to be the child who brought a sparkle to Daddy's eyes or a vibrant smile to Mommy's face. We wanted to be the one listened to the most in family discussions. We wanted to be praised, talked about, and lavished with gifts to the greatest degree. Unless we felt extra-ordinarily secure, attention of any magnitude to another person or activity felt like a diminution of our own self-worth.

## Competition for Star Billing

Sibling rivalry, a common phenomenon in families, is a manifestation of a child's wish to be special and its consequent frustration. While sibling rivalry tends to be initiated by older siblings against their younger brothers and sisters, who are perceived as rivals displacing them from their favored positions, it can be directed toward any sibling viewed as having special status. We can earn special status because of our talents, personality attributes, or handicaps.

In the case of the disabled or behaviorally disturbed child, all of the intense family focus seems to convey that the child in question is very important to the well-being of the family and that this child's needs come first. From the parents' perspective, the needs of the handicapped child come first because the child is so limited or volatile that he or she had to be handled with special care. From the perspective of the other children in the family, the handicapped child appears to be better loved than they are and their own worth seems insignificant in comparison. Besides feeling less loved, the other children often walk around with a heavy burden of guilt. They feel guilty because they are resentful of the attention their brother or sister gets and believe that they should feel kindly instead. If only they were better people (more compassionate, more generous of spirit, etc.), they, too, would love their poor, unfortunate brethren. This message, often overtly and explicitly communicated by parents and other relatives, becomes internalized, thus perpetuating the self-criticism.

Jack and Margaret were two professionally competent people, both university professors, with pronounced difficulty in intimacy. They both chose unlikely romantic partners, reacted to rejection with moderate depression, and generally felt unlovable. In addition, while they both reported having had good and loving parents, both had only one sibling, a profoundly disturbed one, who consumed all of their parents' attention. In the face of the families' stress in coping with their brothers, both Jack and Margaret were expected to be understanding and nondemanding. As a result, their own needs for love and attention got buried under a mountain of guilty concern for their sibling.

In a study comparing children in normal families with brothers and sisters of physically handicapped children, significant differences between the two groups were found.[5] Siblings of handicapped children showed more impulsive and aggressive behavior, conflict with parents, anxiety, depressive symptoms, and psychiatric symptoms in general. The authors concluded that the strain on mothers was the main cause of emotional difficulty in children with handicapped brothers and sisters. In other words, the mothers of handicapped children were often overwhelmed by the care of these children and had less positive, relaxed time and attention for the other children in the family. These mothers, who were worried about the safety of their disabled children, exhausted by the difficult child-care responsibilities, and often guilty about their resentment, had less emotional energy available to tend to their normal children.

## Competing with the "Beauty"

In other families, special status occurs because of unusual talent or beauty. One intellectually gifted woman with strong feelings of competition toward other women had intense feelings of jealousy when her husband's sister won a beauty contest. All of his pride and joy at his sister's success meant to his wife that she was less loved and less important than her sister-in-law. On another occasion, when the woman in question attended a wedding with her best friend, a remark about her friend's attractiveness ruined the wedding celebration for her. The historical antecedents of her reaction lie in an intensely jealous relationship with a younger sister who was viewed as the "beauty" in the family. Comments about her sister's "lovely dimples" resulted in her spending hours as a small child before the bathroom mirror trying to create similar indentations in her own cheeks.

## The Favorite Child

Often, the one child in the family who embodies parental values or strivings more than the other children becomes the favorite child. If the family has musical aspirations, the musical child tends to be the focus of parental attention. In athletic families, the athletic children are more likely to be attended to than the others. In some families, the children who manifest characteristics that the parents value but are themselves lacking become the preferred children. Shy parents favoring an outgoing, extroverted child or dark-haired parents enamored of a blond child are examples of this phenomenon. While the specific characteristics that are admired and loved vary among families and cultures, the admired traits in every family form the criteria by which our own lovability and self-worth are measured.

Regardless of whether we felt loved by our parents in a special manner or not, the desire to be the special person to our intimate partner remains. What does vary as a function of our past success or failure with being special is the intensity of the wish. Ranging from a gentle hope to a powerful, consuming obsession, the desire to be special can occupy center stage in the relationship, or it can be relegated to an occasional murmuring in the back of the orchestra.

While the longings for unconditional love, nurturance, protection, and special status are fairly universal although varying in intensity, these desires often lead to disappointment. No matter how hard our partners try to be all things to us, gratifying all of another's needs is a herculean task for the most part beyond the human calling.

## Chapter 5

# The Masks We Wear

How do people protect themselves from the fears and vulnerabilities of intimacy? What kind of armor do they put on? What kind of shields do they hide behind?

Because intimacy without vulnerability is an absolute impossibility, the most obvious and safest strategy is to avoid intimate relationships at all costs. The loner or the recluse who has long ago given up any hope of having a relationship seldom experiences any intimate stirrings. In response to intense early disappointment, the loner has erected character armor to shield his or her vulnerability. Typically, the loner feels reasonably contented with life and experiences intimacy anxiety only when others put pressure on him or her to get involved. Well-meaning relatives and friends who tease the loner about his or her solitary pursuits tend to be avoided like the plague. Often totally absorbed in work, the loner is frequently the successful workaholic who contributes much to his or her profession.

The total withdrawal from intimate relationships without experiencing loneliness or interpersonal longings tends to be fairly rare. What is more common are limited forays into intimacy followed by rapid flight. How brief these excursions into intimacy can be is illustrated by Ken, who routinely looked at his watch, saying, "I've got to catch a train," just as a new encounter looked promising. He retreated early on, before a relationship could even begin. His cautious moves toward an appealing woman at a party typically lasted an hour or so before a sense of urgency overtook him. While the brevity of Ken's trips into intimate territory is unusual, the phenomenon of retreating once a relationship begins to feel intimate is widespread today. To avoid any of the dangers of intimacy, we retreat or don one or more of the following masks. We bury ourselves in hobbies, tune out, act superior, say little, tell jokes, are promiscuous, or act like we do not need a soul.

A newspaper column in the *Chicago Tribune* by Cheryl Lavin and Laura Kavesh, entitled "When Love Gets Too Good—Well, That's Too Bad," was devoted to examples of men and women "who get close in relationships and then back off. Who can't commit or worse—who commit and run." Felice, Sandra, and Vicky (the women named in the article) all run away when the man begins to look or sound serious. They punt "to avoid the possibility that what starts out good might sooner or later turn sour." To avoid disappointment, they turn off emotionally and feel cold toward their committed boyfriends. Or, they get moody and sarcastic, creating distance in the relationship by verbal sniping.[1]

## Hobbies, Addictions, and Other Games

Eric Berne, in his book *Games People Play*, describes the various kinds of transactions people use to avoid intimacy. He writes, "Because there is so little opportunity for intimacy in daily life and because some forms of intimacy (especially if intense) are psychologically impossible for most people, the bulk of the time in serious social life is taken up with playing games."[2] Berne believes that games (defined as recurring sets of transactions, often repetitious and superficially plausible, with a concealed motivation) are necessary and desirable because people are unequipped to handle much intimacy in their daily lives.

Whether Berne was correct or not in his assessment of how much intimacy people can handle, he contributed much to our understanding of the protective maneuvers people use to deal with their intimate partners. Games such as "If It Weren't for You,"

"Kick Me," "Now I've Got You, You SOB," "Ain't It Awful," and "You Made Me Do It" are permanent fixtures in American culture. Other less well-known games, such as "Frigid Man/Woman," "Harried," "Courtroom," and "Sweetheart," are especially de-. signed to function as barriers to intimacy in the marital situation.

In Frigid Man/Woman, for example, the couple jointly avoids sex to reduce the risk of exposing perceived sexual inadequacies. The man may be fearful that he is not potent enough and the woman may be worried that she is not sexy enough. Instead of dealing with these fears openly, they may resort to the Game of Uproar, loud arguing about all sorts of things except the real issue, right before bedtime. The arguments effectively eliminate any chance for lovemaking to occur.

## Avoidance Maneuvers

Any addiction, preoccupation, or hobby can serve as a means of avoiding intimacy. While it is obvious that not all extrarelational interests are defensive in nature, any involvement that is pursued intently at the expense of the relationship has the potential of being an avoidance maneuver. Watching sporting events on TV continually, cleaning the home constantly, or playing tennis for hours on end can effectively reduce intimate moments. Likewise, working long hours at the office, taking evening courses regularly, or volunteering nightly at the hospital can reduce the amount of time spent together. Harville Hendrix, author of the best-selling book *Getting the Love You Want*, asked his clients, "What does your spouse do to avoid you?" The answers, he maintained, numbered over 300 and included such diverse activities as reading romantic novels, going on weekend fishing trips, jogging ten miles a day, going shopping, and spending time at Mom's.[3]

## Clubs and Causes

While some activities are easy to spot as avoidance man-euvers, namely, the unhealthy, illegal, or foolish ones, it is more difficult to label constructive, healthy, or charitable activities as avoidance strategies. However, even positive activities have the potential to be used in the service of avoiding intimacy, depending upon the extent to which the activity is pursued and the quality of the couple's intimate life together. For example, the recovering alcoholic who spends every evening attending AA meetings may be sincerely trying to stop drinking. Or he may be trying to stop drinking *and* find a substitute for the nightly gatherings at the local tavern, where he spent hours enjoying male companionship rather than being at home with his family. Likewise, the woman who is always at Weight Watchers may have an ulterior motive for her intense involvement other than the obvious goal of trying to lose weight.

The problem with constructive avoidance activities is that they are difficult to criticize. How can a partner be critical of a spouse's intense devotion to a career or time spent in charitable work? Any partner who feels ignored or slighted by such dedicated activity is in a bind. Complaining in these instances seems selfish, childish, demanding, and unreasonable.

Peter was the sort of driven, high-energy workaholic who was always on the go. A recovering alcoholic and ordained minister, Peter spent every moment of his free time doing 12-Step work through AA or pastoral work for his church. While he was running from one worthwhile activity to the next, his meek and rather self-effacing wife stayed at home taking care of their six children. A religious woman, she appeared to be devoting all of her energy to Peter and their family without asking for much in return. However, in encountering his wife on the street, one was struck by the discrepancy between her words, which were filled with proud references to Peter's work, and her tired, disheveled appearance.

And yet, how could she possibly tell Peter that she needed him at home to help with child-rearing tasks and to fill her need for companionship? Couldn't she see that he was busy saving the world, he and many of their friends would say? And so, fearing their condemnation and her own, she said nothing and allowed the weight of her frustration and emotional starvation to consume her. At the age of fifty, she looked seventy-five, while Peter, a sprightly, fit, and energetic man, appeared to be many years her junior. Obviously, Peter's frenetic, virtuous pace agreed with him, while his wife's martyrlike stance robbed her of vitality. Both of them, however, lost out on a warm, mutually rewarding relationship with each other because of their collusion in avoiding intimacy.

## Tuning Out

Tuning out, or withdrawal, is by far the most common of the strategies used to avoid intimacy. By not listening, we can effectively protect ourselves at a moment's notice whenever the going gets rough. Like the turtle's shell, which is always available for easy retreat, withdrawal can be called into service quickly and easily. She starts to complain; he tunes out. He wants more sex; she can't hear. He talks about his work; she's bored and stops listening. The high pitch of her voice may signal that she is upset, so he pulls away. The irritation may be evident on his face, so she switches mental channels to a more blissful station.

Whenever conflict is imminent in intimacy, withdrawal may be used as self-protection. Because our partner's complaints often feel like an assault, we put on emotional armor to reduce the damage. The complaints about our laziness or insensitivity lose their sting when we are miles away, safely sheltered in our mental retreat. Protected, we are free to daydream or pursue another more pleasant avenue of thought until we are interrupted by the harsh, frustrated sound of "You're not even listening to a word I said." Our peaceful reverie jolted, we are reawakened to the harsh reality of conflict.

## Conflict Signifies Rejection

Why is conflict so difficult to deal with? Basically, it is threatening to our self-worth. Like rejection, conflict implies nonacceptance. Something we are doing or not doing is unapproved of by our intimate partner. Thus, our desire to be loved unconditionally is frustrated and we wind up feeling criticized.

In intimacy, conflict is not something we bargained for. Besides wanting to be loved unconditionally, nurtured, protected, and treated as someone special, we want warmth, peace and quiet, joy, and excitement from our intimate relationships. We do not want to be disagreed with, challenged, or told that we are doing something wrong. Essentially, we want to be approved of.

Our expectations of intimacy, which are often reinforced during those early courtship and honeymoon days when blissful togetherness is the dominant motif, are dashed when conflict starts to creep into the relationship. Instead of being greeted warmly when we walk in the door, we are assailed with complaints about our shortcomings. "Why didn't you pick up your towel this morning or put away the laundry last night?" If the assailed were to respond honestly with, "Big deal, why do you make mountains out of every molehill?" the stage would be set for an all-out war. For the next response most likely would be "You never do anything that I ask. All you do is expect me to pick up after you!" To which he most surely would reply with something like, "Never? Why, just last Wednesday, I took the garbage out. You never appreciate anything I do." And the fight would head toward a no-win ending with both partners feeling attacked, unappreciated, and unloved.

Instead, after months or years of nonproductive or violent fighting, one partner learns to tune out rapidly whenever conflict begins. Usually, it is the more passive, withdrawn member of the pair who opts for tuning out as a defense. While tuning out feels much safer to the passive partner, nothing ultimately gets resolved for the two of them. The more confrontational member might stop nagging because of its futility, but the withdrawal from the conflict often results in severe emotional withdrawal from the relationship. In addition, the swallowed resentment can create emotional problems, such as psychosomatic illness or depression.

## The "I'm Better Than You Are" Stance

Looking down on the other from the height of superiority is another self-protective maneuver. Regarding our partner as too fragile, insecure, or emotionally unstable to be on a par with us leaves us smugly protected. With someone who is inferior, we do not have to feel exposed and vulnerable. The inequity between us creates distance in the relationship, which feels safer than closeness.

The sense of superiority may be based on exaggerated or real inadequacies in our partner. A minor failing may be transformed into a major defect so that we can feel superior. For example, our partner's shyness may be seen as basic fragility rather than a minor trait in the midst of other strengths. The tendency to exaggerate and distort negative traits in our partner stems from our need to insulate ourselves from intimacy by standing alone on a hill of superiority. As king or queen of the hill, we may derive self-satisfaction but little in the way of interpersonal closeness.

### *More Reasonable, Sophisticated, and Urbane*

We may feel superior because we see ourselves as more reasonable than our partners. Their emotional outbursts may be viewed as childish temper tantrums indicative of basic immaturity. Or because we prefer classical music to rock 'n' roll, we see ourselves as cultured and refined compared to our crass and unpolished, lowbrow spouses. Or because we enjoy reading and our partners never open a book, we may regard them as uneducated boors. Or because we are older and have traveled more, we may see ourselves as worldly wise compared to our naive, "babe in the woods" partners. The tendency to see the other as inferior, for whatever reason, leaves us safely distant.

Feelings of superiority in intimate relationships can occur with greater knowledge, power, material possessions, money, age, maturity, intelligence, beauty, or higher socioeconomic status.

With a partner who is inferior along any of these dimensions, we can feel protective, nurturant, or parental. The mentor role has clear-cut psychological benefits. Self-enhancement is generally gained with little risk to self-esteem.

## The Sanctimonious Professor

Harry, a portly university professor in his late fifties, fell in love with a bright female student who was twenty years his junior. A pretty, seductive young woman who was intellectually aspiring but unaccomplished, Pat was drawn to Harry's intellectual prowess and academic accomplishments. Their relationship appeared to be the perfect trade-off. She gained intellectual stature and maturity from the relationship; Harry reaped youthful vitality and sexual energy. In addition, Harry's worldly wisdom helped Pat clarify her own career goals and direction.

What could go wrong with such a perfect union? The answer is that there were many factors, both externally imposed frustrations and variables intrinsic to the relationship. The fates seemed to conspire against them by throwing all sorts of obstacles in their path.

At the beginning of their relationship, the fact that they were both married to other people created problems for their families and friends. Their spouses felt betrayed and rejected, their children felt abandoned, and their colleagues, motivated by envy or moral indignation, were critical of their liaison. Relatives on both sides, because of religious convictions, felt that their affair and subsequent marriage were immoral in some way. All in all, their interpersonal environment was nonsupportive. In fact, the critical and hostile atmosphere surrounding them was so aversive that they decided to move to another city. Feeling that a clean start would provide a more benign environment, they were enthusiastic about the move.

Contrary to all their expectations, however, the new city furnished a new set of problems. Because the new university was less prestigious than Harry's original one, he felt humiliated by colleagues of lower intellectual status. Then, too, his new boss, a personal friend of his and his former spouse, was less than warmly accepting of his new bride. Both Harry and Pat were as lonely and socially isolated in their new environment as they were in the town where they met. The new world did not roll out the welcome carpet as they had hoped. In addition, the old world kept intruding upon their idyllic union. The children from their earlier marriages kept showing up on their doorstep at the most inopportune moments.

While the external problems were frustrating and annoying, the most damaging factor to their relationship satisfaction was the nature of the relationship itself. Their Henry Higgins–Eliza Doolittle roles began to show signs of strain when Pat started to grow up. As she started to develop her own sense of professional and personal identity, her admiration of Harry faded. With increasing self-reliance her dependency diminished, and with this loss Harry's sense of superiority was threatened. Besides feeling threatened, he was angry at Pat's lack of gratitude for all his guidance. He believed that if she were truly grateful, she would be content with the more subservient, inferior role they had originally agreed upon. By Pat's yielding to her own healthy developmental striving for autonomy, she was violating the rules of their original contract.

The problem with relationships where one partner is (or feels) significantly superior to the other is that they are stable only if the status quo is maintained. If the so-called inferior partner starts to grow in any way, the balance in the relationship has to shift. Unfortunately, the superior member has more to lose by a change to a more equitable power base. Feelings of superiority, besides protecting against vulnerability, are gratifying.

In Harry and Pat's case, their marriage became increasingly conflictual for them both. Because Harry's identity was so tied up with feeling superior to others, he had difficulty accommodating Pat's emerging self. He was basically a close-mouthed, chauvinistic male, who in the depths of his soul believed that he knew best. His superior status was evident not only with Pat but with his university colleagues, who grew increasingly distrustful of his uncommunicative, paternalistic attitude. As he lost respect and admiration on every front, his health began to falter. When last heard from, Harry was experiencing crippling symptoms of multiple sclerosis that limited his mobility. He and Pat had reached an unhappy truce in which she begrudgingly took care of him while trying to maintain her newly developed professional identity. As for Harry, he seemed demoralized by all his losses and yet resigned to a fate vastly different from the one he imagined five years earlier when he first met Pat.

In Harry's case, he maintained a sense of superiority throughout most of his life by an arrogant and detached manner, criticalness, and a subdued yet boastful style. In his work environment, he had difficulty praising any of his co-workers or acknowledging their contributions in any way. On one occasion, to a member of his staff who had handed him a memo outlining her ideas for change, he had responded, "If there had been a good solution to this problem, I would have thought of it." Frequently, he would remind those around him that he had thirty-five years of academic experience as if such experience guaranteed superior wisdom. In all ways, Harry was a man who could not acknowledge his own limitations, nor could he tolerate anything less than the number one spot in life.

### Superiority Tactics

Harry's tactics are common means of maintaining superiority in intimate relationships. Criticizing, boasting, belittling, and constant correcting are designed to uphold a psychological advantage. It is only by keeping our partner in a one-down position that we can stay on top. Comments such as "Don't you have any taste?", "I'm surprised you didn't know that" (said with exaggerated shock), and "No, dear, we went to Hawaii in 1975, not 1976, and it was a Monday not a Tuesday" (said in a syrupy, condescending tone) are run-of-the-mill verbal snipes that take place in day-to-day intimate encounters.

Karen and Joe came into marital counseling in a crisis. They were about to embark on a lengthy medical fertility treatment program when Joe balked. Out of the blue, he announced that he was unsure that he wanted to remain married. Their power struggles around how to spend their holidays and weekends were so debilitating to him that he felt there was something fundamentally wrong with their marriage. In a more honest vein, he later acknowledged that he felt there was something basically wrong with Karen's personality. He regarded her angry outbursts and emotional demands as extremely childish and self-centered.

A lawyer by profession, Joe felt that any display of emotion was irrational. Silent withdrawal was viewed as the virtuous and mature route to conflict resolution. In Joe's family of origin, his father regularly withdrew, not saying a word, whenever his mother began to shout in frustration. In the eyes of Joe's family, his father's stance was considered both saintly and superior.

Joe's withdrawal during marital conflict intensified Karen's rage. Not only did Joe's cold treatment communicate fury and rejection, but he also conveyed a sense of superiority and contempt by his icy control. When Joe occasionally spoke in the midst of their "fights," he would say something so insulting that the words would stun Karen. "You're nothing but a baby" and "Spoiled brats like you can't always get their own way" were among the most jarring. By his verbal belittling, Joe attempted to cut Karen "down to size," that is, reduce her psychological impact and, in so doing, enhance his own position of superiority.

Provocative and belittling name-calling is designed not only to reduce partners to sniffling children but to exalt our own status. By calling our partners jerks, wimps, idiots, or cowards, we are implying that we do not belong in those maligned categories. As name-callers, we are in a superior, judgmental position, clearly more virtuous and self-righteous than our inferior companions. Whatever our minor limitations, at least we are not as stupid, insensitive, crass, or whatever, as they are. And whatever the quality, it is clearly more damaging to one's value as a person than the insignificant flaws we may possess.

## The Mystery Man Approach

Mystery men and women protect their vulnerability by revealing little about themselves. They believe that when nothing is exposed, their chances of being hurt are minimized. Keeping their cards close to their vests, they attempt to establish and maintain intimate relationships by focusing entirely on the other. Because solicitous concern for others is a trait that is valued by most people, mystery men and women are often regarded as good friends. Their attentiveness communicates affection and interest so their friends feel cared about.

Since most people appreciate being listened to in a nonjudgmental manner, the defensive nature of the enigmatic person's attentiveness is not readily apparent. Just as no one questions the ulterior motives of a virtuous soul, no one looks beyond the surface of a good listener. In short supply in a garrulous society, the good listener is regarded as a rare and valuable commodity.

Why then should the motives of a good listener be suspect? It is apparent that not all great listeners are operating from a defensive posture and that many attentive individuals are concerned and caring persons who do not need to have their own emotional needs met in every relationship. Rather, the problem arises with those good listeners who do not feel intimately connected to others because they refuse to take the opportunity of sharing what is important to them with anyone. In social interactions, they may relate amusing anecdotes or give their opinion about world events. But to talk about their deepest fears, inadequacies, or uncertainties renders them too vulnerable and exposed. For them, the listening stance is much safer than sharing. Unfortunately, the price they pay for this security is a sense of detachment in all relationships, even the most intimate. Besides that, they wind up feeling unloved, essentially because they feel unknown by everyone.

### *One-Sided Relationships*

The lack of mutuality in the mystery man's relationships with others is one clue to its defensive nature. Because there is no give-and-take, the relationship is lopsided. It looks like all giving and no taking. The mystery man or woman tends to be viewed as the nurturant, strong and silent partner in any relationship.

The advantage of the enigmatic "Mona Lisa" stance, besides self-protection, is its great appeal. Not only are we intrigued by mystery in others, but the blank screen allows us to paint the picture any way we choose. In other words, it is easier to ascribe all sorts of positive qualities to a person who has revealed little. The absence of contradictory or disconfirming evidence allows us to project the images of our "ideal person" onto the other without any dissonance. If the quiet, enigmatic person is saying little that is self-revealing, he can reasonably be seen as the strong, wise, deep, and passionate man of our dreams. Our fantasies will embellish the sketchy portrait that sits before us.

## The Accommodating Souls

One variation of mystery man or woman is the passive, accommodating person who is agreeable and easygoing. Having learned early to bury their own emotional needs under a rigidly prescribed role such as good daughter or son, these people are often unaware of their own feelings. They are so busy operating from the dictates of that role that their own emotional needs become alien signals to them. One woman in therapy described how she went from "the good daughter" to "the good wife" role without skipping a beat. Immersed in the role of good wife, she gave up her family, friends, and values without thinking twice about it. Their friends were his friends; the neighborhood they lived in was his; their vacations were spent the way he liked.

It wasn't that he dominated their relationship by his power and control but rather that she abdicated a personal position in their shared emotional arena. She was so good at accommodating his needs and avoiding conflict every step of the way that neither was aware of what was happening until their sexual life deteriorated and he had an affair. Even with these crises, they had no emotional confrontations, no overt conflict. Rather, they drifted apart for several years and then divorced. Since she was essentially a nonperson in their relationship, there was no opportunity to struggle or confront issues. Their relationship ended "not with a bang but with a whimper."

## The Helpers

Groups in our society with a high proportion of mystery men and women are psychotherapists, ministers, and educators. Dedicated to helping or educating others from a very early age, these professionals spend most of their intellectual and emotional energy focused on the people around them. Often from dysfunctional families, they learned very early in their lives that it was in their own best interest to pay close attention to the emotional states of significant others. Because family members were often unpredictable or volatile, exquisite emotional sensitivity to the family's psychological state was necessary to their own survival. If they could anticipate the family's emotional explosions or depressions, they were in a better position to forestall or at least minimize these crises. For example, if they could sense their parent's rage the moment he or she walked in the door, they could stay out of the way, thus defusing the situation.

Along with the defensive focus on the other person, mystery persons develop habitual postures of limiting self-revelation. Because self-exposure of negative feelings or behaviors was likely to lead to attack or rejection in their dysfunctional families, saying little about themselves became the wisest course of action. It was only by blending into the woodwork (with their own emotional needs) that they could hope to escape destructive responses of one kind or another.

Janet, a psychotherapist in private practice, exemplifies "the mystery woman" approach par excellence. A witty, warm, and engaging woman in her late thirties, she had never experienced a mutual relationship in her life at the time she sought help. Always in the role of an attentive and giving person in both her professional and personal worlds, Janet was not aware that her own emotional needs were going unrecognized. "I always felt that it was my job to be there for others," she once said. Her other-centered, interpersonal style, which felt natural and deeply ingrained, was a source of personal satisfaction to her. Being a giving and loving woman fit her view of what an ideal woman should be. Thus, she was clearly behaving in ways that were congruent with her ideal self.

What eventually led to dramatic changes in Janet's view of herself was the emergence of anger. The saintly self-portrait had to be revamped after feelings of rage began to surface. Feelings of anger, which had been experienced only rarely in her life, jarred her unidimensional view of herself. As is common with many women clients, Janet came into therapy following a broken love affair. She had felt very distressed by her boyfriend's abrupt departure from her life, but at the same time she was understanding of his motives for rejecting her. Understanding the reasons why others hurt her had become a lifelong habit.

Growing up with an abusive, alcoholic father and a passive, depressed mother, she took on the role of therapist in her own family at an early age. Listening sympathetically for hours on end to her mother's unhappy life and trying to understand the reasons for her father's drunken rage left her focused on significant others. "It was important to try and help her out—her sadness was deeply upsetting to me," she related about her mother. Her own unhappiness was not apparent to her until she came into treatment and began to explore the torrent of feelings her boyfriend's rejection unleashed. Basically, she felt that she was never loved, heard, understood, or had her own emotional needs attended to in any way. Along with this sense of deprivation was an overwhelming anger that the important people in her life had not been sensitive to her concerns anywhere along the line.

Gradually, however, Janet began to understand her own contribution to this dilemma. While it appeared that her friends and relatives were not particularly attuned to her psychological states, it was equally clear that Janet worked very hard to mask them. On the surface, she appeared to be a happy, mature, independent, and nurturant person, so it was understandable how others assumed that she had not a care in the world. In addition, her other-centered focus was so dominant that it was difficult for her to shift gears and focus on herself. She was so quick to ask the first "How are you?" in any interaction and then proceed to ask for more detail that she bowled the other person over with her attentiveness. While her mystery woman approach left others flattered, it clearly resulted in Janet's feeling unknown and unloved. It was only after she learned how to talk about her own worries and vulnerabilities with her closest friends that she began to experience the satisfaction of reciprocity in relationships. Unfortunately, for many other mystery men and women, the risks involved in self-exposure are viewed as too great to chance, and so they stay safely ensconced in their enigmatic interpersonal styles.

## The Court Jester

Court jesters are the distractors of the intimacy world. Like their counterparts in medieval times, their main function is to amuse and shift the focus away from conflict. Just as medieval court jesters distracted war-weary kings and queens from combat concerns, so do modern-day jesters turn the attention of their intimate partners away from conflict-laden arenas. Because the focus on conflict is too threatening, jesters move rapidly to humor whenever a moment of potential disagreement appears on the scene. They also use a pun or quip whenever high-intensity positive moments occur because high levels of positive intimacy can also be anxiety-arousing to them.

Comic relief is used by court jesters not only to distract but also to disarm their intimate partners. By turning a serious moment into humor, jesters take the upper hand and seize control. Because the change in tone of the communication is momentarily confusing, the partner is temporarily out of commission on the battleground. After the joke, the partner may begin to doubt herself and wonder why she is making such a big deal out of nothing. In effect, the switch in mood results in her feeling off balance as if a rug had been pulled out from under her feet. She is baffled and her self-confidence is shaken.

Court jesters' belief that laughter is the best medicine allows them to avoid resolving interpersonal conflict. In fact, these intimacy comics believe that conflict between intimate partners is basically unsolvable. Growing up in a family where conflict was swept under the rug only to explode episodically, the court jester learned how to put on a happy face in the midst of underground family tension. He or she also learned that while a joke might temporarily alleviate the tension, preventing the recurrent explosions was impossible. No matter how hard he or she and everyone else in the family tried to avoid conflicts, tension would erupt when least expected.

## The Importance of Looking Good

The family settings that are breeding grounds for court jesters are homes where appearance matters more than anything. Because "looking good" is the most important consideration, denial of problems, both inside and outside of the home, becomes the modus operandi. In such homes, the marital unit is often a united-front couple that avoids overt struggle and appears to be in agreement about almost everything. Thus, the familial ingredients in the backgrounds of court jesters appear to be heavy doses of denial, pseudomutuality, emphasis on family loyalty, good appearance above all else, rigid rules, and joking. In contrast to good-natured teasing, the humor in these families is often sarcastic and belittling, a manifestation of hostility rather than affection.

Rick's family had liberal quantities of the above characteristics and was quite emotionally isolated from extended family and friends. (Rick was a forty-five-year-old accountant who came into therapy after his wife separated from him.) His parents basically distrusted others and used feelings of superiority to maintain distance. Their attitude toward others was a smug "Thank God, we're not as unrefined as other people." Pride in the fact that they did not smoke, drink, or eat as much as others and took vitamins, exercised regularly, and were always well-groomed in an immaculately kept house was a source of immense gratification for both parents. Like Rick, his father was the jester in the family who used humor to maintain the facade that all was right and happy in their household.

What wasn't "right" in Rick's family was his father's explosive temper and his youngest sister's schizophrenia, which became obvious as she reached adulthood. As serious as these problems were, they were never talked about openly, not even in the family. In fact, no one outside the immediate family knew about these problems at the time they were occurring. It was only twenty years later when the schizophrenic sister returned from a self-imposed exile in a distant state that members of the extended family began to hear about her. Her reappearance in the city of her birth as a grossly overweight, unkempt, and overtly psychotic forty-year-old woman was a profound embarrassment to her parents, who.had tried to keep her condition a secret all of these years.

In Rick's family, it was more important to maintain the appearance of superior normality than it was to try to resolve any of their interpersonal problems. Besides their need to preserve the illusion of sanity, his immediate family was basically inept when it came to direct and open communication about conflictual matters. They literally did not know how to talk about interpersonal problems.

As might be expected, Rick had pronounced difficulty in openly confronting problems in his marriage. It was only after his wife moved out that he began to consider seriously her many complaints about how unhappy she was. Foremost among her complaints was that she could not talk to Rick about her feelings. According to her, Rick would either explode angrily and counterattack or try to dismiss her complaints with humor. While his comic response—"So you think you have problems, did I tell you the one about . . . ?"—was born out of panic, confusion, and a need to reduce tension, his humorous distractions left his wife feeling misunderstood and belittled. Because she did not feel validated or cherished by either of Rick's responses—the defensive rage or his stand-up comic routine—she gradually withdrew emotionally from the relationship. The pain of her own alienation and distance from Rick was the factor that prompted her physical move from the house and their pursuit of couples therapy.

In therapy, it became apparent that Rick's primary difficulty was in becoming aware of and expressing his own feelings. Because he had learned early in his life that negative feelings of any kind were unsafe, shoving aside such feelings and replacing them with a cheerful patter had become an ingrained style. Thus, the basic therapeutic task for Rick, before he could ever learn how to respond empathetically to his wife's sadness and rage, was to tolerate his own negative feelings without running away into humor. Fortunately for their marriage, Rick was able to change. After therapy, the only vestiges of his earlier comedic posture were puns of all kinds that regularly elicited good-natured groans from his children.

## The Art of Distraction

Besides humor, changing the topic or the focus of attention is another time-honored distraction technique. Whenever the emotional climate starts to heat up in any intimate setting, distractors shift gears rapidly. They chatter away on a happier note or turn up the volume. By their antics, they are trying desperately to shift attention away from the conflict-laden monster that has just walked into the kitchen. Essentially, the distractors are saying to their families, "Hey, look here, don't look there. Maybe if we don't pay attention, it'll go away and we'll be safe from catastrophe for another day."

The art of distraction goes back a long way developmentally. Children as young as three years of age change the topic boldly and shamelessly whenever their behavior is questioned in any way. "Hey, look, I can stand on one foot or roll my eyes or whistle" is a standard kind of retort when critical questions are directed their way. The childlike wish is that distraction will result in the unpleasant accusations disappearing from view permanently.

As children, habitual distractors hope that a change of topic will result in conflicts disappearing from sight and memory forever. Often feeling very responsible for solving the family's problems, the distractor has not the foggiest idea of where to begin. Confused about alternatives, he or she believes that doing anything is better than nothing. So, he or she may talk nonstop about the fight in the schoolyard, knock over his or her glass of milk at dinnertime, or sing loudly, all in hopes of changing the focus of attention whenever the going is rough. While these antics are meant to alleviate the tension of a quarrel about to begin, the distractor frequently winds up as the family scapegoat because of his or her annoying and distracting behavior. It is easier to focus on a glass of spilt milk, for example, than on Mom's drunken appearance at the family table. So, the distractor ends up feeling misunderstood, angry, helpless, and yet somehow responsible for it all.

Jean's first sessions in therapy were memorable because of her rambling verbal style. Her presentation was a litany of neurotic "sins" which ranged from insecurity and perfectionism in her professional world to demandingness and criticalness in her personal life. She seemed quite willing to blame herself for every imaginable failing and was intent upon uncovering as many personal transgressions as she could. However, it was difficult to follow her tale of unhappiness because of the frequent shifts in the focus of her self-blame. Just as one would start to understand a particular point, she would introduce some new interpretation of her behavior. Her distracting style was designed to keep others from noticing what was *really* important about her.

Her distracting posture was also evident in the anecdotes she used to describe her familial role. Growing up as the middle child in an alcoholic family of five, she was always worried that her parents would fight when her dad was intoxicated. Typically, her parents were involved in a cold war and did not speak much to each other except for perfunctory remarks such as "Pass the salt." However, when her father was inebriated, the probability of a violent quarrel between her parents became quite high. Like most alcoholics, her father's alcohol-related behavior was unpredictable and took the form of verbal and occasional physical abuse toward his wife or son. Jean's way of coping with the tension related to her father's drunkenness was to become the sacrificial lamb in a distracting manner. For example, on one occasion unbeknownst to her parents, she stayed overnight at her girlfriend's house so "that they would worry about her whereabouts rather than focus on themselves." At other times, she simply tried desperately to change the topic to whatever felt like safer ground. In her family, she was both the distractor and "the responsible one," who felt it was her duty to solve parental problems.

A hypervigilant woman constantly worried about potential catastrophes, Jean had difficulty enjoying the present moment. Idyllic moments of romance would be interrupted by unpleasant memories of bygone days. At age thirty-three, she came into therapy because of anxious overconcern about her three-year marriage. She was fearful that her husband would leave her because of her insecurities and criticalness toward him or, conversely, that she would leave him because of his shortcomings. While her multifaceted worries were significant concerns to her, her worries were also distractions because they made it difficult for her to focus on deeper aspects of herself. In addition, the rapidity with which one worry would be supplanted by another, more pressing concern before anything was resolved was distracting. Therefore, the main focus of treatment with Jean was on helping her to stay with a therapeutic topic through all its uncertain meanderings until resolution. It was important for her to discover that one can face conflict and live through it without any permanent disability.

## Don Juan and Jezebel

Like court jesters and other distractors, Don Juan and Jezebel, symbolic of untrustworthy and promiscuous seducers, are not what they appear. Looking carefree as they move from one relationship to another, they are careful to hide their vulnerabilities from even the most discerning eyes. Often the objects of envy, they look confident and successful with strings of broken hearts worn like trophies around their belts. Because they appear to lead such exciting and rewarding lives, it is hard to spot what is missing for them.

The missing elements, however, are fundamental to emotional well-being. Having split off sexual from emotional intimacy, Don Juans and Jezebels obtain only transitory gratification from their interpersonal relationships rather than lasting satisfaction. For them, a one-night stand tends to be as meaningful as a longer relationship. In fact, since most of their emotional satisfaction comes from the conquest, a succession of lovers is more rewarding than one person. Being victorious in the pursuit of a sexual relationship appears to be the primary factor that contributes to their emotional pleasure. Victory validates physical desirability, a cornerstone of their self-esteem.

While the wish to be admired for physical beauty is a universal desire, the Casanova and the temptress are more highly invested in this longing than the rest of us. For them, the admiration of others is a mirror that validates their very being. Essentially, they believe they have value only as long as they are admired and desired. Without that, they feel empty and worthless.

## The Importance of Tangible Reality

The need for external validation, reliance on the senses, and preference for action are characteristics of the Don Juan–Jezebel defensive style. Often impulsive, nonreflective people, they spend little time and energy thinking about their own motives and those of others. They are more comfortable in the world of action than of the mind because the tangible, concrete reality of action is more trustworthy than thoughts and feelings. Likewise, what is seen and touched directly through the senses is believed more than words or feelings. For these reasons, a sexual connection has more validity than a verbal outpouring of everlasting love. The physical touching is emotionally reassuring, even if only temporarily, whereas language, seen as a system of hollow symbols, is disquieting.

Early in their lives, Don Juans and Jezebels learned to distrust words as well as the speakers of those words. Similar to Lord Byron's Don Juan, who was sent abroad by his mother, they suffered early abandonment and betrayal at the hands of their caretakers. Whether or not they were actually physically deserted by a parent who died or departed the family home, they typically experienced emotional abandonment in some form. Abandonment in the shape of parental emotional or physical illness, marital conflict, parental overwork or job loss, the death of a significant relative in the family, the birth of a sibling, the injury or illness of a brother or sister, or any other source of severe familial stress took its toll. For whatever reason, the womanizer and the siren came to believe that people could not be relied on because they were not available in any consistent manner. Thus, emotional closeness to others is viewed by Don Juans and Jezebels as an unreliable and potentially dangerous state. Sexual contact divorced from emotional connectedness is as far along the intimacy path as they are comfortable in going.

Emily, a married, thirty-five-year-old fashion designer, came into therapy because of excessive use of alcohol and diet pills. An extremely attractive and stylishly dressed woman, Emily kept glancing at her reflection in the office window in a fascinated and self-satisfied manner throughout most of her therapy hours. When she came into treatment, she was on the verge of ending a two-year affair with a married man and beginning another one. She maintained that her marriage to an older professional man was basically one of convenience in that he provided for her financially. However, their sexual relations and his inattentiveness were very unsatisfying to her.

Throughout her single adult years and her five-year marriage, Emily had gone from one affair to another without coming up for air. According to her, she was looking for someone who "needed and adored" her. The fantasy of having a man need her intensely began in childhood as a frequent daydream with which she soothed herself whenever she was lonely. There was never any conscious awareness of the converse, namely, that she needed men desperately for her own validation.

Emily's choice of men was designed to maximize the likelihood of being adored. In all cases, she was extremely special to her male lovers, not only because of her beauty but also because of some demographic difference that they valued. Either she was significantly younger (fifteen to twenty years), of a different skin color (they were black and she was white), or more educated. She referred to them all as her "victims," a term that reflected her hostility toward men. While she inflicted much pain on her lovers with her sudden rejections, it was apparent that she was also suffering. Her excessive alcohol and drug use was a clear-cut manifestation of this inner turmoil. In addition, while her lovers were all obsessed with her, some of them were obvious losers who treated her badly. Their lower intellectual, socioeconomic, and psychological levels of functioning reflected her own self-denigration.

Emily was the only child of a critical, depressed mother and a distant, proper father. Her mother, who was sixteen years older than her father, was emotionally unavailable to Emily throughout her life. Whether it was due to her mother's emotional absence or other factors, Emily believed that she was worth little in relation to her female peers. She believed that she could not compete in that arena and so sought out situations where she had an advantage. Her fascination with older men related not only to an unresolved Electra complex (she adored her father) but also to her need to have an edge in competition with other women.

Unfortunately, Emily's promiscuous, seductive style provided her with little enduring gratification interpersonally. Likewise, her impulsivity and impatience with the verbal tools of therapy did not permit her the opportunity of staying in therapy long enough to make significant gains. Her pattern of changing lovers frequently to avoid the dangers of intimacy extended to therapists. There, too, she moved on rapidly whenever the going got too rough or too close. At last count, she was on therapist number five with little evidence of significant change.

The pursuit of multiple lovers, either simultaneous or consecutive partners, provides not only narcissistic gratification and an outlet for hostility but also a measure of control over the risks of intimacy. By limiting involvement with others, the chances of being exposed and hurt are minimized. Likewise, if we reject before being rejected, the risk of abandonment is minimal. To play it safe, Don Juans and Jezebels need to play it superficially. From their perspective, deeper emotional involvements are too risky.

## The "I Don't Need Anybody" Attitude

When viewed from a distance, the superindependent stance looks emotionally healthy and mature. Often moving through life successfully, the highly independent person appears free and unencumbered. He or she may be committed to a career, to the care of an elderly parent, or to a political movement, while pursuing an active social life. Capable of spending time alone or in the company of others, the superindependent individual is conveying the message that all is well on every front.

What then is unhealthy and defensive about all this independence? As John Donne wrote a long time ago, "No man is an island unto himself." We are basically social creatures in need of intimate relationships to satisfy our longings for love and companionship. Without such intimacy, most of us feel lonely unless we have made a commitment to religion or some larger-than-life cause.

For paragons of self-sufficiency, however, the loneliness and emptiness are hidden by an "I don't need anybody" attitude. Basically insecure about intimate relationships, the superindependent person is like the boy who whistles whenever he is afraid—he keeps a stiff upper lip and steels himself against fear by pretending he is not worried. Having been taught early to bury inadequacies under a facade of bravado, the superindependent person acts in ways opposite to his or her concerns. He or she believes that by acting strong and tough, the underlying tenderness will be transformed.

The underlying vulnerability for the superindependent person consists of strong and frustrated dependency longings. The desire to be taken care of, loved, and protected was thwarted early in life and changed beyond conscious recognition into premature maturity. Disappointed by the inadequacy of caretakers who told them repeatedly to grow up and be big boys or girls, pseudomature children learned to count on themselves rather than others. In the process, they gave up any conscious hope of ever being cared for. However, unbeknownst to them, these buried dependency wishes remained alive and ready to be reactivated whenever a relationship became intimate.

## Avoiding the Regressive Pull

The pseudo-independent individual avoids intimate relationships because the desires for nurturance, whenever they are consciously experienced, feel intense and infantile. The threat of regressing to a childlike state when closely involved with others is anxiety-arousing. Most people do not like to feel childlike and needy; it lowers their level of self-confidence. Feeling grown-up, rational, self-sufficient, and in control of life are clearly preferred by most of us.

Typically, pseudo-independent people move through adult life comfortably until one day, out of the blue, they fall in love. Struck unexpectedly by intense feelings as if hit by a bolt of lightning, they are left reeling. Their neat and orderly world is jarred by the obsessiveness of their thoughts and the intensity of their feelings. Having decided much earlier that they did not need people, these lovestruck, formerly autonomous people find their current neediness unsettling. Whether they will be able to integrate feelings of passionate love over time and be transformed into wiser, more vulnerable, and less rigid people will depend on many factors.

## The Outcome of Intimacy Forays

Chief among the factors is the outcome of the love affair. A successful expedition into intimate territory, that is, discovering that intimacy has more joy than pain, bodes well for future success with intimacy. After learning how to tolerate the disappointment and dependency of intimacy, the formerly superindependent person may be able to conclude that intimacy is preferable to solitude. If, however, the first foray into intimacy led to intense heartbreak, the stage is set for more permanent withdrawal from love relationships. With the pain of a recent betrayal, severe childhood disappointments, and the success of total self-reliance throughout most of life, superindependent character armor begins to be forged.

Marge, a thirty-nine-year-old human resources specialist for a large computer firm, gave the impression of being tough, strong, and "in charge" on first encounter. A tall, large-boned woman with a firmly set jaw, she looked as if she had no trouble taking care of herself and others. In her case, however, appearances were clearly deceiving, for she began to sob within minutes of sitting down in the office for her first therapy session. As she began to tell her story, it was clear that depression and loneliness had been frequent companions over the past ten years. It was ten years ago that her husband had left her for another woman, leaving her with three small children to raise. Since that time, she had spent all of her life buried in work, family, and church responsibilities. Not a moment was available for any kind of leisure or social life—a state of affairs that she preferred. Marge believed that she was unable to negotiate relationships, and so she avoided intimacy whenever possible.

The second child in a family of nine, Marge saw herself as least favored by her mother. Feeling criticized for being "too mean," competitive, and aggressive, Marge had been involved in a power struggle with her mother for as long as she could remember. Her relationships with her siblings were no better. With her sisters, she was somehow "the odd one out," and with her oldest brother, the competition for their mother's affection was a contest she never won. She felt loved only by her father and paternal grandmother to whom she was "the favorite." Throughout her life, she had very few girlfriends and no boyfriends except for Barry, whom she eventually married. She commented that men in general found her "too independent."

When Marge's intimacy venture failed and Barry left, she resumed her earlier superindependent style. She spent all of her time and energy conveying to others and to herself that she could manage alone. All household chores, whether plumbing, carpentry, electrical work, wallpapering, sewing, or cooking, were within her domain. What did not fit into her world were relationships and all that they entailed. What she had not counted on, however, was the overwhelming sadness and loneliness she was left with.

For Marge, the aspect of intimacy that was most problematic was talking about feelings and criticism. To expose vulnerabilities, like hurt feelings, was to risk criticism. And being criticized, which was experienced by Marge as a psychological assault, resulted in a sense of humiliation and/or outrage. Either feeling—hurt humiliation or defensive anger—was upsetting to her and resulted in further retreat from relationships. In essence, she had no idea how to get close to others without disastrous consequences. And yet, some degree of intimacy in her life was necessary to reduce the sense of painful isolation that she felt.

The solution to Marge's dilemma lay in learning how to risk criticism and rejection in small doses so as to build up tolerance. A "tougher hide" develops gradually by learning how to handle negative feelings and interactions with close friends. As we learn to say routinely to our intimate others, "Hey, I was hurt by your behavior," the likelihood of being overwhelmed by hurt and angry feelings decreases. In addition, with better communication skills, we feel less helpless and more in control.

All of the masks we wear to protect ourselves from the risks of intimacy have their psychological benefits. With hobbies, addictions, and other games, there is intrinsic pleasure involved in the participation. Tuning out gives us a breather as we marshal our reserves, while a superior stance provides a temporary boost of self-esteem. Cloaking ourselves in a veil of mystery makes us more attractive, and laughter, for whatever reason, is like music to our ears. Seductiveness and desirability enhance our self-image, while superindependence provides feelings of mastery, an important component of self-esteem. While there are advantages to the defensive interpersonal styles we pursue, the disadvantages, in terms of loss of intimacy, are greater.

# Chapter 6

# Sex Differences and Attraction

---

"Why can't a woman be more like a man?" bemoaned Henry Higgins and countless other men before and after him. Similarly, women have been asking that same old question about men, more vocally in recent years. Are men and women destined to babble away in different tongues, forever doomed to understand only a fraction of what the other is saying? What makes us so different in terms of what we want from relationships?

## Different Intimacy Styles

Current beliefs and research attribute the majority of male-female differences in intimacy requirements to socialization practices, role models, and peer influence. From a very early age, according to psychologists Eleanor Maccoby and Carol Jacklin, authors of *The Psychology of Sex Differences,*[1] boys in our culture are socialized to be more competitive, task-oriented, and goal-directed than girls. Their play is typically more aggressive and physical in nature than girls' play, with an emphasis on spatial and motor skills. Girls, by contrast, are more verbal and socially oriented than boys, focused more on conversation, relating, and the caretaking of others. It has been said that boys are concerned with achievement and girls with relationships. While boy-girl differences during the infancy and toddler years are not that apparent, by the time children hit grade school the majority of each sex has diverged from a common developmental road to a separate path.

What do these early sex role differences have to do with adult sexual and intimacy needs? A great deal. Because the most glaring adult intimacy differences between men and women are apparent in young boys and girls, it is obvious that these sex differences are fairly deeply ingrained by the time adulthood arrives. The early focus of young girls on feelings, conversation, and relationships explains why verbal intimacy is such a critical component of emotional intimacy for women. Talking about important feelings and values is the vehicle for closeness for women, while physical closeness is more highly valued by men. Because physical closeness, either sexual, affectional, or spatial (sitting or doing things together), is more tangible than conversation, physical activity of some kind tends to be the preferred mode of maintaining closeness for men. She wants to talk; he wants to have sex or be in the same room with her.

Most women want to feel close emotionally before being sexual, while men use sexual activity to bring about emotional closeness. That is not to say that all men feel emotionally connected to their partners after sexual activity but rather that sexual contact is their preferred avenue for achieving emotional intimacy. According to psychiatrist Joan Shapiro, "For men, sex is connection—sexual acceptance is necessary in order for them to feel emotional acceptance."[2] When men and women in intimate relationships feel distant from each other, women want to talk about the distance, while men try to reduce the distance through sexual contact. It is the difference between the "Don't just stand there and talk, let's do something" orientation versus the "Stop doing that, let's talk" point of view.

## Thinking versus Feeling

While some of the sex differences are related to differing points of view on a verbal-action continuum, other dissimilarities have to do with the distinction between a "thinking" emphasis and a "feeling" orientation. While it is obvious that both sexes think and feel, women as a group prefer the feeling mode, while men value logic and rationality more highly. The preferences have to do with skill and comfort in each of these modalities.

Possibly because of their overinvestment in relationships, women are better at identifying both their own feelings and those of others. Like their mothers before them, women are more tuned in to the emotional subtleties of relationships, the underlying currents and dynamics. As a result of their greater aptitude for the emotional substratum of interactions, they are more likely to evaluate the worthwhileness of a particular activity on the basis of its impact on feelings. Men, by contrast, are more likely to utilize more objective criteria, such as logic, propriety, or protocol. Of all the virtues, mercy or kindness would probably be at the top of the female list, while justice or fairmindedness would head the male list.

It is not that women are fuzzy-headed sentimentalists and men tough-minded rationalists, but rather that each sex tends to emphasize one modality over the other. The differences are humorously illustrated in the classical interchange between a woman and her husband of many years. The wife was complaining to the marital therapist that her spouse never tells her he loves her. To this her husband replied, "I told her that I loved her when we got married. If the situation had changed, I would have informed her." So much for logic and reason!

### Inside versus Outside

Another male-female difference lies along the internal versus external dimension. Not only do women pay more attention to their own inner thoughts and emotional states than do men but they are more internally focused in terms of their own bodies. They are more in tune with bodily aches, pains, and other sensations in both a positive and negative manner. For example, they are more likely than men to see a doctor for genuine physical distress, and yet be more hypochondriacal along with it. The fact that a woman's major sex organs are partially (the clitoris) or totally hidden (the vagina) inside the body, while the primary male organ (the penis) is external and visible may contribute to her unique orientation.

The location of the primary sex organs may also be a factor in accounting for sex differences in the association between physical and emotional intimacy. Women tend to link emotional with physical closeness, while men are more adept at keeping these two components separate. Women prefer sexual intimacy with partners they are emotionally involved with, and sexual contact adds to their feeling of emotional closeness. Because sexual intercourse represents a penetration of body space for women, the man's physical presence in their inner bodily world may be a more emotionally intimate experience for women than the act of penetration for men. The experience of having our body space entered appears to be emotionally different from the experience of entering.

### Self-Esteem through Approval

Another intimacy-related difference between men and women is the extent to which relationships are a source of identification and self-esteem. Women tend to derive more of a sense of self through intimate relationships than men. Since more of their identity and ideal self are tied up with being "good, obedient, and helpful" than is true for men, women derive more self-esteem gratification from being sensitive and nurturant to others.

The problem with women defining themselves through their positive impact upon others is that they become dependent upon the approval of others for their self-worth. To view themselves as loving and giving, their helpfulness must be acknowledged and appreciated by others. Nurturance that is falling on deaf or critical ears hardly qualifies as self-esteem enhancing. Then, too, with all the emphasis on nurturing relationships, academic and artistic achievement with its more reliable provision of self-esteem tends to take a back seat. If women are so busy tending to the needs of others in hopes of obtaining approval, the likelihood of being successful in the more impersonal world of academia and high finance is less for women. As William Fezler and Eleanor Field, the authors of *The Good Girl Syndrome*, wrote, "You sacrifice your own personal satisfaction in return for being told how nice and sweet you are by the men whose approval you are seeking."[3]

Another drawback to women's high investment in relationships is that the vicissitudes of intimacy get exaggerated. When her self-esteem is riding every moment on his ups and downs, his every emotional and behavioral nuance becomes pregnant with meaning. His momentary indifference or surliness has greater significance to her than it would to a casual acquaintance. It is not just that he is tired from overwork or irritable because of traffic, but rather that he is unhappy with her and having significant doubts about their relationship. While she may be accurate in identifying his emotional states, her interpretation of his motives may be overly personalized. Her greater need for intimacy—and women *do* have higher levels of intimacy motivation[4]—colors the attributions she makes of his behavior.

## The Greater Importance of Intimacy for Women

Women's greater need for intimacy is manifested in a preoccupation with relationships and a stronger desire to maintain intimate contact. Women spend more time thinking about relationships; they also converse more and write more letters. In addition, they show higher levels of self-disclosure and express feelings more openly.[5] Their perceptions of intimate relationships also appear less conflictual. Men, by contrast, are more comfortable talking about sports, business, politics, and sex than they are about their private thoughts and feelings. They tend to fear intimacy more than women and are more pessimistic about the outcome of intimate relationships.

Because men have to separate from their first love object, their mothers, in order to become men, closeness with women is experienced as more regressive in nature. Prolonged intimacy for men is thought to stimulate anxiety associated with the infantile longing to be dependent and taken care of. Wanting to be held and caressed is more likely to be experienced as childlike and threatening by men. Because women identify with the first object of their affection, they do not have the same need to be separate from men in order to feel like women. Intimacy does not have the same regressive potential for women.

Men's greater tendency to roll over and fall asleep after lovemaking may be related to a greater need for distance after intimate contact. Conversely, women's greater need to stay intertwined for periods following sexual contact can be viewed as an attempt to prolong the intimate connection. For one sex, too much intimate contact is threatening, while for the other, too little contact is the greater danger.

With all these sex differences it is amazing that men and women get together for any length of time. Not only are men different from women in their orientations to the world, but they clearly have different intimacy requirements.

## Is There Love at First Sight?

The answer to that question is fairly easy: No, if we define love as Sternberg does. Because Robert Sternberg, a Yale psychologist who has researched the concept of love, sees love as having three dimensions—passion, emotional intimacy, and commitment[6]—love needs time to develop. However, if we are talking exclusively about passion when we ask that question, then the answer is yes, since it is clear that strong sexual attraction can occur at a moment's notice. The sight of an enchanted stranger across a crowded room can signal with a fluttering heartbeat the beginning of a supercharged affair.

Where does all that intense emotion come from? And how can we possibly discern what that stranger is all about at first glance? And why is the person who turns on one individual so different from the one who ignites another's passion?

The nature of sexual attraction is in many ways still a mystery to us. We are well aware of how powerful a force sexual attraction can be and how broadly it impacts upon us. When we are strongly attracted to another person, it is as if we are under a spell. All of our thoughts, motives, and feelings are dominated by the sexual attraction, and other emotional or reality-based considerations (job, friends, family) take a back seat. Dorothy Tennov, in her book *Love and Limerence: The Experience of Being in Love*, uses the term "limerence" to refer to the powerful emotional and sexual forces unleashed by sexual attraction.[7]

While the all-consuming nature of sexual attraction has a clear-cut biological or procreational imperative, psychological factors predominate in both object choice and the intensity of passion. The reasons why some people are attracted to shy, retiring souls, others to talkative, life-of-the-party types, and still others to bold, daring adventurers reside in the deep recesses of our past. The neurotic factors that account for repetitive, self-destructive patterns, such as the abused wife who chooses yet another abusing husband or the rejected boyfriend who finds cold, unavailable women especially appealing, are also found in our individual histories of intimacy.

## The Primary Ingredients of Passion

Regardless of the specific qualities that turn us on, familiarity is a key ingredient affecting our sexual choices under normal conditions. Her smile, the sound of his laughter, the twinkle in his eye, her body build, or her shyness may remind us of a favorite person—someone who provided us with warmth or pleasure at one point in our lives. The most likely candidates for "the favorite person" category are parents, grandparents, siblings, or special aunts and uncles because they tend to be important figures at developmentally vulnerable times. We gravitate toward old, familiar sources of pleasure, provided the degree of pain and conflict associated with them was not too great.

## Attraction to Similar Types

One woman remembered her enjoyment of the good-natured teasing she received from both an affectionate grandfather and a playful uncle when she was growing up. As a result, a teasing, playful manner became a major factor determining the intensity of sexual attraction she felt toward men. For others, it may be a certain physical characteristic (blue eyes, long legs, large breasts) or intelligence or strength of character reminiscent of a much-loved person that provides the titillation. The surge of sexual adrenaline that comes "out of the blue" when we encounter a stranger is a signal that an emotionally charged quality from the past is making a reappearance.

The qualities that we find sexually appealing may relate not only to favorite persons but to powerful and conflictual figures as well. A person may be powerful for us because they have authority, money, status, or charisma. Or they may be powerful because they are explosively angry or emotionally manipulative. For whatever reason, they have had a significant impact on our lives, and the characteristics they manifested became emotionally and sexually charged for us. Power, even if destructive, tends to have appeal.

## Other Sexually Appealing Factors

While the qualities we are attracted to vary from person to person, what they have in common is the high degree of emotional significance they have for us. They may be (1) traits directly associated with our favorite people, (2) nonconflictual qualities that were highly valued in our families, such as intelligence, musical talent, or sports ability, (3) interests and values similar to our own, (4) characteristics that are appealing or powerful along with being conflictual, (5) traits or values that are the opposite of what we experienced, (6) qualities that relate to the gratification of our emotional needs, and/or (7) ideal qualities that we hope will make up for our deficits. The first three categories of sexually appealing attributes are based on familiar positives, while the last four relate more to conflictual past experiences.

The common factors that contribute to conflict around sexual choice are intense attachment to and idealization of a parent, unresolved Oedipal/Electra complexes, early parental loss, severe rejection, sexual abuse, harsh criticism, and extreme unpredictability in a parent. In attempting to resolve such conflicts, we seek out carbon copies of the conflictual parent or opposite types. Whether we are more intent upon mastering, rejecting, or bypassing the source of conflict will affect the degree of similarity of our object choice. When we're determined to master the old pain, we seek out similar partners; when rejection of the past is our dominant motive, we look for opposites. And when we are trying to pretend that this new partner is nothing like the old, we search out partners who look different but behave in fundamentally similar ways.

## Attraction to Opposites

Whether we are attracted to familial figures or opposite types (in terms of cultural, ethnic, or racial characteristics) is a function of the amount of pleasure and degree of conflict associated with the family members involved. When the conflict was minimal and the number of positive experiences high, sexual attraction toward familial characteristics tends to prevail. However, whenever there was significant unpredictability, ambivalence, or withdrawal in a family member who was loved, the attraction to opposites may occur. The attraction to opposites also occurs when the longing for a highly valued and attractive parent or sibling runs into head-on conflict with the incest taboo. Because strong sexually tinged feelings toward family members are culturally and religiously prohibited, the attraction is transformed into its opposite.

Ruth, a forty-eight-year-old single woman who adored her father, remembered how she followed him around the house as a young child. His outdoor and mechanical activities were more exciting to her than her mother's domestic chores. His sudden death of a heart attack when she was in her teens left her feeling deserted and deprived of an important source of joy and happiness. However, rather than trying to replace him after his death with similar men, she found herself attracted to men who were physically opposite of her father. They were dark and swarthy while he was fair-skinned; they were large-boned while he was small; they were hairy while he was balding. More importantly, they were from a different ethnic (non-Jewish) background and socioeconomic level than he was. The only remnant of her earlier longing for her father in her sexual choices was age. With few exceptions, they were older men (by fifteen years or more) who held positions of authority in relation to her. While her lovers did not look like her father, their fatherly status was obvious to even the most skeptical eye.

Beatrice, a Jewish woman of forty, was also attracted to older men from different ethnic groups. The only child of two elderly parents, both of whom died before she was twenty-five, Beatrice was sexually turned off by Jewish men, even though her own father had been a very positive person for her. He had been a refined, scholarly man, who shared his love of the arts with his daughter. Their relationship had been a warm, loving one, albeit somewhat distant because his intellectual style added an element of aloofness to his personal manner. Here again, as with Ruth, the longing for a relationship with a highly positive parent is thwarted by death and becomes permanently transformed into an attraction toward opposites. The permanency of the loss seems to intensify the idealization, the desire and the pain attached, thereby rendering the wish for a relationship with a man like the father a more conflictual one. Also, the permanent loss makes it difficult for the desire to be close to the father to be transformed by reality and maturation into a less powerful motivation.

Even in situations where there is no parental loss, sexual attraction toward a different ethnic or racial group often occurs when there is strong attachment to a parent or sibling. Because the lover's physical appearance is so dissimilar to that of family members, the incest taboo is bypassed. The person who is attracted to opposite physical characteristics is lulled into believing that there is no similarity to the beloved familial figure. However, a significant but less obvious similarity, like age, clearly exposes the underlying dynamic.

Jose, a thirty-year-old, upper-class Mexican-American, was strongly attracted to a forty-two-year-old, white American woman, who was cultured, professionally accomplished, and financially solvent. Jose met her at a time when he was recovering from a three-year bout with alcoholism and struggling to get on his feet financially. Like an angel of mercy, she came to his rescue in a nurturant, maternal fashion.

As one might expect, Jose's relationship with his own mother was very close and supportive. The youngest child in a family with three much older siblings and a frequently absent father, Jose and his mother spent long hours together involved in artistic and musical pursuits. The companionship they shared was a source of intellectual and emotional gratification for them both. It was not surprising, then, that at a time of vulnerability Jose would be attracted to a woman with strong maternal qualities. The fact that she was of a different ethnic class made it easier to overlook the personality characteristics that were similar to his mother's.

## Rejection of Familial Values

Not all cross-cultural, interracial, or interclass relationships represent a retreat from the incest taboo. In some cases, cultural diversity is a strong familial value that is adopted. In upper-class families, for example, where there is travel abroad and intimate exposure to different cultures, a spirit of adventure and quest for novelty may be the underlying motivations for cross-cultural attraction. More frequently, however, the attraction to opposite cultural or physical characteristics represents a rejection of familial values. Because an important family member was seen as rejecting, critical, inadequate, or absent (and without redeeming value), the qualities they represented were discarded. A decision was made, typically on an unconscious level, to have nothing to do with any of the values or characteristics that the rejected family member represents.

Larry, a middle-aged English professor, after experiencing repeatedly cruel and blatant rejection at the hands of his mother, decided in his late teens to have nothing to do with her again. Not only has he not seen her since then, but his sexual choices stand in marked contrast to her, both ethnically and emotionally. They have been generous and caring blonde Scandinavians, dramatically different from his mother's cold and brooding Mediterranean demeanor. His healthy resolution appeared to be facilitated by a total lack of ambivalence. Once he made his final decision to reject his mother, he never looked back with regret or nostalgia (or so it has seemed).

In contrast to Larry's lack of equivocation was Martha's conflict-ridden rejection of her mother. Involved in an emotionally charged power struggle with her mother from an early age (she was a picky eater who refused to eat her mother's cooking throughout childhood), Martha's sexual choices were rejecting of maternal values and clearly self-destructive.

Martha's mother, a rigid WASP with upper-class standards, drank too much. She was somewhat bigoted and overly concerned about manners, propriety, and appearance. Not surprisingly, then, when Martha reached adolescence she became attracted to impulsive, rebellious, lower-class black men who were abusive to her. Not only were her choices markedly opposite to her mother's values, but Martha's own conflict about her sexual choices was apparent in the abusiveness of her lovers. Her choice of men who were cruel and aggressive toward her strongly suggested that she felt guilty and self-punitive about her rejection of maternal standards. However, another possible explanation for Martha's choices lies in the idealization of her father, who left the family for another woman when Martha was twelve. The incestuous conflict around her strong positive feelings toward him may also have contributed to Martha's maladaptive choice of men.

## *Attraction to Familiar, Maladaptive Types*

While the attraction to opposites is one outcome of highly conflictual familial relationships, another possibility is the compulsive repetition of the earlier frustrated longing, that is, being drawn to similarly depriving or maladaptive types. The person who has been rejected repeatedly is often drawn to cold, distant lovers or to safely unavailable married partners, who have no intention of leaving the marital bed. The woman whose relationship with her powerful, manipulative mother has been a source of turmoil marries a strong-willed, manipulative man. Battered women are forever drawn to battering men; ex-wives of alcoholics are attracted to alcoholic partners a second and even third time around.

Are we such creatures of habit that we are doomed to repeat forever the same old patterns? Once programmed, do we have no choice but to repeat the same old drama on yet another stage? At times, it certainly seems that way.

While the concept of familiarity is a partial explanation for repetitive, self-defeating patterns of sexual attraction, it does not tell the whole story. It may explain, for example, why Carol, a lesbian (see the "Fear of Loss of Control" section in Chapter 2 for more detail) with a history of rejection dating back to infancy, would continue to "fall in love" with unavailable or rejecting women. In her last self-defeating relationship, she was involved with a childlike, married woman who had intense ambivalence about her homoerotic feelings. Because of the ambivalence, she routinely bounced in and out of the relationship with Carol.

Even though rejection was painful, Carol seemed resigned to the idea that a loving relationship was not in the cards for her. One day, when asked in therapy if she believed that anyone could ever love her, she seemed astounded by the idea and replied that she thought it was impossible because "no one ever had." She had come to expect and seek out that which was known to her. It was only after she started to consider love as a real possibility that her sexual choices began to shift in a more adaptive direction. Currently, she is involved in a committed relationship with a kindly, older woman, who genuinely seems to care about her.

Besides familiarity, mastery motivation is another facet of maladaptive patterns of sexual choice. We repeat old patterns in hopes of altering the drama; that is, we want to rewrite the story with a happy ending. Even though our past experiences have been a source of intense emotional pain, the hope is that this time around it will be different. We want to achieve some sense of mastery over an old wound, to right an old wrong, in order to reduce our own sense of impotency and failure. And so, we desperately want to believe that this new, drug-abusing boyfriend will go straight or that this unfaithful lover will never stray again.

The attraction to appealing but conflictual familial characteristics often results in intense emotionality. Because there is both great appeal and deep disappointment or frustration, these familial qualities become very important. The combination of intense positive and negative emotion results in these familial traits becoming highly cathected. Then, when we are on the lookout for romantic partners, our emotional radar searches out these highly charged features. Like iron filings drawn to a magnet, we are attracted to these highly ambivalent, unresolved characteristics from the past in hopes of getting them settled once and for all.

**Unfaithful Types.** After a long history of neurotic or characterologically disturbed lovers, Kay (see the "Fear of Disappointment and Betrayal" section in Chapter 3 for more detail) finally met the man of her dreams (same ethnic and cultural background) and wanted to settle down with him in married stability. Unfortunately, he combined the worst qualities of each of her parents. He had her mother's dishonest, egocentric side along with her father's roaming and unfaithful eye, characteristics that had caused considerable pain and turmoil as she was growing up.

Why then was she attracted to these same burdensome qualities? Was it the hope of rewriting the childhood script or blatant naivete that led Kay toward another emotionally unavailable and rejecting man? The former motivation is more plausible, for in spite of her father's infidelity and desertion he had some strikingly appealing qualities. Like her fiancé, he was charming, highly intelligent, articulate, and professionally successful. Also, her father was more emotionally available than her mother, whose self-absorption left little room for anyone else. So, the glitter (and some substance) on the package was attractive and dazzling enough to blind her to his serious failings. After several breakups and reconciliations over three years, Kay finally ended the relationship when it became apparent that her dream man could not make an enduring commitment to one woman.

**Withdrawn Types.** Rosemary (see the "Fear of Losing Autonomy" section in Chapter 2 for more detail), too, was attracted to emotionally uncommitted men, but their kind of unavailability took a different form. Rather than being unfaithful, they tended to be emotionally withdrawn and distant, characteristics that were similar to both her father and her favorite brother. Her ex-husband had been a brooding, iconoclastic soul, who would retreat whenever Rosemary was needy or affectionate. What had been attractive about him, however, was his unconventionality and musical talent. As with her brother, who had been a musician before his death, her ex-husband's artistic intensity and mysterious aura were powerfully appealing. Unfortunately, his inability to maintain emotional closeness led to battles and, ultimately, to their divorce.

Another example of the power of unfinished business is Laura's highly charged, twenty-year fantasy relationship with Tim. An adolescent "first love," Tim's and Laura's relationship had many tragic elements. He was a boy from the wrong side of the tracks whom Laura's mother, in particular, objected to. Then, too, there was Laura's unwanted teenage pregnancy and abortion, which added dramatic emotional intensity to their union. Their on-again, off-again relationship continued for five years until each of them married someone else. Their emotional attachment, however, never diminished in intensity, and the fantasy of finding each other someday warmed many of Laura's lonely nights over the years.

When Laura and Tim finally met again fifteen years later, after they had gotten divorced from their respective spouses, the emotional and sexual fireworks were still there for both of them. The qualities that had earlier attracted Laura to Tim were very much in evidence in his middle age. He was still gregarious, manly, athletic, and self-sufficient. He had become successful at running his own plumbing business in their childhood hometown, while she had earned a doctorate and was a highly respected educator in a distant city.

While their relationship had all the markings of a perfect romance except for the professional disparity, Tim was an emotionally distant and ambivalent man, just as her father had been. Their sexually charged weekends together were followed by little ongoing communication on Tim's part until he abruptly stopped calling one day about six months after their reunion. His failure to answer her phone messages or to say much except "I've been busy" when she did reach him by phone left her hurt and baffled.

While Laura had been having doubts throughout their reconnection about Tim's emotional shutdowns (e.g., he seldom talked about feelings) and the paucity of shared intellectual interests, his sudden departure from her life was very confusing. What was clear, however, was the extent of Tim's similarity to her father. Both had the same appealing personality attributes—a kind of macho sociability and bravado. In addition, the socioeconomic disparity between Laura and Tim was similar to the one between her parents. Her father had been a coal miner while her mother came from an upper-class, professional family. The romanticized image of the hard-working, self-reliant man with ties to the soil fit both Tim and her father in Laura's eyes. Unhappily, along with these qualities was a pronounced emotional withdrawal and unavailability in both cases.

## Other Fueling Factors

### The Search for Wholeness

Regardless of whether we are attracted to similar or opposite types, sexual attraction often occurs in response to characteristics of our ideal self. We are attracted to qualities that we highly value and want for ourselves. When we are lacking the valued qualities, the wish to become a whole or complete person by merging with someone who has these characteristics (the completion hypothesis) is often in operation. The longing to compensate for our deficits by mating with an ideal partner becomes a powerful basis for sexual attraction.

Very often, the characteristics that constitute our ideal self are positive qualities, such as warmth, strength, and joviality, possessed by the important familial figures in our lives. These valued qualities borrowed from a variety of persons become fused into an ideal conglomerate that becomes the standard by which our intimate partners are judged. It is as if we are saying, "If only this partner had my father's intellect, my mother's patience and sensitivity, my grandfather's sense of humor, and my brother's good looks, then I could be happy." While this belief is unrealistic, this sort of expectation often festers underground until it can be examined in the light of reality.

The desire to make up for deficits is manifest in couples where a significant difference exists in emotionality, for example. In these cases, one partner is typically inhibited and overcontrolled, and the other, spontaneous and undercontrolled. The emotionally constricted member is attracted to the liveliness of the other, while the spontaneous member finds rationality appealing. Emotional spontaneity, on the one hand, enriches the drab existence of the overcontrolled member; the reasoned predictability of the controlled partner, on the other hand, adds security to the relationship.

Other examples where the completion hypothesis is at work are in the pairings of serious-funny, practical-idealistic, and adventuresome-complacent types. The desire to balance or control one personality characteristic by being attracted to its opposite is often in evidence. The dreamer falls in love with a practical soul as a way of keeping his feet on the ground. The serious person delights in her partner's humor, which adds emotional spice to her life. Adventuresomeness brings excitement; complacency introduces a measure of stability to the relationship mix.

Sex differences in attraction, with men as a group being

drawn to beauty and women to power and financial success, appear to be manifestations of the completion hypothesis. Those qualities that we as a sex lack have the greatest appeal. As cultural changes blur some of these sex differences, particularly as women attain more professional success on their own, the emotional factors governing sexual attraction should change to some degree. For example, when women discover that they are powerful forces in their own careers, they may be less attracted to men who are potent magnates and more attracted to men with other qualities, such as kindness or generosity.

## The Desire to Play Big Daddy or Momma

Sexual attraction is also powerfully influenced by our emotional needs at any given moment in time. The emotional desires that are in ascendance, such as needs for nurturance, dominance, submission, control, or a strong wish to be a caretaker, will affect our sexual responsiveness. Of the group, the most salient needs with aphrodisiac properties are the need to take care of someone, and, its converse, the wish to be taken care of.

Taking care of others typically boosts our self-esteem. Not only do we feel like decent human beings when we are loving and protective, but the nurturant stance has an added payoff—the feeling of being needed. Because others come to depend upon our generous outpouring of emotional goodies, we do not have to fear abandonment to any significant degree. The likelihood of being rejected by someone who is dependent upon us is small.

Marty, a talented sculptor and homosexual in his early forties, was attracted to younger versions of himself. In fact, several of his friends had commented on how much Marty and his most recent lover looked like brothers or "father and son." Marty was a recovering alcoholic who had given up alcohol use and the accompanying promiscuity (the one-night stands at the local bar) five years earlier. As part of his recovery, he was attempting to develop stable relationships in addition to being more productive artistically.

While he was successful careerwise (in fact, sobriety and artistic attainment went hand in hand for him), his intimate relationships continued to flounder. His choice of younger, more rebellious, and stereotypically masculine "sons" as lovers left him in the role of Big Daddy trying to rescue them from the consequences of their impulsive actions. The role was rewarding in many ways but also exhausting.

Growing up in a family with a patriarchal, distant father and a soft-spoken, kindly mother, Marty, the second son of four children, was familiar with the role of rescuer from his earliest days. While his older brother, who was the father's favorite, was pursuing traditional masculine activity (e.g., sports of all kinds), Marty was involved in artistic pursuits and in being the big brother to his younger sisters. His selection of younger, physically similar men seemed to represent both the search for an ideal self (younger, more "virile") and the desire to play a rescuing, fatherly role.

People who derive self-esteem gratification from the nurturant role, typically first-borns, are often sexually and emotionally attracted to helpless or psychologically vulnerable people who need them. Because each member of such an intimate pair is getting what he or she needs, the emotional and sexual turn-on is mutually reinforcing.

Because first-borns have had the most experience with the role of nurturer in their families of origin, this kind of relationship is a natural one for them. As a result of earning parental approval for performing the caretaking role with their younger brothers and sisters, taking care of others becomes an automatic source of self-esteem. Unfortunately, their own needs to be nurtured get buried in the process.

One brilliant young man who grew up in a demanding, intellectually gifted family dropped out of a doctoral program in chemistry at the age of twenty-one to marry a handicapped, highly dependent, and obese young woman from a lower socioeconomic level. A mathematical genius from early childhood, Max was the oldest son and the apple of his brilliant father's eye. The pressure to succeed academically, which was evident throughout

Max's childhood, was fueled in part by his father's personal frustration at not winning all the university accolades he had hoped for himself.

Max's turning his back on his father's professional dream to marry a woman who appeared to offer little seemed to be motivated by the rejection of his father's values and a strong need to nurture others. The rejection hypothesis is bolstered by the fact that Max and his wife became ardent fundamentalist Christians, while his parents were staunch atheists.

After ten years of marriage and four children, Max's life as a patriarch and primary caretaker of his family left him feeling worn out. To the observer, his life seemed chaotic and devoid of pleasure. He was regularly in debt as a result of poor financial management (rather than low earning power) and in conflict with school authorities because of a religiously based home tutoring program for his children. Max's extreme caretaking stance coupled with his wife's dependent helplessness had serious negative consequences for both himself and his family. While Max was overloaded and overworked, his wife had serious bouts of depression which required hospitalization. Although it is too soon to tell about their adult development, all four children appeared needy and somewhat unsocialized in childhood.

Sexual attraction to psychologically needy or downtrodden individuals is often a manifestation of a savior complex. Self-esteem gratification is derived from rescuing "damsels in distress" and others from their own impulsivity, drug dependence, or mental illness without risking too much. By being sexually attracted to individuals who have lower self-esteem than we do, the threat of abandonment or criticism is minimized. We can feel virtuous without exposing ourselves, as more egalitarian, intimate relationships require.

## Times of Vulnerability

Vulnerability is another factor that adds fuel to passion. At those moments in our lives when we are feeling particularly lost or overwhelmed, we are more likely to experience intense sexual attraction. Psychological vulnerability renders us more receptive to passion. Then, too, vulnerability increases the desire to be taken care of, often a strong component of sexual attraction.

The state of being raw, exposed, and undefended is more likely to occur after severe loss or rejection. After the death of a parent, for example, when our defenses have been dealt a severe blow and our sense of immortality permanently destroyed, we are more open to attachment. On the lookout for someone to fill the void, we are eager to bond with the first available person who crosses our path. If that person has the potential of being a caretaker and/or makes us laugh when we are sad, the stage is set for intense attraction.

Another time of great vulnerability occurs when we are rejected by an important lover. Reeling with self-doubt and feelings of inadequacy, we are wide open for the validation that takes place when someone is attracted to us. We are in need of a healing balm of some sort when we are smarting from the pain of rejection. Another's attentiveness soothes our troubled psyches and we are grateful. The road to a new intimate merger frequently lies on the rebound from rejection. The combination of emotional states (sadness, inadequacy, gratitude, liking) increases the emotional arousal available for sexual attraction. When several emotions or motives fuse, the potential for intense sexual bonding exists.

The blending of several emotional states into sexual attraction also occurs under certain circumstances with liking and fear. Psychologists Dutton and Aron have shown that fear magnifies interpersonal attraction,[8] while other investigators have demonstrated that physiological arousal in general enhances sexual responsiveness.[9] Whether we have difficulty in distinguishing one kind of arousal from another or whether there is a blending of emotional states with sexual arousal is not clear. What is clear is that intense sexual attraction often occurs in anxious people who have strong feelings of inadequacy. For some of them, sexual attraction takes on the quality of an obsession. Overwhelmed by intense sexual feelings fueled by anxiety, these neurotic, psychotic, or characterologically disordered individuals have difficulty putting these emotions into perspective or letting them go when the feelings are unrequited.

## The Impact of Defensive Style on Arousal

Why does one anxious person experience intense feelings of sexual arousal and another equally anxious person feel sexually inhibited? Why does one inadequate-feeling individual jump into a new intimate relationship shortly after being rejected while another insecure person retreats from intimacy for long periods after being burned? Since self-confidence and emotional stability do not explain the difference, what does?

One of the basic factors appears to be the dominant defensive style we use to process internal conflict. Whether we fight or flee in response to dangerous threats to our self-esteem is a function of where we sit on the approach-avoidance continuum. When we are anxious, do we ruminate about the problem for hours on end or avoid thinking about it as much as possible? In response to novelty and conflict, approachers tend to think about and confront situations (even when it would be better to avoid them), while avoiders tend to retreat rather than risk rejection, failure, criticism, or humiliation again.

With other factors being equal, approachers are more likely than avoiders to experience strong sexual feelings if they allow themselves to get involved in a relationship. One complicating variable, however, is degree of behavioral inhibition. People who approach conflict in their head but are behaviorally inhibited may not act upon any sexual urges that are experienced. Avoiders, by contrast, who repress conflict but are behaviorally impulsive may act out sexual feelings and be promiscuous. The most sexually inhibited person would likely be a repressed, behaviorally inhibited individual, while the most sexually integrated person would be an approacher with a moderate degree of expressivity. Depending upon defensive style and degree of behavioral control, sexual arousal is intensified or minimized by anxiety and feelings of inadequacy.

## The Intensity of First Love

Sexual feelings tend to be magnified a hundredfold during adolescence and early adulthood. Novelty, unpredictability, vulnerability, idealization, and merger fantasies provide fertile soil for the development of passion. This combination of factors, all of which magnify sexual feelings, sets the stage for the drama of our first love with all of its romanticism and occasional tragedy—witness Romeo and Juliet!

First experiences of any sort tend to be imbued with more emotion than subsequent ones. Our first day at school, first best friend, first party, and first date tend to be remembered more vividly than the later events, which lose their distinctiveness. The novel sensations of a first experience—the sights and sounds of a new world—are sometimes overwhelming, essentially because they represent uncharted territory. We have not been down those roads before.

Our first love is colored not only by the emotional impact of all first experiences, but it has the added emotionality of new tactile and bodily sensations. Being touched, hugged, kissed, and fondled in our newly adult bodies is intensely stimulating. We discover body zones that we never knew we had, reacting in ways that we never suspected. Added to the multiplicity of sensations clamoring to be heard is our vulnerability. Adolescence and early adulthood are times of uncertainty and change. While we may have been clear about where we stood in our families of origin, we do not know how attractive or lovable we will be to strangers. Our own insecurities make us an easy target for even the most casually attentive eye.

Coupled with our vulnerability is our tendency, when we are young and idealistic, to see the world in terms of polarities: good and evil, strong and weak, black and white. We long for a world where love, peace, justice, and beauty prevail. Anything less is unacceptable. When this need for perfection is dominant, our first love, whose beauty, goodness, and strength of character seem to outstrip even our grandest expectations, appears on the scene. What we are unaware of, however, is that it is the projection of our ideal qualities onto this loving stranger (and not his or her reality) that transforms him or her into a knight in shining armor or a beautiful maiden unsurpassed in goodness. The rose-colored glasses, which minimize negative qualities, add a spiritual or larger-than-life uniqueness to our first loves. Because they are seen as God's uniquely created soulmates for us, first loves are often felt to be irreplaceable and matchless. No one coming later can compare, which is why first loves frequently have long-lasting, emotional power in fantasy and memory.

The longing to become a whole person by merging with this ideal soulmate is frequently a part of our experience with first loves. Because our own identity as adults is incompletely formed at the time we encounter our first loves, the desire to become a better self by taking on the other's positive qualities is often intense. The intertwined bodies of young lovers and their constant touching of each other appear to be attempts to override the boundaries of skin and get inside. We want to become the other person, thereby enriching our own meager selves.

Laura (who was discussed in detail earlier in this chapter in the section "Attraction to Familiar, Maladaptive Types") maintained an intense attraction to her first love for over twenty years. In spite of marriages to other people and different career directions and lifestyles (she was a school principal in an urban area, he a plumber in a rural community), the fantasy of being reunited one day provided hope and comfort to both of them during periods of turmoil. While time, distance, and other intimate relationships failed to diminish their passion, reality turned in a harsher verdict. It was only Laura's anger at Tim's rejection that was powerful enough to dismantle and defuse the mystique of her first love.

## *Piecemeal or Whole-Person Attraction?*

Since much of sexual attraction is based on unconscious emotional components, sexual passion often appears fragmented and irrational. The question might be raised: Are we ever attracted to whole people rather than emotional pieces?

The answer is: Yes, over time! Initially, sexual attraction tends to be based on rather discrete physical and/or emotional characteristics, but the sources of attraction can expand gradually. As we get to know a person better and the enjoyment increases, the number of appealing characteristics can multiply until the whole person is encompassed.

At the beginning of a relationship, however, especially when passion or sexual attraction is high, we tend to be affected by specific qualities and by our own elaborations. Because we do not know a new love well, our own associations and projections affect the intensity of sexual desire. Our emotional responsivity to discrete qualities, our vulnerability, and our specific needs at a given moment in time all fuse to determine the sexual intensity. The combined emotionality of these elements often results in overwhelming passion that has little to do with the object of all this adoration.

With slower-developing intimacy, however, realistic factors tend to be the determining variables affecting the intensity of sexual attraction. Gradually, we begin to derive pleasure from different aspects of the other's personality until there is more of a total appeal. If the other is beginning to reciprocate in kind, their enjoyment of us is added to our enjoyment of them. The gradual growth of passion, intimacy, and commitment in an unfolding relationship adds staying power. Quick-starting fires burn out quickly, while slow-burning embers, fueled by reality, can last a lifetime.

*Chapter 7*

# Intimacy and Alcohol Abuse

For a substance, alcohol has achieved remarkable notoriety. Probably both the most widely acclaimed and the most vilified liquid around, alcohol has a unique place in our romantic, historical, and scientific literature. It is the substance most written about in our poetry and law books, and Demon Rum has prompted the greatest degree of ambivalence accorded to a nonliving thing. The poet Ogden Nash heralded alcohol as the means to fast romance ("Candy is dandy but liquor is quicker"),[1] while Shakespeare cautioned us about its illusory effects ("provokes the desire, but it takes away the performance").[2]

## Needs Served by Alcohol

Alcohol serves many psychological masters, which is one of the reasons for its perennial popularity. Not only is it a readily available tranquilizing or relaxing drug, but it has an opposite, or energizing, function. After adrenaline starts to flow with a few drinks, people report feeling more alive and integrated. Alcohol's tendency to depress the social regulatory or inhibitory mechanisms of the brain (the conscience or superego part of our personality) results first in an increase in the number of thoughts and feelings we experience. With the demise of our negative injunctions (the shouldn'ts or don'ts), we are free to converse effortlessly about a broad range of topics. Alcohol as a social lubricant increases conviviality and camaraderie.

## Increased Spontaneity and Impulsivity

Along with its disinhibiting function, alcohol decreases conflict. Since we care less after a few drinks about what others may think about our behavior, we are more likely to say or do anything we feel. The diminished concern about social approval and punishment results in greater spontaneity and impulsivity. Also, with the decrease in social control and concern about consequences, we are freer to be outrageous, angry, or seductive. In that way, we are more likely to get our affectional, exhibitionistic, sexual, or aggressive needs met. We are also more likely to feel powerful rather than frightened or inadequate, at least early on in the drinking sequence. Thus, the initial rewards of alcohol intake—greater sociability, expansiveness, spontaneity, and power, along with decreased anxiety and conflict—render it a highly reinforcing drug.

## Increased Depression

As we continue to drink, however, there is greater withdrawal and passivity. After five or six drinks, the depressant effects of alcohol begin to be experienced and the world takes on a somber tone.[3] Because negative experiences and feelings from the past get magnified by alcohol, we start to cry in our beers and wallow in self-pity. With increasing alcohol consumption, we recall feeling unloved, unappreciated, and/or abandoned by the important people in our lives. Such thoughts routinely lead to sadness, feelings of worthlessness, and depression. Thus, in one drinking sequence, we may go from hilarity and garrulousness to depressed withdrawal and despair.

## Costs and Benefits

In both the energizing and depressing phases of alcohol use, there are pluses and minuses. While we can get our sexual and affectional needs gratified with a bit of disinhibition, there is always the morning after, when the results of our impulsivity and lapses of judgment are apparent. Likewise, when alcohol frees us up to behave aggressively, there is a price to pay. Our victims with injured psyches or bodies will often rise up the following day to retaliate or leave us. In sum, while we achieve greater emotional freedom with alcohol, there is often a corresponding loss of sound judgment.

The depressing phase of alcohol use, while seeming to be all negative, also has its positive side. Our passivity allows us to behave in a more helpless and dependent manner than we ordinarily would. When we are slowed down, we do not have to be superresponsible and worry as much about everything. The comforting or soothing effect of alcohol can (almost literally) rock us to sleep. This nurturant effect of alcohol with its dependency-need gratification has a regressed, infantile quality to it. A case in point is the skid row alcoholic comfortably asleep on the curbstone in the middle of the day.

The retreat from the cares and responsibilities of the world into a near-comatose state at the end of a heavy drinking bout and in later-stage alcoholism appears to be primarily psychopharmacological, that is, related to the physical effects of the drug. Withdrawal seems to be an end point of drinking rather than the motivation that instigates alcohol consumption. What seems more important motivationally than the wish to retreat into passivity is a desire to reduce internal conflict in some fashion. For some people, conflict reduction occurs by withdrawal, while for others, behavioral expression or acting out of impulses is the dominant method.

## Acting Out Anger

Ed, a thirty-seven-year-old marketing manager, sought help for his excessive drinking, essentially because his live-in girlfriend of four years was threatening to leave him. Ten years his junior, Sylvia was described by Ed as a beautiful, naive woman with whom he had great sex. He enjoyed playing the role of Henry Higgins with her, teaching her about manners, music, and culture, and was very attached to her. Sylvia was an uneducated waitress, who grew up on the other side of the tracks.

The problem in their relationship was Sylvia's suspected infidelity. There were many secret phone calls with whispered phone responses and early morning returns from nights out with her girlfriends. Sexual paraphernalia and undergarments that were unfamiliar to him provided even more tangible evidence. In spite of all this, he was unable to confront her with his suspicions except when intoxicated. At those times, he was verbally and, occasionally, physically abusive to her.

When sober, Ed felt that being loving and understanding was the best way of keeping Sylvia around. He also had a great deal of difficulty in expressing his feelings honestly to her or anyone else for fear of alienating people to the point where they would reject him. Alcohol gave him permission to be more straightforward but impaired his impulse control. For Ed, the therapeutic task was learning how to be more direct in expressing anger, hurt, and disappointment when sober. Happily, he was successful in doing so and, concomitantly, learned how to control his drinking.

## Reducing Sexual Conflict

Besides facilitating the expression of negative affect, alcohol is also used to reduce sexual conflict. The sexual conflict may be related to religious/moral dilemmas about sexual behavior, unconscious homosexual impulses, sexual identity confusion, and/or sexual adequacy concerns. In Wendell's case, both homosexual feelings and deep concern about his own manliness were the basis of his heavy drinking. Wendell was a single, forty-year-old accountant with a long history of daily drinking, whose entrance into therapy was precipitated by physical distress (headaches, gastrointestinal symptoms) and concentration and memory problems.

Wendell's heavy use of alcohol began in college as a way of reducing social anxiety and shyness in groups. However, he began to drink in a more solitary fashion shortly after he developed potency problems with a girlfriend, who was only interested in occasional sex, not a more total relationship, with him. Her rejection of him (he had wanted to marry her) coupled with his own disturbing, masturbatory fantasies of wearing a diaper brought to the surface deep-seated feelings of inadequacy as a man. Incidentally, the fantasy of being diaper-clad that accompanied his masturbatory activities was related to a memory fragment of being erotically stimulated accidentally by his father while his diapers were being changed.

Wendell's concerns about masculinity and sexual adequacy had their roots in a competitive relationship with a good-looking, athletic older brother, who was the family star. In contrast to his brother's appearance and behavior, Wendell was a tall, thin, bookish-looking man with spectacles. His serious, shy, and clumsy manner was the antithesis of his brother's charming gregariousness. "No matter what I did, I was never as good as Tom," he once said. It was not surprising, then, that Wendell had strong doubts about his own manliness with his brother as a comparison norm. It was only after he began to resolve his feelings of inadequacy and develop greater self-esteem that his drinking was brought under control. Currently, he seems to be happily married with no evidence of alcohol problems.

## Boon to Creativity?

In contrast to Wendell's drinking, Martha's early alcohol use allowed her to be sexually promiscuous without conscious guilt. A shy, inhibited woman who grew up in a strict religious home, Martha went through a rebellious phase that began as soon as she left for college. Wild parties with other artistic free spirits, reckless motorcycle rides in the middle of the night, cigarette smoking, heavy alcohol use, and sexual promiscuity were prominent in her early and middle adulthood.

Martha came into therapy at age thirty-two to stop drinking.

She had been married for a year and a half to a quiet, conservative architect, and they were considering having a child. Over the years, her alcohol consumption had climbed to two six-packs of beer daily, which she felt was necessary in order to help her create artistically. According to Martha, alcohol freed her to focus deeply on her artistic endeavors. She saw alcohol as a boon to her concentration and creativity. However, with the pressure from her husband to have a baby, she was in conflict about her alcohol use at the time she came into therapy.

With the ongoing support of AA and intermittent psychotherapy, Martha did give up alcohol use and has remained abstinent throughout the past seven years. Unfortunately, her story is not one that can be concluded with "and she lived happily ever after." Because abstinence starkly exposed the marital problems that her alcohol use had swept under the rug, she became depressed about the lack of communication and companionship in her marriage. Alcohol had cast a rosy glow on her marriage and made it palatable. Now, without illusions, she had to confront the reality of being married to a very withdrawn and inhibited man, who was insensitive not only to her emotional needs but to his own as well.

Then, too, the arrival of a baby three years into her sobriety further strained their marital relationship. With a very colicky and demanding infant daughter and a husband who had retreated further, Martha was on the verge of emotional collapse when she returned to therapy five months after the birth of her baby. She had struck her infant daughter several times and was frightened by this loss of control. In addition, she felt no maternal attachment to her child and, in fact, was overwhelmed by anger and dislike for her. Motherhood was experienced as an ever-present demand from which there was no escape.

Over time, AA, individual therapy, couples therapy, and a course in parenting skills brought her some relief but little enduring happiness. She seemed to enjoy the companionship of other young mothers and found some satisfaction in her artwork and comfort in her church, but as of this writing, has continued to feel inadequate and burdened. For Martha, sobriety exposed more intrapsychic and intimacy problems than it resolved. Without the liberating effects of alcohol, Martha was left with a rigidly controlled personality that permitted little spontaneity and pleasure.

## Alcohol Use and Avoidance

In an established intimate relationship, alcohol is more likely to be used as a means of avoiding emotional and sexual intimacy than as an aphrodisiac. Drinking nights out with the boys at the local pub and solitary drinking at home late into the night are often substitutes for intimate contact. Rather than confront the fears and dangers associated with prolonged intimacy, the drinker tries to avoid the nagging wife or critical husband altogether. The camaraderie of drinking buddies or solitary peace and quiet are preferred.

What exactly is being avoided by excessive alcohol use? The confrontations, accusations, rejections, exposed inadequacies, demands for greater closeness, disappointments, and/or guilt that arise in intimate encounters are being avoided like the plague by one drink too many.

### Avoiding Conflict

When problems arise in intimate relationships (as they inevitably do) and tension over unresolved conflicts mounts, the possibility of an explosive encounter increases. Facing an angry partner who is all too eager to scream at us about our shortcomings may have about as much appeal as standing in front of a firing squad. Or the prospect of talking to our wounded partner who is devastated by our unfeeling words or actions is anticipated with as much pleasure as we mustered for our disciplinary sessions with the school principal. Or when the thought of making love to an intimate partner who is perceived as emotionally uptight, lacking in passion, or sexually unappealing turns us off, then having a drink or two seems like a pleasurable alternative. It feels better to find solace in liquor than to deal with a potentially unpleasant encounter.

Barbara and Tom came into couples therapy because of Tom's excessive drinking. Since the birth of their first child five years earlier, their close and companionable relationship had begun to deteriorate. Tom's job stress (he was in the highly demanding and cutthroat world of international finance), his disappointment that he had two daughters rather than sons, and his sense of inadequacy as a father all contributed to the acceleration of his drinking. His daily drinking of several bottles of wine, which began at noon with his business associates, left him exhausted and ready to collapse by the time he got home for dinner. Too tired to talk much, he retreated into his den soon after arriving home and fell asleep shortly thereafter. His daily retreat into an alcoholic stupor left his wife, who also had a professional job, feeling abandoned and resentful. Not only did all of the household and emotional chores of the family fall on her shoulders, but she felt deprived of the emotional contact with him that had been a gratifying part of their earlier relationship.

Tom's excessive drinking and avoidance of his family would have continued had not Barbara taken a strong stand. Her calm announcement during their first therapy session that she would leave him if he did not stop drinking and spend some time with her was jarring to him. Visibly shaken by this pronouncement, Tom had never even considered this a possibility. He was obviously still very much in love with Barbara and wanted their relationship to continue. Using therapy sessions to regain verbal and emotional contact, they quickly worked out alternate means of reducing stress, ways for Tom to spend conflict-free time with their daughters, and a new division of labor. Along with these changes, Tom significantly reduced his alcohol consumption.

## Gregarious Alcoholics

For men who are problem drinkers or alcoholics, the nightly stop at the local watering hole is both avoidance behavior and a search for easy companionship. In the dimly lit, noisy atmosphere of a club or bar, light banter and free-flowing conversation can be found without much risk. Typically, no criticisms are offered nor judgments made (at least early on in the evening). There are no demands for greater closeness or increased sensitivity. Rather, the easy acceptance, effortless give-and-take of conversation, merriment, and music create an atmosphere of play and pleasure. The feeling of male bonding also brings back pleasant memories of all-male group activities that took place on the playing fields in childhood and adolescence.

Contrast this relaxed scene with the more aversive scenario that typically greets the male drinker when he sets foot on his home doorstep. His long-suffering wife, who is tired, depressed, and bored, acknowledges his arrival with an icy glare or a weary nod. Whether she has been taking care of the kids all day or holding down a full-time job, she is exhausted and angry. Working at full capacity to keep the home fires burning with little support or appreciation, she feels drained of emotional resources with nothing to give. Her husband's late arrival with alcohol on his breath unleashes the torrent of rage that she has been holding back and the angry confrontation begins.

In the midst of tears, she accuses him of neglect, insensitivity, selfishness, and irresponsibility while he defends himself loudly by self-justification or counterattack. In either case, the onslaught of accusations leaves him feeling misunderstood, hurt, guilty, or angry—and ready to hit the bar again the following day. For the thought of facing his wounded and angry wife again leaves him feeling cold and anxious and beset by the feelings of inadequacy that have haunted him all his life. He will need that "one drink," he tells himself, to take away the edge he is feeling so that he can greet her with open arms. Unfortunately, the one drink will lead to four or five, and the stage is set for a repeat performance.

Once this kind of vicious cycle is set up, it is difficult for either partner to stop. The adverseness of their confrontations renders it difficult to anticipate reunions with pleasure, and the building sense of hurt betrayal creates a wedge between them. He begins to see her as a punitive, withholding mother, and she starts to view him as an irresponsible, self-centered boy. Since neither perception is ordinarily accompanied by romantic or sexual feelings, avoidance of intimacy becomes the dominant interpersonal strategy.

## Solitary Drinkers

The solitary drinker (usually a woman) who is involved in an intimate relationship is also avoiding closeness, but rather than seeking solace in the company of others, she derives comfort from being alone. Typically an introvert, the solitary drinker uses alcohol to retreat into a safe, inner world where she can ponder the universe, human nature, or relationships. Often, alcohol facilitates her getting in touch with feelings and ideas more profoundly than she experiences in a sober state. Thus, alcohol has both a soothing and a liberating function for her early on in her drinking pattern.

The inner world into which the solitary drinker retreats is a haven from the dangers of intimacy. Needing more space from the demands of intimacy than most people, the solitary drinker is ordinarily (when sober) too conscientious to withdraw from intimacy for any length of time. She feels the responsibilities of intimacy (the listening, conversing, and caring functions) keenly. It is only through alcohol use that she can escape guilt-free, temporarily at any rate. While drinking, she can avoid the risks of intimacy and derive psychological gratification at the same time. Unfortunately, however, her alcoholic retreat does not always remain comforting. Many times, feelings of rage, terror, or sadness interrupt the pleasant reverie and transform the experience into a nightmare. Nevertheless, she continues to seek the soothing high that occurs at the beginning of a drinking episode and forgets about the terror-filled moments that occasionally follow.

## Choosing Withholding Men

The solitary woman drinker tries to avoid intimacy because the kind of man she married (or is involved with) highlights her own insecurities. Worried about her own adequacy as a woman and sexual partner, she frequently chooses a withholding, controlling, and critical man much like her own father (or mother, in other cases). While she was trying to recreate and master earlier conflicts about lovability and self-worth in her selection of an intimate partner, her choice of men and her drinking keep her in a one-down or inadequate position.

The woman drinker's concerns about sexual adequacy and self-worth get magnified in a relationship with a nonaffectionate man, who has difficulty in appreciating or validating her. The more she seeks out approval from him, the more likely he is to reject her. For the intimate partner in such a relationship is often unable to tolerate emotional demands of any magnitude. Her neediness overwhelms him, and so he withdraws further into icy self-righteousness. Marian Sandmaier, in her book *The Invisible Alcoholics*, wrote:

> The "feminine" woman who becomes alcoholic is likely to have married a man who keeps her at an emotional distance, which serves her needs to the extent that she tends to put little trust in the affection of others and thus fears relationships that require real intimacy. But ironically, her choice of husband only serves to perpetuate her intense, lifelong loneliness and her conviction that no one could truly care for her.[4]

Left to her own devices, then, the woman drinker increases her alcohol consumption and avoids her partner just as he avoids her. Unfortunately, her drinking provides him with a valid reason for avoiding her even more. And so, they get locked into a battle of emotional withdrawal from each other that is interrupted periodically by overt conflict, until a crisis demands change in one, the other, or both.

## Power Struggles around Autonomy

With a male gregarious drinker, the dynamics are similar and, yet, different. He, too, has struggled with inadequacy concerns related to masculinity all of his life and, frequently, chooses a nondemonstrative, critical, and controlling woman for an intimate partner. Trying desperately to win the approval of a woman who has difficulty giving it, the male drinker often gets into a passive-aggressive power struggle with her around his drinking. The more she tries to stop him from drinking, the more vigorously he asserts his independence in deciding when, where, and how much he will drink. His drinking becomes the battleground on which he protests and protects his autonomous masculinity ("Drunk and Proud").[5] His drinking also becomes the vehicle in which he manifests his rage at his partner's attempts to control him. Thus, for male problem drinkers, drinking is often accompanied by violence toward their intimate partners.

In contrast, women alcoholics are more likely to be depressed and suicidal than violent when intoxicated. "Studies repeatedly show that alcoholic women suffer significantly more guilt, anxiety, and depression than alcoholic men, have lower self-esteem, and attempt suicide more often," wrote Sandmaier in *The Invisible Alcoholics*.[6] As drinking becomes more and more maladaptive, the positive aspects of solitary drinking are replaced by self-loathing and hopelessness. The more self-punitive and passive behavior of women frequently results in a tearful, self-blaming intoxicated state, where the primary verbalized concern is about being unloved. This is not to say that women do not become angry and violent when drunk, but simply that they are more likely to be depressed, whereas the opposite possibility is more likely for men.

## Strong Need for Approval

Typically, both male and female alcoholics have self-esteem problems, sexual adequacy concerns, strong fears of intimacy, a family history of alcoholism, and an intense need for approval and affection. One alcoholic scribbled on the blackboard of an inpatient alcoholism treatment unit: "Alcoholics have a sick need to win the approval of others who have a sick need to withhold it." While his comment has more than a grain of truth to it, what is not clear is which comes first. Does the alcoholic's excessive need for approval overtax the intimate partner, who becomes more withholding over time? Or does the alcoholic's drinking turn off the affectional behavior of the intimate partner? Or does a depriving spouse intensify the alcoholic's insecurity, need for approval, and alcohol consumption? Or, as is usually the case, is there a mutually reinforcing and reciprocal system at work in the alcoholic couple so that the answer to all three questions is yes? It certainly seems that way! Our own personality predispositions get reinforced by the responses of our intimate partners, and we do likewise for them, so that it becomes difficult, if not impossible, to separate the person from the interpersonal environment in which he or she resides. We become to some degree what our intimate partner desires and/or fears.

## Alcohol Use as Marital Glue

Alcohol use can also serve to keep a dysfunctional couple together. If drinking becomes a way of reducing the motivation to complain, leave, or make changes in the relationship, then it can have a stabilizing effect. Dissatisfactions can be buried and passivity can reign supreme!

When the complaints about relationship unhappiness repeatedly fall on deaf ears, the drinker has several options. He or she can attempt to accept the partner's limitations, seek help, or leave. Since the request to seek out couples counseling is often rejected by the intimate partner who is convinced that the root of the marital problems resides in the drinker, accepting the situation or leaving become the other viable alternatives. Of these two possibilities, acceptance or resignation is usually preferred because the thought of ending the relationship is filled with fears about loneliness and doubts about sexual attractiveness and competence in handling life alone. Then, too, the drinker is often still very emotionally attracted to and attached to his or her more adequate-appearing partner.

Over time, then, the drinker tries to adapt to the partner's more repressed, controlled, and conservative style and lead a "normal life." In this type of alcoholic pairing (which is a fairly typical pattern), the partners tend to be the security-minded, pragmatic members, while the drinkers are the ambitious, somewhat grandiose dreamers. The drinker tends to provide excitement, humor, and playfulness to the relationship, while the partner brings security, reality, and consistency to the system. The drinker keeps reaching for the stars, while the intimate partner tries to keep both their feet planted firmly on the ground.

In this kind of relationship, frustration at not finding the spontaneity, affection, or adventure the drinkers had hoped for in their lives fuels their drinking. However, if their drinking is not too disruptive, and their partners have minimal needs for intimate contact, the drinking may stabilize the relationship. The alcohol use may keep drinkers guilt-ridden enough to doubt their ability to maintain any other intimate relationship and also robs them of the energy necessary to leave. So, they are caught in an ongoing cycle of dissatisfaction leading to drinking leading to guilt, which leads to more drinking.

If the partner has his or her own conflicts about intimacy and a high need for distance in the relationship, the spouse's drinking can be ignored. Because the drinking allows the partner to engage in his or her own solitary pursuits, the drinking may be viewed, with a sigh of relief, as a way of keeping intimacy demands at a minimum. The intimate partner who falls asleep intoxicated most evenings is in no bargaining position to insist upon greater sexual or emotional contact, so the spouse can relax. At times, the drinking also serves to keep the drinker blind or only dimly aware of the partner's extramarital affairs. Even if the drinker is aware of the infidelity, the suspicions of a mind clouded by too much alcohol can easily be dismissed by both partners.

## Heavy-Drinking Cultures and Intimacy

In some heavy-drinking cultures (e.g., the Irish in Boston are seven times as likely to develop alcohol problems as other ethnic groups),[7] the husband's daily drinking may be ignored by his wife, who has little interest in emotional or sexual contact with him. Whether the woman's lack of interest in intimate contact is a consequence of the husband's drinking, an antecedent of it, or an interactional effect is not always clear. What is apparent, however, is that her husband's inebriated withdrawal is both an expectation and a relief. Having grown up in households where men regularly drink heavily, these women appear to view the drunken behavior of men as a routine occurrence, which reduces intimacy demands for them.

Harriet and Chester were first-generation, blue-collar Polish-Americans, whose families of origin were headed by heavy-drinking fathers. In addition, two of Chester's three older brothers were alcoholics. Not surprisingly, then, Chester, an intelligent and ambitious man with strong feelings of inadequacy, began to manifest alcohol problems early in his marriage. A proud, rigid, and dominating man, Chester often came home intoxicated from his factory supervisory position to berate his wife for not loving him enough or to complain bitterly about not being appreciated sufficiently on the job.

Harriet's initial response to Chester's verbally abusive drinking was depressive helplessness. A mild-mannered, childlike, and passive-dependent woman with limited intellectual resources, Harriet initially played the role of martyr. As the helpless victim of an angry husband, she was often reduced to tears and unable to see any alternative course of action for herself. She would often wring her hands and ask no one in particular, "Oh, what should I do?" While Harriet was a warm and pleasant woman when not depressed, she once confessed that she never liked sex and was relieved that Chester passed out shortly after walking in the door at night.

When both their children were in grade school, Harriet got a part-time job as a sorter in a department store. The job turned out to be a godsend for her because it provided her with companionship along with an escape from her marital woes. She loved getting out of the house each day and enjoyed being in the company of other women. For thirty years, the job added stability to her marriage. As long as she could leave the marital situation for some time each day, she could tolerate Chester's daily drinking.

Over the course of this thirty-year period, Chester's drinking continued at the same frequency as before, but there were fewer associated emotional outbursts. His drinking seemed to lose its emotional intensity. Also, the couple gave up sexual contact, essentially at Harriet's doing, and slept in separate rooms. The price of this more tranquil phase was minimal intimacy.

When Harriet retired, she began a daily pattern of solitary drinking. Earlier in her life, it was apparent that she enjoyed social drinking, but there was no evidence that she was drinking in any problematic manner. However, with the absence of daily structure upon her retirement and the increased contact with her spouse, she began to use alcohol in a decidedly self-destructive manner. While Chester maintained a daily drinking regime (he would drink from 11 a.m. till 2 p.m. at the local tavern with his buddies, come home staggering drunk, fall asleep for several hours, have a shot or two of whiskey with dinner, watch TV, and retire early), Harriet would sip vodka surreptitiously throughout the day. By early afternoon, she was slightly incoherent, but no one in her family was clearly aware of her drinking.

Harriet's drinking behavior was not apparent to her alcoholic husband who lived with her, nor to any other relative, many of whom were frequent visitors. It was only when her health began to deteriorate dramatically and the diagnosis of cirrhosis was made that her condition was made public. Sadly, she died shortly thereafter from complications related to her liver condition. Her sudden death at age sixty-eight, years before Chester's demise, was a shock to her family and many friends.

In Harriet and Chester's case, alcohol use, while clearly self-destructive, also served to keep their marriage together. If either one had stopped drinking, the sober partner would have had to face the emptiness of the relationship and do something to change the situation, for it was apparent that few of their intellectual, sexual, and emotional needs were being met. Chester seemed to need a lustier and brighter woman to match his sexual and intellectual needs, while Harriet appeared to need a quieter, gentler man who could have given her the attention and affection she required. Unfortunately, as is often the case, their marital choices were determined by unconscious issues that had past origins rather than by their current emotional requirements.

## Alcoholism and the Family

One of the legacies of alcohol abuse is significant damage to the ability of family members to be intimate with others. Because parental alcohol use creates unpredictability and instability in the family system, nothing and no one can be trusted. The parent who is drinking problematically undergoes dramatic mood swings as the level of blood alcohol rises and falls; the nondrinking partner, who is reacting to the drinker's emotional and behavioral changes, is also behaving in untrustworthy ways. The drinker may be loud and abusive one day, remorseful and affectionate the next, while the partner's behavior ranges from moody withdrawal to forced cheerfulness. The lack of stability fuels anxiety and uncertainty in all family members, who feel buffeted about by the emotional turmoil around them.

Another factor that contributes to the distrust and uncertainty is the lack of credibility. The adults in an alcoholic home cannot be believed—not the drinking parent, who keeps promising to abstain, nor the nondrinker, whose words of reassurance have a hollow ring. Because denial of conflict tends to run rampant in alcoholic families, the children are required to distort their perceptions. Putting on rose-colored glasses, they are asked to see, hear, and speak no evil. Mommy or Daddy is sick with the flu, not a hangover, and the bruises on Brother's arm were caused by an accidental fall, not by abuse.

Because of the instability and dishonesty in the family, the children often need to create predictability and certainty for themselves. By acting within fairly circumscribed roles, they can reduce their own anxiety. In that way, they can learn to depend on themselves rather than on others. Since they cannot trust others, they are hoping that they can trust themselves.

The familial roles that children in alcoholic homes adopt have been described in detail in recent years. Claudia Black[8] wrote about the "Responsible One," "Acting-Out Child," "Placater," and "Adjuster" roles, while Sharon Wegscheider[9] described the roles of the "Hero," "Scapegoat," "Lost Child," and "Mascot." Both writers identified children assuming a parental or pseudomature role (Hero/Responsible One), a distracting role (the Acting-Out Child or Scapegoat) that draws attention away from the marital conflict to the child, and a distancing role (Lost Child/Adjuster) where the child tries to remove himself or herself from the family turmoil and spend more time with friends. While these particular roles have not been determined to be the only ones found in alcoholic families or to be unique to them, they resonate with adult children of alcoholics and appear to have experiential validity.

While roles of any sort are helpful in reducing confusion, they also restrict the self. For example, if we have to be helpful and tuned in to parental needs at all times, our own confusion, anger, helplessness, and desire for nurturance will get buried, only to resurface in other intimate relationships. Or if we need to play the scapegoat as a way of deflecting our parent's anger from each other, our needs for love, appreciation, and approval will get put on a back burner until they are resurrected with great intensity at a later time. Typically, the rigidity of the role keeps emotional needs at bay until intimacy appears on the scene in adolescence or early adulthood.

Alcoholism in the family is also damaging to the self-esteem of spouses and children. No matter how hard everyone tries to avoid family conflict (by burying oneself in schoolwork or athletics, for example), there is literally no escape. If the alcoholic has violent outbursts, everyone will be a victim at one time or another. According to James Milam and Katherine Ketcham, who wrote *Under the Influence,* alcohol is involved in 60 percent of known child abuse cases,[10] while Claudia Black estimates that 66 percent of the children of alcoholics have been physically abused or witnessed such abuse in the family. In addition, she estimates that over 50 percent of known incest victims come from families where at least one member abused alcohol.[11] Spouse abuse is also believed to occur more frequently among alcohol-abusing couples.

Even with a quiet, withdrawn alcoholic, someone in the family, usually the spouse, will become verbally abusive on occasion because emotional needs are not being met and frustration tolerance is down. Then, too, the guilt that arises because of the drinking—the feeling of being responsible somehow for the drinker's unhappiness—contributes to the lowering of self-esteem. If only we were more considerate, helpful, or compassionate, our mommy, daddy, husband, or wife would not drink.

Thus, the impact of alcoholism on the family is multifaceted and pervasive. It has been estimated that every alcohol abuser or alcoholic negatively affects a minimum of four other people's lives.[12] In addition to the lack of trust, high level of anxiety, stereotypical role behavior, denial of emotional needs, guilt, and lowered self-esteem, the family member in an alcoholic home is also prone to addictive behavior of one kind or another. As a result of physical, emotional, or sexual abuse, psychological deprivation, and maladaptive coping skills learned from parents, the children in these families are vulnerable and at high risk for addictions. When these children grow up and have to contend with the demands of intimacy, they will find that a multipurpose drug like alcohol is a particularly appealing first choice for self-soothing and conflict resolution.

## Chapter 8

# Intimacy and Violence

As the statistics indicate, violence of all kinds abounds in intimacy. For example, the FBI has reported that a woman is battered in this country once every eighteen seconds.[1] About 7 percent of wives and about 1 percent of husbands experience severe beatings, or other physical abuse.[2] Besides the violence between intimate partners, abusive behavior toward children in families is staggering, with annual estimates ranging from 1 to 1.4 million cases.[3] Because most domestic violence occurs under the influence of alcohol and other drugs (estimates range from 50 to 75 percent of cases),[4] it is clear that we are dealing with a multidimensional problem.

Why do we hurt the ones we love? Essentially, because we have allowed our lovers into our intimate zone and they have profoundly threatened our self-esteem. Intentionally or inadvertently, they have penetrated to the core of our identities. They may have exposed our painful inadequacies, rubbed salt in old wounds, or taunted us about our shortcomings. They may have refused to do as we said, making a mockery of our position as head of the family. Or they were unwilling to love us or have sex with us in what appeared to be a cavalier disregard for our needs. Whatever the alleged crime, it cuts deeply into our fragile sense of self-worth, and we react with overwhelming rage at times.

We also abuse our partners because we feel entitled to certain intangibles in the relationship. We may feel that love, affection, respect, and sexual gratification are owed to us, that they are our birthrights in intimacy. Then when our partners fail to deliver, we feel justified in attacking them for depriving us of our due.

## Power and Control

The need to dominate intimate partners stems from two motivations: powerlessness and narcissistic entitlement. When the abuser feels ineffective in getting his emotional needs met, coercive attempts increase in frequency, intensity, and irrationality. These attempts include insistence, begging, pleading, and/or the use of physical force. When these increasingly vocal or physical demands are ignored or rebuffed, the violent act ensues, born of frustration, despair, and the terror of abandonment. In the act of violence, which seems a last-ditch effort to maintain intimate contact, the abuser seems to be saying, "I hate you for not loving me as much as I want" along with "I need you desperately to fill my emptiness, so don't leave." Feeling diminished by the rejection and frightened by the possibility of being deserted, the abuser is desperately trying to hang on to his or her partner.

Abusers' inability to control their partners is usually accompanied by a general feeling of powerlessness. Often, they do not feel in control of any aspect of their lives: job, children, or social life. They may be unemployed or working at a low-level job; their children may be the wrong sex or not as smart, athletic, or sociable as they had hoped. They may be lacking in friends and isolated from the community in which they live. All in all, they are experiencing more stress in their world than a nonabuser is.

However, whatever the abuser is feeling—tension, sadness, despair, or powerlessness—is quickly transformed into rage. With softer feelings, like hurt, sadness, and disappointment, there is usually an accompanying sense of helplessness that further intensifies feelings of inadequacy. In contrast, there is potency in anger and violence. As one schizophrenic man said after recovering from a catatonic episode, "Madness is better than sadness.

When you're mad, you can do something while when you're sad, you don't feel like doing anything at all." What he seemed to be saying was that anger spurs action, which feels more potent than passivity. There is greater psychological power in action even when the behavior is destructive in nature.

## Role Models of Violence

Besides feeling powerless, the male abuser has typically observed violence in his family of origin and so regards domination and violence as part of his role as breadwinner and head of the household. For example, the chances of being a wife-abuser are ten times greater if a man grew up in a violent rather than a non-violent home.[5] There he not only observed violence being perpetrated on others but he was often the victim himself. Thus, he learned how to discharge the rage that was fueled by the cruel treatment inflicted upon him by abusing others.

As a result, the abuser is convinced that control over the family is both his lot and responsibility in life. Hitting wives is somehow viewed as a duty that is necessary to show wives who is in charge. According to sociologists Richard Gelles and Murray Straus, who wrote the book *Intimate Violence*, "The most telling of all attributes of the battering man is that he feels inadequate and sees violence as a culturally acceptable way to be both dominant and powerful."[6] Not only is domination viewed as role-appropriate, but the violent man often feels that he is more intelligent, wiser, or more knowledgeable about the ways of the world and, thus, deserves to make all the decisions for the family. Grandiosity and feelings of superiority frequently alternate with feelings of inadequacy.

Besides control, the abuser also feels entitled to affection, respect, and sexual gratification from his partner. When she refuses, he is astounded. "How dare she?" he may bellow, as he prepares for battle. Her refusal is viewed as a callous disregard of his birthright because he feels entitled to love on demand.

What the abuser is confused about is the distinction between

desires and rights. We may hope to be loved and desire consideration from our intimate partners, but we are not entitled to love and
care. Likewise, we may desire emotional and sexual gratification,
but our wishes, hopes, and desires do not constitute the domain of
inalienable rights. The abuser, however, operates as if his desires
were entitlements. He does not understand that love has to be
freely given to have deep and lasting significance. While it may be
prompted by duty and responsibility, love cannot be delivered on
demand. The abuser does not grasp that angry insistence deprives
love of its sources of vitality, namely freedom and spontaneity, and
transforms the loving impulse into a lifeless, duty-driven obliga-
tion.

## Pride and Rigidity

In addition to the sense of entitlement, the abuser often manifests excessive pride and rigidity—not healthy pride as in "pleasure or satisfaction taken in something done or belonging to oneself," but false pride as in "high or inordinate opinion of one's
dignity, importance, merit, or superiority." This pride and accompanying rigidity (the inability to consider opposing viewpoints)
are major stumbling blocks to the give-and-take of a mutually
satisfying, intimate relationship.

The proud man is convinced that God is on his side and that
*truth* resides in his corner. Any deviation is threatening and tends
to be regarded as heresy. There is only one way, and that is the
proud man's way!

In intimacy, where we are faced with potential conflict on
every front, essentially because a different and separate person is
inhabiting our space, the proud and rigid person has difficulty in
accommodating these differences. If there is only one way—his
way—then it follows that the partner must yield. The proud man
cannot compromise because it is viewed as subscribing to false-
hood. "Giving in" is tantamount to committing grave error or, at
the very least, being humiliated.

When the proud person overwhelmed by righteous indignation encounters a resistant partner, rage often erupts. There is no room for flexibility or alternate perspectives in the ensuing argument. Like the Crusaders who were determined to rid the world of "heresy," the proud person in a moment of angry passion tries to stamp out the voice of dissent. By forcing his partner into silent submission, he will regain control and certitude. To this end, violence is used.

Chester (see the section "Alcohol Use as Marital Glue" in Chapter 7 for more detail) became enraged whenever his wife or children disagreed with him. No matter how gently an opposing argument was presented, Chester would fly off the handle and become verbally abusive. Different viewpoints were threatening because they implied to him that he was wrong, a position he could not tolerate. Being wrong was synonymous with inadequacy or worthlessness, feelings he tried desperately to keep at bay.

Likewise, disobedience and even inconvenience were perceived as threatening to his rigidly defined view of himself as family patriarch. When his elderly mother-in-law dropped a clothespin on the lawn and he almost ran over it with the mower (he was convinced it would have ruined the mower), he ranted for days about her inconsideration. Similarly, a slammed door jarring his solitude or kids playing noisily outdoors would trigger explosive rage. He was an arrogant man with a short fuse, who could not tolerate disruption of any magnitude.

Like other proud individuals, Chester never said that he was sorry for his abusive behavior, according to family members. Apologizing for interpersonal insensitivities or cruelties was ego-alien to him. Because he was convinced of the error of others' ways and the correctness of his own, he saw no need to apologize. Even when his wife or children were devastated by his abuse, he appeared to be convinced that the problem was theirs, not his. His externalizing style, wherein the responsibility for his behavior fell on shoulders other than his own, created havoc, excessive guilt, and low self-esteem in family members.

For example, Chester attributed his violent beatings of his

children to their misbehavior. By their noisy chattering, slamming of doors, or reluctance to eat the food on their plates, they came to believe that they were responsible for his rage. Their mother, Chester's wife, agreed with this assessment, and after they were severely beaten, would tell them to apologize to their father for angering him. As a result, both daughters became cautious about exposing their most intimate selves to anyone because they were convinced they were intrinsically bad. They felt they were destructive and had the power to set off explosive rage by their most insignificant actions.

Since all negative interpersonal outcomes in the family were their fault, vigilance and guilt became their daily companions along with diminished self-worth. In addition, the anger that normally occurs in response to maltreatment appeared to be directed toward the self in both their cases because they both had drinking problems and low-grade depression as adults. The failure of either parent to take any responsibility for family conflicts left the burden of accountability falling squarely on the daughters' shoulders.

## The Partner as a Thing

The abuser's sense of entitlement results in depersonalization of his partner. If his own needs are all that matter at any given moment, the partner exists not as a person in her own right but as an extension of the abuser. She is seen in a utilitarian or unidimensional manner as either providing or denying gratification. "If you're not with me, you're against me," is the black-and-white, dichotomous thinking that abounds in such a household, frequently in both partners.

Tom, a burly, physically imposing, forty-eight-year-old man, was referred by his company's employee assistance program for an evaluation of his drinking. While Tom initially was more interested in unloading twenty-five years' worth of hurt feelings and complaints about his wife, it was quickly apparent that alcohol contributed significantly to the loss of control and violence he displayed toward her (e.g., he had broken her ribs several years previously and regularly shoved her). However, alcohol was not the only factor in their conflictual relationship. During a three-year period several years earlier when Tom had abstained from alcohol, he maintained their relationship had still been marked by frequent quarrels, verbal abuse, and temporary separations (his wife, Sophie, would leave for days and spend time with her parents when their conflicts became violence-tinged).

While most unhappy couples quarrel and blame each other, what was unique about Tom and Sophie was the intensity of their rage toward each other, their marked inability to see the other's point of view, the extent to which the police were called to provide control, and the blatant use of their two adopted children as pawns in their conflicts. Tom and Sophie were joined, not in marital harmony, but in marital battling that began even before the nuptial ceremony. Sophie's parents, who had been vehemently opposed to Tom because of religious differences (they were Catholic and he was Greek Orthodox), were convinced that from the time of her engagement their daughter had made a serious mistake in choosing Tom.

After their marriage, the first area of combat was Sophie's inability to conceive children. Unable to provide consolation to each other for their mutual disappointment, they blamed each other for the infertility until a medical verdict definitively established Sophie as the cause. Tom, whose manhood was narcissistically wounded by Sophie's barrenness, kept attacking her for her childlessness whenever he was intoxicated. As a man, he felt entitled to offspring and blamed Sophie for depriving him of his legacy. At these moments, she was nothing more to him than a barren womb humiliating him before the whole world.

The sexual arena was another area of strife—Tom liked oral sex but Sophie did not. Problems arose when he forced her to go along with what he wanted. When she got free, she often cried and screamed obscenities at him until he became verbally or physically abusive. The police were frequently called (by neighbors, Sophie, or their adopted children) during these violent encounters because the intensity of their shouting and name-calling frightened even the calmest of bystanders.

Besides sex and alcohol use, Tom and Sophie fought about in-laws, child-rearing, and Sophie's separations. Sophie would frequently scream at the children for hours when they disobeyed her, much to Tom's dismay. At other times, she tried to engage the children as allies in her war against Tom by sharing intimate details of his behavior with them. An angry, dependent woman who was very attached to her parents, Sophie would run to her parents' home whenever the marital conflicts escalated. Sometimes when Tom was fed up, he would insist that Sophie go to her parents' home and drove her there, thereby humiliating her in front of her parents. While they were both masters at hurting each other and trying to gain control, Tom's malice was born out of narcissistic entitlement and frustration of his emotional needs. Sophie's verbal attacks, by contrast, stemmed from powerlessness, impulsivity, physical abuse, and affectional deprivation.

After the psychosocial evaluation, Tom was referred to a three-week, inpatient alcoholism program with the recommendation that both he and Sophie pursue marital counseling after discharge. A three-month follow-up call from Tom revealed that he was sober and attending AA regularly but that he and Sophie were not communicating. Sophie was going to Al-Anon regularly but was not particularly interested in interacting with him. It appeared as if they had agreed to an uneasy truce and were living like strangers under the same roof.

## Competition

The abuser tends to view his intimate partner as a competitor rather than an ally. Because of his own insecurity, he has difficulty in rejoicing in her good fortune. By her enhanced stature, he feels diminished. Her accomplishments highlight his failures; her strengths magnify his weaknesses. It is only when he is with someone at or below his psychosocial level that he feels comfortable.

The status inconsistency between intimate partners is a source of frustration for the abuser, who is generally low man on the status totem pole. If his partner works, she generally has a better-paying job or is better educated, according to Gelles and Straus.[7] For example, violence is less common when a wife is at home than when she works. Having a wife with an independent source of income and prestige is threatening to a man with strong doubts about his own adequacy, especially when he is unemployed or working at a meager job.

Besides differences in income and education, status inconsistency can also occur on the social dimension of popularity. The spouse who has more friends or seems better loved by the world runs the risk of violence from an isolated partner who feels cheated of affection. Begrudging her the popularity she has achieved, he attempts to cut her down to his size by verbal or physical abuse.

## Reducing Psychological Disparity

Verbal putdowns and physical assaults are both misguided attempts to reduce psychological inequity. Envious of the psychological advantages of the partner, the abuser tries to diminish the partner's power and reduce the status differential. One man felt threatened and became verbally abusive to his wife at the time of her birthday each year. The number of birthday cards she received (ten to fifteen) was in sharp contrast to the one or two he managed to get. Because her popularity was a painful reminder of the lack of friendship in his life, he retaliated by loudly pointing out her shortcomings. Only when she was brought down a peg or two did he feel they were at the same level. Thus, feelings of inferiority are often the triggers to abusive behavior, which, in turn, reduces psychological disparity.

One woman became enraged whenever her husband got more attention than she did at a social gathering. She was envious of his greater social appeal and conversational ability, and she believed the attention given to him diminished her. She believed they were competing for a limited supply of psychological rewards; his victory was therefore her loss.

## Dependency and Isolation

In addition to the need for power, pride, rigidity, and competition, the abuser is frequently a highly dependent man with few other meaningful interpersonal contacts. All of his emotional eggs are placed in his partner's basket, and he relies on her for validation. Having been disappointed repeatedly by significant others in his life, he does not trust others sufficiently to allow them access to his vulnerability. When he got emotionally involved with his intimate partner, the floodgates opened for the first time and his neediness was exposed.

Ordinarily, the abuser is hypersensitive to his partner's approval and quick to take umbrage at any perceived insensitivity. Easily insulted, he walks around with a chip on his shoulder and dares her to knock it off by her indifference or hostility. Psychologically, he is always in the boxer's stance, ready to fight at a moment's notice.

When his partner is preoccupied with other things, he is jealous. When she is angry and critical of him, he is threatened and enraged. When she is ill, he is frightened and resentful. Because he has no emotional life that is differentiated from hers, he is always reacting, usually angrily, to her. Insofar as he is capable of loving another human being, she may be the most important person in the world to him. However, because his capacity to love another is limited, he has inordinate difficulty in seeing her as a person separate from himself. He is dependent on her for his own emotional well-being, and not particularly tuned in to her concerns. His regular, emotional temperature-taking of her is an attempt to find out where he stands with her rather than a way of trying to meet her needs.

## The Paradox of Isolation and Overcrowding

His isolation from others, both emotionally and geographically in some cases, further adds to the intensity of his preoccupation with his mate. With no extended family or good friends around to provide perspective, diversion, or balance, the abuser and his partner are locked into a small, suffocating interpersonal space where every emotional nuance gets magnified. Every minor failing becomes a cardinal transgression; every offense is viewed as a sin. In addition, daily frustrations are displaced onto the partner because there is no other release valve around. Their relationship becomes the dumping ground for every life disappointment because there are few other tension-reducing mechanisms in place. In this highly charged emotional atmosphere, the stage is set for explosiveness. Regular spouse-battering then becomes a vehicle for tension reduction and a means of trying to maintain intimate contact.

Whenever the abuser feels alienated from his intimate partner by his own anger or the frightened partner's distance, the separation anxiety engendered by the distance spawns desperate attempts to regain contact. He wants her to know his despair, hear his frustration, and see his rage. To this end, he shouts loudly, believing that the intensity of his voice and manner will ensure an attentive hearing. Frightened about being alone, he wants to reconnect with her as quickly as possible. Unfortunately, as he raises his voice, she, fearing another assault, retreats even further. Becoming more frustrated, he grabs her with more intensity and tries to convince her to accept his rendition of their relationship's reality. The physical contact, delivered in an angry rather than a loving form, is a means of desperately trying to hang on to her while punishing her for her withdrawal or insubordination at the same time. As the pitch of emotional intensity gets higher, the escalation into physical violence is just a matter of time.

## The Battering Cycle

After beatings, many abusers, though unfortunately not all, are consumed with guilt and abandonment anxiety. Begging for forgiveness and promising never to deliver another blow, they try to make amends. Phone calls, flowers, candy, and other romantic paraphernalia are part of the seduction attempt. If the partner succumbs, they are on their way to a cycle of beating, reconciliation, tension buildup, and further violence that may last a lifetime. Because this pattern can become entrenched, with each partner losing self-respect and the motivation to change in the process, physical separation, divorce, psychotherapy, and/or death are ordinarily the only foolproof means of interrupting this battering cycle permanently.

## Violence on the Fringes

While all violence is uncivilized and destructive, sado-masochistic behavior is more unnatural. The fusion of pain with sexual pleasure or domination-submission with sexual arousal represents a perversion of the sexual drive. Rather than being turned on by loving behavior, the sadist and masochist are sexually aroused by aggression.

Why does the giving or receiving of pain enhance sexual arousal? Because sexual arousal is profoundly influenced by other psychological motives and emotions, most notably anxiety, feelings of danger can add to sexual excitement. In sadomasochistic behavior (whippings or beatings, for example), there is potential danger every step of the way because the risk of injuring one's partner is high. The thrills of sadomasochistic behavior may be similar to the excitement of climbing a steep mountain, driving in the Indy 500, or going over Niagara Falls in a barrel. In the case of sadomasochistic behavior, however, the dangerous excitement of the activity magnifies sexual arousal.

In addition to thrill-seeking, the sadist has a strong need to dominate, while the masochist seeks to be overpowered. For the sadist, domination intensifies feelings of manliness and sexual potency. By contrast, for the masochist, the act of yielding renders the partner stronger and more attractive as an object with which to merge. The sadist directly enhances his sense of potency, while the masochist hopes to gain power indirectly or passively by uniting with a powerful partner. Rape fantasies of women represent this same masochistic phenomenon—the desire to be overpowered by men, whose strength they hope to borrow or absorb by osmosis. In both sadomasochistic behavior and rape fantasies, sexual drive is influenced by low self-esteem and the desire to make up for ego deficits by sexual unions.

## Where Does Sadomasochism Come From?

In some cases of sadomasochism, sexual arousal occurred early in life in the context of punishment, so the sex drive becomes conditioned to pain. For example, a child may have been spanked in such a way that stimulation of the genitals regularly occurred. In other cases, the mechanism of reaction formation, wherein impulses and feelings are transformed into their opposites, and counterphobic behavior, in which feared objects are sought after, may be the explanatory factors for sadomasochistic behavior. The fact that high emotional arousal tends to occur in both states of sexual arousal and severe pain and that all emotions have a common pathway—the reticular activating arousal system—in addition to their distinctive correlates may be a factor in accounting for the fusion of pain with sexual arousal in some cases. Also, at high levels of emotional arousal, the distinctions between emotional states tend to blur.

One man, who was seen in couples therapy for retarded ejaculation (inability to have an orgasm during intercourse), reported that the sensate focus exercise used in sex therapy (gentle touching of the body by a partner) was revolting to him because it felt like he was "being petted like an animal." He preferred to be scratched with some force, a sensation he described as distinctly pleasurable. While this masochistic quality was fairly circum-scribed, he did have pain and pleasure reversed in some way. The vast majority of people find the gentle fondling of sensate-focusing exercises pleasurable and the rough scratching he described as unpleasant and painful. Whether his revulsion to fondling was a reaction to anxiety associated with incestuous wishes (he was unusually attached to his mother, whom he described as very physical in her demonstrations of love) or some other factor was unclear.

Some sadomasochistic practitioners report that intense emotional intimacy accompanies their sexual encounters. The intensity of the sexual experience and the amount of attention that needs to be paid to their partner in order to reduce the likelihood of injury appear to increase feelings of closeness. While heightened intimacy may be true for some people engaged in sadomasochistic behavior, the provision of pain along with sexual pleasure is an aberration of the usual loving pathways to emotional intimacy.

## Garden-Variety Violence: Verbal Sniping

The most common form of violence in intimacy is clearly verbal assault. While verbal abuse is not as destructive as physical violence, words do hurt. Being called pejorative names, accused unjustly of wrongdoing, or categorized unfairly are painful occurrences in intimacy. While we can shield ourselves from the emotional sting of strangers' insults by discounting their knowledge or intelligence, it is more difficult to defend ourselves from attacks hurled our way by people who know us well. The verbal assault of our intimate partners, to whom we have exposed our shortcomings, has intense power to damage our self-worth.

Because we are so vulnerable in intimacy, the verbal swords thrust in our direction cut to the core. In addition, we reason, there must be some truth to the hurtful accusations, seeing as they come from such reliable sources. Maybe we are an "idiot," "creep," or "fool" in some way. Since our self-worth is seldom set on a foundation of steel, it totters under an avalanche of verbal attack. Also, since verbal abuse is only a stone's throw away from physical violence, our very life feels threatened by an onslaught of angry words. *War of the Roses*, a contemporary movie about a warring couple, illustrates the short distance that exists from verbal to physical violence.

Beverly and her husband were frequently involved in name-calling, shouting, and shoving matches. While they managed to stop short of serious physical abuse (she reported a bruised arm on one occasion), their verbal abuse of each other was clearly destructive to their relationship. Each partner would leave the battle scene feeling hurt, misunderstood, and uncared about. Also, they wondered out loud whether their marriage could survive such assaults over the long haul.

Where was all their anger coming from? For Beverly, the underlying source seemed to be frustration of the desire to be loved unconditionally and the wish to be the most important person in Don's life. While it was clear to Beverly that Don loved her, he was very attached to Beverly's competition, a son from his first marriage. Like many other divorced fathers who are geographically distant from their children and see them infrequently, Don lavished his son with gifts and showered him with unconditional love. In Don's eyes, his son could do no wrong.

In contrast, Don was often critical of Beverly and unempathic. Growing up in a household where conflict was swept under the rug, he frequently became defensive in response to Beverly's angry accusations. Rather than sensing that her underlying pain was related to her feeling left out or unloved, he reacted to her criticisms by angry counterattack. Her fury about the amount of money he spent on his son was perceived as an assault on his judgment rather than a cry for reassurance or loving attention. She would shout angrily, "You're stupid for buying him such expensive clothes" (underlying message: "You don't care for *me* that much"), and he would reply, "You're neurotic, insecure, and trying to control me" (underlying message: "You're belittling me by your criticism").

To reduce these sorts of misunderstandings, they both needed to learn how to communicate their feelings more directly and be more sensitive to the other's psychological pain. Don's difficulty in being empathic, however, was a major stumbling block to their communicating with less hostility. His most frequent response to Beverly's verbalization that she felt hurt, unloved, or inadequate was to dismiss her complaint as invalid by saying, "You shouldn't feel that way." In effect, he was implying that there was something wrong with her, further adding insult to injury. It was only after he learned how to respond in a less provocative manner that their interactions improved. A more neutral response, such as "I didn't know you felt that way," reduced Beverly's defensiveness and propensity to counterattack.

Clearly, the frustration of psychological needs and desires is the most common underlying cause of intimacy violence. Because we want to be loved unconditionally, criticism is painful. Because we want to be the most important person in our intimate partner's life, competition for that special status is threatening. Being misunderstood thwarts our desire to be known perfectly; being ignored frustrates our wish to be attended to and protected. Whether the frustration of these needs becomes the catalyst for the transformation of these wishes into more realistic desires or the fuel for violent eruptions is a function of the individual's emotional health and growth potential. The healthier person, who experiences life as an ongoing process of change, regularly modifies expectations in the light of new information. For the more psychologically damaged individual fixated at earlier developmental levels, however, the frustration of emotional needs often turns into violence.

*Chapter 9*

# Minimizing the Risks

While intimacy is dangerous in a variety of ways, it is obvious that intimate relationships have many advantages over solitude. Most people would agree that it feels good to have someone around to share life with, and when there are love, kindness, acceptance, and patience to boot, life could hardly be better. And so, we gamble at love, hoping to grab the brass ring or to find the pot of gold at the end of the rainbow. Leading with our hearts rather than our heads, we venture out into intimate territory with nary a thought about our idiosyncratic blind spots and vulnerabilities. Because the contents of our intimate zones are often buried, we have no idea what we will expect, desire, or fear once we get involved in an adult intimate relationship for the first time. While we all hope for the best and fear the worst—that is, we desire everlasting love while worrying that rejection, criticism, or betrayal will befall us instead—we have not a clue as to how to minimize the risks.

## Identifying Vulnerabilities

Because earlier intimacy left us with specific needs and fears waiting to be realized or resolved in new relationships, one of the most important tasks for each of us is clarifying the unfinished business from the past. What kind of emotional issues were we exposed to in our families and how did these needs and fears get resolved? If we had a critical, nonaffectionate father and a hysterical demanding mother, for example, what was their combined impact on us? Were we left with an attraction to these types or to their exact opposites? In general, do we find ourselves shying away from or rushing headlong into intimate relationships? What is the fear of intimacy that dominates our consciousness and keeps us awake at night? In short, what are the dimensions of intimacy that are unique to each of us?

## Tracing Fears to Their Beginnings

While the fears and emotional needs aroused in intimacy tend to be universal, the intensity and relative importance of one need or fear over another vary as a function of our experiences with caretakers. If we grew up in a family with a highly unpredictable parent (a schizophrenic, a manic-depressive, an alcoholic, and a drug user are the primary occupants of the category of "unpredictable parent"), the fear of losing control would be a major intimacy concern for us. Because the lack of predictability in the family led to high levels of tension, we would consciously vow to stay away from this kind of turmoil while being drawn to it at the same time. So many of us have passionately uttered the phrase, "I'll never marry that kind of person" (referring to a parent who has been a source of significant emotional pain), only to find ourselves attracted to similar types, much to our chagrin. For example, we may be drawn to an explosive woman like our mother or an erratic alcoholic like our father in spite of our conscious resolutions.

Fear of exposure tends to be dominant in families where humiliation and shame were used extensively to control behavior. When our inadequacies have been exposed regularly to ridicule, we are afraid that new intimate experiences will provide us with the same kind of embarrassment cloaked in new forms. Experiences of being laughed at or taunted because of our foibles and ineptitude result in a sensitivity to exposure and humiliation.

The fear of losing autonomy occurs regularly in intrusive, smothering, or enmeshed families, while the fear of attack is common in physically or verbally abusive homes. We often fear a reoccurrence of that which we experienced. Similarly, the fear of disappointment and betrayal can be traced to experiences with caretakers in which there was a significant breach of trust. Promises were broken repeatedly and commitments not honored. The philandering or gambling parent along with other unavailable types, such as workaholics whose careers take precedence over family responsibilities, provide fertile breeding ground for the development of mistrust and concerns about betrayal in intimacy.

The fear of guilt in intimacy develops in families where the children are regularly blamed for the sins of the parents. Rather than taking any responsibility for family conflict, such parents use their children as scapegoats for their own frustrations. As a consequence of the displacement of responsibility, these children fear that intimacy will bring nothing but finger-pointing and guilt their way.

Fear of rejection, the most common of the anxieties in intimacy, can be traced to profound experiences of disapproval and/or desertion. When our parents or other significant caretakers turned their backs on us, giving us the cold shoulder for days on end, we were left fearing that they would never relate to us again. Initially, we had no idea when the silent treatment would end, and so we worried that we had lost them forever. Just as toddlers panic initially when their parents leave for an evening outing, so we, too, feared that we would be permanently deserted when our parents withdrew affection from us for any length of time.

In situations where a parent left the family when the children were young (six years and under), fears of abandonment in intimacy can be intense. Even when the desertion occurred through no fault of the parent's, as in death, lengthy illness, or military service, children feel abandoned and often blame themselves for the loss. If only they had been better children, they reason, this terrible misfortune would not have occurred. In Dorothy's case, where her father ran off with his secretary when Dorothy was six (see "Fear of Rejection" section in Chapter 3 for more detail), she thought at the time that her father "left because I was naughty." In adult intimacy, then, the fear of being deserted anew coupled with a sense of guilty responsibility for the impending loss can haunt our relationships. It is easier to believe that history will repeat itself than to trust that new beginnings will have different endings!

## Which Emotional Needs Are Important?

The emotional needs that get resurrected in adult intimacy also have their origins in early experiences. The intensity and relative importance of needs for unconditional love, nurturance, protection, and special status are primarily a function of which emotional needs were frustrated in the course of development. If we seldom felt loved unconditionally, understood, appreciated, or nurtured in our families of origin, then the desire for these qualities will have passionate intensity. Having been thwarted in our wish to be loved during childhood, we are determined to get the pot of gold the next time around.

While some people who were unloved by their families gave up hope of ever being loved early on, most of us keep searching for perfect love. When disappointed in this quest the first time around, we intensify our efforts. Modern-day multiple, sequential marriages give witness to this unremitting journey in pursuit of love. However, most of us do modify the desire of attaining ideal love someplace along the line and become realistic (or cynical) about the chances of finding a perfect partner. Instead, we accept whoever comes our way, warts and all, and become resigned to the bittersweet, imperfect love that seems to be our lot in life.

The desire for protection in intimacy tends to be strongest in adult children coming from families with few rules, chaotic discipline, and loose organizational ties. In these families, the absence of structure is often experienced as a lack of caring and concern. Because these children had to fend for themselves, they became self-reliant rather than dependent on others. However, the missing experiential component—a trusting reliance upon others for need gratification and protection—becomes the primary ingredient of the adult wish for protection in intimate relationships.

Mary grew up in a household of ten children where both parents' heavy drinking resulted in erratic parental involvement in child care. The younger children tended to be cared for by the two oldest girls (the oldest of whom was Mary), who took turns feeding, dressing, and scolding their siblings. As a consequence of this premature caretaking assignment, Mary's own needs for nurturance and protection were almost totally ignored until adulthood when she found an older, domineering man who was eager to play the patriarch for Mary and her children.

As for the desire for special status, families where competition between siblings was intense tend to be the primary breeding grounds. When a brother or sister regularly got star billing in the family, we are left with a strong sense of inadequacy and the accompanying wish to be the "favorite child" in any new intimacy. Anything less than "number one" is too painfully reminiscent of our earlier, inferior status.

Besides strongly competitive families, only-child households are prone to develop their fair share of children for whom special status is an important consideration in intimacy. Some of these only children have grown accustomed to undivided consideration and have difficulty in sharing attention with anyone. Others, while feeling entitled to special status by virtue of their positions as only children, believe they did not receive their due. In these cases, parents may have been too busy with their jobs, their own parents, or each other to have much emotional energy left over to give their child.

## Choosing Suitable Masks

While our intimacy needs and vulnerabilities are related to interactions with parental figures for the most part, our interpersonal and defensive styles are adopted from a broader arena that includes siblings, cousins, and childhood friends. We seem to have more individual choice with our interpersonal and defensive styles than with our needs and fears. The latter more directly mirror our experiences.

The strategies we adopt in relating to others (interpersonal styles), many of which are designed to protect our vulnerabilities, are a function of the styles we have observed, the rewards associated with them, and temperamental factors. Basically, we try to select interpersonal approaches that are effective in gaining love and/or power (importance, influence, and respect). In doing so, we scan our interpersonal world, looking for role models of successful living. These models, along with our parents, influence the interpersonal and defensive approaches that we ultimately adopt in accord with temperamental factors, such as activity level and approach-avoidance tendencies.

## Combining Our Interpersonal History

Thus, in trying to ascertain what our intimacy parameters are, we need to look at our interpersonal history and determine the sources of influence on our needs, fears, and interpersonal styles. For example, in the case of a young woman with a hysterical, intrusive mother and a cold, critical father, the resultant intimacy factors may be as follows. If we assume that her basic sexual orientation was heterosexual and that she viewed her parents' marriage as reasonably satisfying, the most likely scenario would be that she would adopt her mother's interpersonal style (as a result of same-sex identification) and look for a man similar to her father. In searching out such a man, she would be hoping to undo the self-esteem damage suffered at her father's hands and rewrite her intimate, heterosexual script.

In intimate relationships, such a young woman would be particularly sensitive to the issues of intrusiveness or loss of autonomy brought about by her mother's style and criticism or fear of attack introduced by her father. Mostly, she would be hoping for unconditional love and protection from demands in adult intimacy. Most probably, her own interpersonal and defensive style would be seductive or prone to acting-out (as in addictive behavior or psychosomatic illness). Essentially, if there are no other mitigating factors and the amount of familial conflict is not high, we take on same-sex interpersonal styles and choose adult intimate partners to work out unfinished business from our earlier years.

## Other Complicating Factors

However, because intimate behavior is influenced by a whole host of other emotional variables, additional factors need to be considered. If, for example, we saw that our mother's histrionic, demanding style resulted in unhappiness for her and few interpersonal rewards from her husband (our father), we might decide to act differently in our relationships with others. While our adult intimacy requirements (unconditional love and protection, in this case) and sensitivities (fears of losing autonomy and of attack) would be the same, we could be more thoughtful and less demanding. As a result, our defensive behavior would take on a different, quieter tone. For example, "tuning out" and/or the "mystery woman" approach would be more compatible with a passive, interpersonal style than the "court jester" or "Jezebel" defensive styles would be.

The existence of brothers and sisters further complicates the picture. In addition to our assessment of parents' interpersonal efficacy, we are continuously observing our siblings to see who is getting the most attention and by what means. We are trying to determine which qualities and/or behavior elicit the most approval and by whom. Is it athletic prowess, scholarship, musical talent, or politeness that brings a twinkle to Daddy's eyes and a smile to Mother's lips? If at all possible, we will attempt to modify our own behavior to earn more beams of approval from the people whose attentiveness we value. Very often, however, once an area of accomplishment is established as one sibling's territory, the other children in the family shy away from that arena and try to find less competitive ground. Rather than emulating the interpersonal styles that our more successful siblings adopted, we often try to find our unique niches in modified or opposite directions. If

the quiet, studious role is taken, for example, then we might highlight the coquettish, witty, or mischievous sides of our personality.
By taking on somewhat different roles, we minimize the competition and reduce the risk of losing out on love and attention altogether.

## Clues to Intimacy Parameters

Our intimacy dimensions (needs, fears, and defensive styles),
while not readily apparent, are manifest in both our day and night
dreams and in the partners we are attracted to. What kinds of
people inhabit our fantasies? Are our love objects mysterious,
unattainable types; doting, protective parental figures; or dashing,
good-looking people whose physical beauty will enhance our self-
image by association?

As for interpersonal terrors, which ones are paramount for
us? In our dreams, are we spinning out of control, in danger of
drowning, or being abandoned on a deserted country road in the
middle of the night? Are we being exposed and ridiculed or attacked with such ferocity that our very life is in jeopardy? When
we are running breathlessly with heart pounding through the
streets of our dreams, what are we fleeing from? The answers to
these questions can provide us with valuable insights into our
unique intimacy road maps and suggest those intimacy components that are overdetermined, magnified by the past, and therefore, unrealistic.

## Giving Up the Impossible Dream

The realization that we may never attain that which we have
desperately hoped for is a poignant yet sobering awareness. This
harsh reality, while jarring when encountered for the first time,
can also have a calming effect. There is more than a grain of truth
to Hickey's belief in Eugene O'Neill's play *The Iceman Cometh* that
getting rid of self-delusion is liberating.[1] Because freedom from

self-deception enables us to devote emotional energy to more attainable pursuits, truth does, in fact, set us free.

After infancy, the chances of being loved unconditionally by anyone are small. No matter how far-reaching our efforts are to achieve this sort of perfect love, the reality is that we all have limitations in our capacity to love. Our own needs and preoccupations get in the way of our ability to tune in to another person, see the world from their perspective, and give unconditionally. Our own emotional and intellectual agendas keep interfering with an external or other-person focus. At a particular time, we may be too emotionally drained or too worried or absorbed in our jobs to pay much attention to another person. Because we live in our own minds and bodies, self-absorption seems more natural and adaptive in some ways than other-centeredness. At least we can be successful at meeting our own needs, whereas the likelihood of meeting someone else's is minimal.

Even when love appears to be selfless, the lover is usually getting his or her own needs met in the process. He or she may be getting affection, sexual gratification, emotional stimulation, or self-esteem enhancement, at the very least. Larry, a thirty-five-year-old college graduate, was the primary giver in a ten-year marital relationship with a demanding, insecure woman who was also physically fragile; that is, she would tire easily and had frequent migraines. In addition to his full-time position as manager in an accounting firm, Larry came home after work to make dinner for his family, wash dishes, straighten the house, and read to the children while his wife recuperated from her daily struggles as housewife and mother. In the mornings, Larry also bathed all four children before heading off to work and was regularly involved in most household and child-care tasks. While the lion's share of familial duties fell to Larry, he appeared happy with his marriage. His wife was a physically beautiful woman who needed Larry for her own emotional stability. Thus, Larry felt valued and important to the well-being of his family in the process.

Under the best of circumstances, a romantic relationship has emotional and sexual intimacy, mutual need gratification, an agreeable quid pro quo contract about duties/responsibilities, affection, and companionship. As for altruistic and selfless love, it is rare indeed. Thus, emotional needs for unconditional love, perfect understanding, large-scale nurturing, parental protection, and "number one" status are doomed to frustration. Realistically, we can ask our partner to be committed to love, to have a strong desire to be understanding, and to provide occasional chicken noodle soup along with moments of reassurance and support. We can also hope to be among the most important people in our partner's life, but in all probability, our ranking will be variable, going up and down as satisfactions and disappointments change with each passing day. While we can be cherished by our partners, being the be-all and end-all of their every waking moment is unlikely. Eternal and unchanging love, a topic poets write eloquently about, is elusive on a day-to-day basis. Shakespeare's hauntingly beautiful sonnet—"Love is not love which alters when it alteration finds, or bends with the remover to remove, oh, no it is an ever-fixed mark that looks on tempests and is never shaken"[2]—resonates with our deepest longings but clashes head on with what is possible.

## Learning to Tolerate Criticism, Disappointment, and Rejection

Since our intimate partner will never be perfect in meeting all our emotional needs, what is reasonable to expect? The British psychoanalyst D. W. Winnicott, who was convinced that mothering could never be perfect because of the mother's own emotional needs, coined the phrase "good-enough mothering" to refer to imperfect, though adequate, provision of emotional care that was not damaging to children.[3] In a similar vein, is there a level of imperfect intimacy that is good enough to live and grow on? How much criticism, disappointment, and rejection should we tolerate in the name of reality?

In imperfect but good-enough intimacy, we are reasonably happy and growing. The relationship is providing us with enough emotional security and/or nurturance that we are free to test our wings and explore our own possibilities. Painful encounters do occur, but they are balanced by the strength and pleasures of the relationship. We are able to absorb hurt feelings and tolerate our partner's shortcomings because the positive aspects of the relationship outweigh the limitations. We can ignore slights and swallow disappointments, essentially because the relationship is on a solid footing.

Criticism, disappointment, and rejection are not ignored but rather they are put into a broader context. When seen as part of a larger mosaic that includes joy, companionship, sex, and security, self-esteem barbs lose their sting. These negative interpersonal behaviors also become less personalized and tend to be viewed as a function of extrinsic rather than relationship factors. For example, before it is perceived as a personal affront, his irritability might be attributed to job pressures or her withdrawal to fatigue. This broader perspective provides for multiple interpretations of behavior and a spirit of generosity that give the other the benefit of the doubt.

Because criticism, disappointment, and momentary rejections are a part of intimate life, developing a thicker skin can be a healthy means of not simply surviving, but thriving in intimacy. While these negative behaviors will never feel good, accepting their inevitability can reduce our outrage and narcissistic injury. Besides, occasional (not constant) criticism can be growth-inducing because it challenges our typical ways of behaving. Likewise, periods of inattention can foster self-reliance and reduce dependency. As for disappointment, which is ever-present in intimacy, learning how to discriminate when to modify our expectations in the light of reality and when to insist upon sensitive and respectful treatment is a maturing process. Frederick Perls's (the father of Gestalt therapy) somewhat cynical but realistic commentary to us about relationships is worth keeping in mind:

> I am not in this world to live up to your expectations, and you are not in this world to live up to mine. You are you and

I am I, and if by chance we find each other, it's beautiful. If not, it can't be helped.[4]

## Self-Exposure in Graduated Doses

During the courtship and honeymoon phases of an intimate relationship, we are on our best behavior. Fearful that our darker sides will lead to outright rejection, we reveal little about our shortcomings and imagined weaknesses. Rather, to play it safe, we present a limited perspective, a unidimensional view of what we are all about. Then, when we are further along the intimacy pathway, we reveal all and risk significant disappointment or rejection. The more emotionally involved we are, the more the dangers of intimacy will hurt.

If we were to test the waters early on in any potentially intimate relationship to determine how accepting our partner is, we would be in a better position to retreat before the damage was significant. Obviously, we are not going to parade our inadequacies in front of total strangers—we need to feel trusting before exposing ourselves. But waiting until the symbolic knot is tied prevents us from learning whether we are compatible with each other insofar as self-esteem enhancement is concerned.

More important than compatibility with respect to hobbies, political views, and/or religious values is mutual self-esteem gratification. Are we able to feel good about ourselves in the relationship and does our partner feel likewise? Do we feel valued and accepted with our inadequacies showing, or do we need to play a role in order to gain approval? When we let our hair down, does enjoyment or derision come our way as a result? In short, have we chosen someone whose valuing of us will enhance our self-worth, or the opposite?

Just as we inch our way into freezing cold water, so self-exposure can be a slow and gradual process. Rather than saving all our secrets for one momentous, cathartic experience, we can share our important hopes, values, and disappointments with potential intimate partners from day one. Letting someone know the deeper dimensions of ourselves and then experiencing their reactions to our self-disclosures is a sound means of evaluating their potential as intimate partners. Also, the degree of our interest and acceptance of their self-revelations will be a measure of our ability to be self-enhancing to them.

## Sharing the Daily Negatives

Among the revelations that can be shared with a potential intimate partner during the beginning phases of a relationship are day-to-day worries and frustrations. While we would prefer to present ourselves in the best possible light and talk about our brilliant insights or accomplishments, disclosing the daily disappointments and hardships is a better test of intimacy potential. For example, when we complain about how hard we worked all day and our boss's indifference, what is our partner's reaction? Is the subject quickly changed to a more pleasant topic or do we receive a minilecture about the pressures of upper administration with the implicit exhortation that we should be more tolerant? Or do we feel listened to nonjudgmentally and understood in the process? In essence, is our potential partner able to hear our negative feelings and be empathic, or does he or she shift gears whenever possible? In addition to support, consideration, and generosity, empathy is one of those qualities that goes miles in validating the self and in promoting healthy intimacy.

## Talking about the Relationship

Another category of self-revelation that is invaluable in assessing a partner's intimacy potential is relationship disclosure. When we talk about our feelings about the relationship (our hopes, doubts, pleasures, and disappointments), what do our partners do? Are they able to comment with a similar degree of openness, or do they try to avoid the topic altogether? Honesty is typically a positive sign of involvement, while avoidance is suggestive of defensiveness.

While most columnists advocate some degree of "playing hard to get" to their lovelorn readers (and there is some advantage to being a "mystery man/woman"), the disadvantages of playing our cards close to the vest are great. Research has shown that lack of emotional expressiveness in premarital communication is associated with less marital satisfaction later on.[5] In the tentative atmosphere of early courtship, reticence to express feelings is easy to misconstrue as indifference. Because we feel so vulnerable and insecure early on, our partner's subtle, positive cues about us are easy to ignore. We need the more overt signs of enjoyment, such as, "I really had a great time tonight," to give us the courage to go on with the relationship. Without clear-cut, encouraging signs, we are left to muddle around in our doubts and convince ourselves that the situation is hopeless.

Expressing feelings about the relationship, even negative concerns, is a means of clarifying our status and resolving ambiguities. The comment "I like you a great deal but I'm not sure whether you care about me" opens the door to several possibilities, all of which are positive in the long run. The most hoped-for response, a very emphatic declaration of affection, will quickly allay our doubts and leave us floating on a cloud of elation. An ambiguous response, while disappointing, can serve as a warning sign for us to retreat momentarily and clarify the ambivalence before venturing further. And even the most dreaded response, namely, "I don't care about you at all," is usually a clear indicator that we are wasting our time and need to move on. Whatever the response to our exploratory probe, the relationship is clarified to some degree and we are free to make a decision about staying or going.

Often in the course of verbalizing our feelings or concerns about the relationship, we come to a new realization that was not possible before. The very act of uttering a misgiving may make us aware of how trivial the doubt really is. Or our protestation of love may sound hollow and inauthentic, forcing us to reexamine our commitment. The process of putting our feelings into words gives them a new, and sometimes different, reality that has to be contended with before the relationship can progress to a new level or be ended.

## Confronting Our Worst Fears

As a relationship becomes more intimate, greater self-exposure usually occurs. Before any irrevocable steps are taken, confronting our worst intimacy fears or risks is often a wise course of action. First of all, we need to determine whether our partner would be available and nonrejecting of us under our imagined "worst circumstances." Second, we need to know how we would survive these fantasied catastrophes if they did occur. For example, if we fear that expressing anger will lead to rejection, then we need to experience our partner's reactions when we verbalize our angry upset. Is our partner able to take our anger in stride and deal nondefensively with the issues, or does he or she bolt in horror at our departure from a loving stance? If the former, we can breathe a sigh of relief, secure in the knowledge that we can be genuine in this relationship. By contrast, if our partner scolds or avoids us when we are angrily upset, we need to determine how we can cope with this limitation in our partner. Can we live with these rejections, or will this lack of acceptance undermine our self-esteem and ultimately destroy the relationship? In any event, knowledge of the outcome of our catastrophic intimacy fears enables us to make wiser decisions about pursuing or ending a particular relationship.

## Maintaining a Degree of Control and Autonomy

No matter how promising a relationship appears, diving into it impulsively, without a glance in any direction, is likely to result in psychic bruising. Our deep desire for a soulmate who will meet all our needs is readily triggered by a stranger who arouses intense emotion. Convinced by the strength of our feelings that Mr. or Ms. Right has just arrived on our doorstep, we give up everything for the sake of love. The "everything" might be our schedules, our same-sex friends, our families, and our entertainment preferences. Somehow, we are convinced that the more we give up, the more favorably disposed the fates will be to grant us this love.

In fact, the opposite is more likely to occur. The more we give up of ourselves, the more likely we are to be taken advantage of and discarded. Our constant availability diminishes our worth, both in our own eyes and in those of our partner. Because we appear to have little going on in our lives other than this single-minded devotion to a new love, we lose our desirability and appear desperate in some way.

In addition, the chances of a new, intense love affair becoming a permanent liaison are lessened by the fact that our out-of-control feelings of attraction have more to do with our own needs than with characteristics of the other person. Because we do not really know this stranger around whom our emotions storm, we are at great risk of being disappointed. Once our romantic hero topples to the ground from our pedestal, we are left face-to-face with a person different from what we had envisioned.

### Keeping a Separate Life

To reduce the impact of our disappointment, maintaining a life apart from the relationship is imperative. Keeping our emotional energies invested in an array of other people and activities helps to balance us. We can take the fluctuations in the relationship in better stride when we have other emotional connections to buffer the blows. These other relationships help to keep us less dependent on one person and reduce our emotional vulnerability. In addition, other people can serve as sources of emotional support when we are feeling devastated by intimacy assaults of one kind or another.

Maintaining a separate life also reduces out-of-control feelings and helplessness. We can take charge of professional and social activities even when the opportunity for control in our intimate relationship is more limited. For example, deciding how, where, and with whom to spend leisure time provides us with a sense of autonomy and direction. Our lives feel less at the mercy of outside forces when we are exercising some degree of decision-making in our extrarelationship pursuits.

## Keeping Control Some of the Time

We also need to maintain a degree of control within the relationship to get our emotional needs met and reduce the fear of smothering. How much affection, sex, communication, and/or distance we need to feel intimate and autonomous has to be negotiated with our partner. If all that we are doing in the relationship is accommodating the other's needs, we will lose ourselves in the process, becoming a blurred or indistinct *self*, not marching to our own drummer, but walking like a shadow in our partner's footsteps. Out of touch with our own needs, feelings, and values, we become reactive—operating from the surface of our personality rather than its depths. In this uncentered state, our needs are unknown to our partner, who, unfortunately, is unable to plunge to the depths of our being with mind-reading techniques. Thus, the possibility of getting our healthy needs met when we are involved in an accommodating merger is unlikely.

The need for greater distance in an intimate relationship often occurs when our partner's needs are so intense that they overshadow ours. They either talk more, demand more, or otherwise so overwhelm us with logic or emotional intensity that we feel like we are suffocating in the process. Unable to speak up and be heard, we frequently move away emotionally to gain some breathing room. Whether we withdraw permanently or simply take regular furloughs for self-restoration will depend on how much gratification the relationship provides. If some of our needs are met, we will stay; otherwise, a death knell will sound for the relationship.

## Shedding Unnecessary Guilt

The guilt-prone among us tend to find intimate relationships unhappy affairs rather than joyful encounters. Because we carry every intimacy problem on our own shoulders, we feel burdened and weary much of the time. The imperfections in the relationship are not evenly distributed; rather, the bulk of the breast-beating comes our way and we are left uttering litanies of mea culpas ("It's all my fault"). We blame ourselves for everything from our partner's irritability to his flu symptoms.

Because the guilt-prone among us tend to see self-blame as part of intimacy, we either avoid close relationships altogether or suffer needlessly. Unable to discriminate clearly the reasons for interpersonal failures, we find it easier (from force of habit) to assume responsibility ourselves. In contrast to blamers, who externalize the responsibility for all their dissatisfactions, we become the scapegoats instead. Whenever a relationship dissatisfaction is in search of a culprit, we volunteer.

### We Cannot Be All Things to All People

Attributing excessive responsibility for intimacy failures to ourselves is both unrealistic and unnecessary. Even if we were perfect people, our partners could be dissatisfied with us because of their own expectations and emotional programming. We may be kind, gentle people; they may prefer chaotic, nongiving types because they like excitement and are more comfortable in a helping role. We may be refined, cultured souls, while they prefer loudness and flagrant sexuality. Or we may have black hair and dark eyes while they are more sexually attracted to blue-eyed blonds. No matter what our sterling attributes are, our partners may be looking to complement themselves (e.g., add emotional vitality to their dreary lives) or for someone to work out unfinished business with. Because emotional needs, sexual preferences, and intimacy fears are closely linked to interpersonal histories, our own reality (personality and behavior) is not the determining factor influencing our partner's level of relationship satisfaction. More important is whether our partner's unique—and frequently neurotic or unrealistic—needs are being met.

Then, too, if our partner is deeply dissatisfied with the relationship, for whatever reason, there are limitations to how much we can change. We can certainly modify our behavior to some degree, but we cannot turn ourselves inside out. Quiet, studious types have difficulty in transforming themselves into sultry sirens, and the opposite metamorphosis is also unlikely. Even with extended psychoanalysis, our basic temperamental and personality characteristics remain constant. No matter how hard we try, we cannot always become what our partners expect.

## Differentiating Needs from Wishes

Guilt also occurs when we feel that we are "too demanding" in an intimate relationship. Because we believe that our emotional needs are whimsical rather than legitimate, asking for what we need feels like we are pushing our own agendas onto the other person. To feel like a "good person," we would prefer trying to make our partners happy rather than insisting upon our own requirements. However, if we are going to be reasonably satisfied in intimacy, our emotional needs will have to be met at least some of the time.

What adds to our confusion is the failure to distinguish emotional wishes or preferences from more substantial needs. As adults, we do not *need* any particular emotional sustenance to survive, but to feel reasonably satisfied and emotionally connected in intimacy, we need to feel cared about in some way. While the need to matter or be valued by our intimate partner can be satisfied in countless ways, the needs for love and autonomy in intimacy appear to be fundamental.

Thus, the status of "emotional need," as differentiated from wish or desire, can be reserved for these two basic, opposing drives. To thrive in intimacy, we need to feel cared about and, yet, separate from our intimate partner. Any issue that relates to these basic needs is thus important and worthy of unhurried attention; all other considerations are decidedly secondary.

Most interpersonal conflicts can be resolved by determining whether these two needs are involved in the conflict and to what degree. If Mary wants the two of them to spend the holidays with her family but Bill wants to travel to Europe with her at that time, how important is either outcome to each of them in terms of autonomy and feeling cared about? In this example, Mary's desire, which appears to have more psychological significance because it is associated with family and holiday time, would have higher priority. In another instance, Bill's need for autonomy, manifested in a desire to spend a weekend alone fishing, would take precedence over Mary's less emotionally charged wish to spend the weekend furniture shopping with Bill.

While any desire can have psychological significance and relate to feeling cared about, some wishes have more importance and greater emotional meaning than others. However, reaching agreement about the relative importance of one desire over another can be an arduous task requiring the wisdom of Solomon. One couple contemplating divorce attributed the beginning of their relationship deterioration to a Christmas conflict that occurred during their courtship. He wanted to spend the holidays (as he usually did) skiing with his family in Utah, while she wanted him to be a part of her family's Christmas festivities. They battled back and forth over the phone (he had gone skiing) until he finally acceded to her desire. Unfortunately, a plane delay caused by a snowstorm resulted in their spending Christmas day apart, thereby spoiling their reunion. Years later, they both believed that their difficulty in reaching agreement about that holiday portended their tumultuous, battle-scarred marriage.

## Mutual Causality

Regardless of whose desire is more psychologically important in a given situation, excessive guilt for intimacy problems is unrealistic because both partners contribute to their mutual problems. Circular rather than linear causality is involved. In linear causality, a reaction is thought to be determined by a single cause, while in circular causality, each reaction is regarded as both cause and effect. Interpersonal systems, especially intimate ones like families, operate along circular lines because every member influences and is influenced by every other member. Thus, our behavior in intimacy is a function not only of what we bring to the interpersonal table, but what our partner brings as well. "I nag because you neglect me" is often as valid as "I neglect you because you nag."

Thus, each individual's responsibility for intimacy conflict is often difficult to determine. If our hostility toward our partners is a function of their insensitivity, then who is to blame for the ensuing negative interaction? Similar to the old paradox, "Which came first, the chicken or the egg?" the question cannot be answered easily. However, rather than conceptualizing interpersonal conflict in terms of responsibility or blame, an alternate and more valid psychological perspective is the determination of each person's role. Since we all play a part in escalating or reducing intimacy conflict, our individual task is to determine our options in any given interaction and choose the most adaptive ones.

## A Multifaceted View of Responsibility

For example, if our partner walks in the front door intoxicated and two hours late for an anniversary dinner that we have spent all day preparing, we could deal with our hurt and angry feelings in a variety of ways. Most of us would agree that the inebriated spouse in this scenario was rude and insensitive to his mate and bears the major responsibility for the battle that followed. But even in this rather clear-cut vignette, the wounded partner plays a role in the tension-filled moments that follow his arrival. Of all her possible responses—shouting, crying, name-calling, the silent treatment, angry door-slamming and leaving the scene, accusatory comments such as "How could you?"—some responses are healthier than others in communicating her feelings and in dealing with him. By the way, in this situation, the fewer the words and the lower the intensity of emotional expression, the better! Essentially, because he is intoxicated, he is emotionally unstable and not likely to remember much of what was said.

Further complicating any determination of blame in a particular situation are the motives of the transgressor. Why did he come home late to his anniversary dinner? Among the most likely possibilities are alcoholism, severe and recent work-related disappointment, and/or unexpressed resentment of his wife from days, months, or even years earlier. While his motives may diminish or intensify his culpability, should his wife feel guilty for not providing an ideal environment that would rid her interpersonal world of alcoholism and other maladaptive coping strategies? Most of us would answer no without much hesitation. However, as part of her husband's intimate environment, she does play a role. Her attitudes and behavior are contributing factors to his responses, not determining or causal influences. His drunkenness is a function of biological factors, level of self-esteem, degree of interpersonal conflict, coping strategies, and current psychological environment, of which his family is a part. The complexity of factors that influence behavior argues for a multidimensional and circular view of causality rather than a simplistic, unilinear model.

Even in severe psychological and behavioral disorders, such as schizophrenia, manic-depressive illness, and alcoholism, that are profoundly influenced by genetic factors, stress and interpersonal conflict play a role. These latter variables have been shown to affect the frequency and duration of relapse, particularly in addictive behaviors.[6] Thus, while we all have an impact on one another, the responsibility for any given behavior is ordinarily shared. If our partner is drinking too much, he has to bear the major responsibility for this maladaptive coping strategy, but our emotional unavailability or criticality may contribute to his unhappiness. Unfortunately, we do not know the degree of our influence. In response to this ambiguous state of affairs, one couple humorously assigned days of blame. Everything that went wrong on Mondays, Wednesdays, and Fridays was Don's fault, while Gladys took Tuesdays, Thursdays, and Saturdays. Happily, on Sundays, their blaming took a day of rest.

*Chapter 10*

# Identifying the Pitfalls

Intimacy foibles can be put into either of two categories: run-of-the-mill or abusive. The former insensitivities and minor cruelties can be attributed to the limitations of human nature, while the latter are more psychopathological in quality and frequency. All of us make interpersonal errors, but the severity of these blunders determines whether we are safe for intimate cohabitation or not.

## Run-of-the-Mill Transgressions

The common intimacy errors are sins of omission that we all commit. Because we are entrenched in our own psychological worlds, we may have difficulty understanding our partner's verbalizations, let alone their latent messages. Tuning out part of the time, either because we have heard it all before or our own world is more absorbing, results in our missing part of the communication. Thus, misunderstanding what our partner wants or expects from us is inevitable. The daily disappointments—the forgotten gifts or chores—often result from this sort of half-hearted listening.

Another sort of impaired communication occurs in situations where we have no experiential basis for understanding what our partner is trying to convey. No matter how hard we try to grasp our partner's words, the message eludes us. For example, they may be trying to communicate how upset they were at yesterday's party because we were the center of attention while they were being ignored. While we may understand the gist of what is being said, we do not grasp (because of our own gregariousness) why they did not initiate conversation if they were interested in attention. In a similar vein, our partner's moodiness may be incomprehensible to us because of our lightheartedness and easygoing nature. Or their suspiciousness may be alien to our trusting nature. We all have a hard time relating empathically to qualities and experiences that are foreign to us.

## Minor Scapegoating

The displacement of everyday frustrations onto our intimate partner is another common intimacy error. While it is difficult to put aside the irritability brought about by daily disappointments, taking it out on our partner, who is often an innocent bystander, has negative consequences. All of us resent being treated rudely because our partner has a proverbial "bad day at the office" or got caught in an hour-long traffic jam. However, none of us is capable of putting our anger where it belongs all of the time, and so spillage into the intimacy area frequently occurs. If brief periods of moodiness, sullen withdrawal, or a few sharp retorts are the only manifestations, this sort of displaced frustration can be regarded as a minor flaw in an otherwise solid relationship.

## Routine Conversational Differences

Other routine intimacy problems revolve around differences in conversational style and self-awareness. We may need to talk endlessly about our daily experiences, while our partner is content with a cursory exchange. Our enjoyment of conversing may occur because we have the ability to translate mundane occurrences into amusing anecdotes, while our partner lacks that skill. Or we are acutely aware of our own thoughts and feelings and eager to share them, while our partner has a diminished capacity for self-observation. Similarly, talking about the meaning of life and other philosophical issues might be our forte, while our partner is more concretely tuned into the world of work and sports. While all of these common differences, including closeness-distance requirements, have the potential for creating tensions that erode the relationship, these common intimacy problems occur in most intimate relationships to one degree or another.

## Plain Old Frogs or Potential Princes

To evaluate how entrenched an intimacy problem is, potential for change needs to be examined. Is our partner capable of growing up and becoming a reasonable facsimile of our prince or does his or her behavior appear fixed in stone? Similarly, are we able to change sufficiently to accommodate our partner's needs and maintain our own happiness and sanity in the process? The basic question is: Where are the growing edges in this relationship?

Our first adult, intimate relationship of long duration ordinarily is the most treacherous, but at the same time filled with interpersonal insights. We learn not only what our fears, needs, and interpersonal styles are but discover our capacity to change. We find out how much we can absorb and/or adjust to while maintaining our integrity as a person. Are we able to accept his or her discomfort at social gatherings, poor table manners, or long hours spent watching TV without experiencing disgust, contempt, or resentment? In other words, how much can we learn to tolerate and still feel basically loving?

Similarly, are our partners capable of changing in the directions that are important to us? If we love classical music and they prefer rock 'n' roll, are they able to attend an occasional classical concert without complaining? If we like to talk but they do not, are they willing to initiate conversation sporadically to meet our needs? In short, how much can each of us yield, compromise, or change to meet the other somewhere along the common relationship pathway?

Clearly, the answer to these questions will depend on the

importance of the behavior in question and the adaptability of each partner. While most of us can learn to adapt to our intimate partner's idiosyncrasies, more unusual or pathological behaviors require maladaptive coping strategies. If a partner is physically abusive, for example, learning to tolerate the abuse requires low self-esteem and self-destructive potential. Similarly, if our partner has a strong need to dominate or control, we would have to be withdrawn, dependent, or depressed to tolerate the suspiciousness, interrogation, and ongoing surveillance that would be involved.

With extreme personality traits and behaviors such as voyeurism, exhibitionism, drug abuse, grandiosity, and sexual promiscuity, maintaining the relationship requires fine-tuning of our denial mechanism or ongoing battles. Excessive denial, on the one hand, constricts and dulls both partners intellectually and emotionally; continual warfare, on the other hand, exhausts them. Thus, in order to enhance our own emotional development, we need to avoid intimacy partners who have the potential of crippling us.

Karen, a forty-five-year-old housewife, ignored her husband's frequent business trips and late nights away from home because of her emotional dependency on him and fear that she could not survive financially without him. By ignoring Larry's regular absences, Karen was able to protect herself from worries about rejection and abandonment. Unfortunately, because ignoring the obvious takes it toll, Karen began to overeat and limit her social world to a few friends. By the time she allowed Larry's infidelity to become apparent to her, she had gained almost 100 pounds and was suffering from increasingly serious bouts of depression. Her denial had served to protect her from confronting her worst fear, namely, Larry's desertion, while hastening his departure by her self-destructive weight gain and loss of vitality. Karen eventually faced her problems in therapy; however, her marriage ended.

In addition to severe psychopathological conditions, there are personality types who have limited capacity for intimacy. Sometimes, these "poor risk" intimacy candidates have emotional needs that are so overwhelming that they have little energy left over to pay attention to anyone else. At other times, they lack salient interpersonal or personality skills. They may have difficulty being empathic, taking on adult responsibilities, or hearing a point of view that is different from their own. Regardless of whether their interpersonal skill deficits are a function of early psychic damage, inadequate opportunities for learning, or severe emotional immaturity, these "poor risk" candidates are to be avoided because of the misery they inflict on their partners.

Of all the contenders for the "poor risk," psychologically abusive category, the most common are emotional hermits, passive-aggressive types, blamers, narcissists, and immature personalities. While physical violence is usually not involved, the degree of frustration and unhappiness that these partners engender is profoundly damaging to self-esteem. With emotional hermits, blamers, and narcissists, the self-esteem damage occurs as a result of verbal assault or severe neglect. Passive-aggressive types, by contrast, are so indirect and frustrating that we wind up feeling helpless and immobilized. Immature personalities, lacking the capacity to give much emotional nurturance and yet requiring ongoing support, deplete us.

## Emotional Hermits

While these personalities often avoid intimacy altogether because of their basic mistrust of others, emotionally withdrawn persons are found in intimate relationships in significant numbers. Often intellectually and professionally gifted, they are more comfortable in the neatly ordered and pristine world of ideas than in the messier and more mundane realm of emotions. Logic and reason are not likely to betray or hurt them, while with people, there is no such guarantee. Basically introverted, they prefer books and other solitary pursuits to people. Emotional hermits abound in academia, scientific laboratories, and the ministry.

Easily identified by the paucity of their close relationships, emotionally withdrawn individuals typically arrive at intimacy's doorstep later in life than their peers. They may have had a couple of brief, sexual relationships in late adolescence or early adulthood, and drinking companions, if alcohol use is part of the picture, but characteristically they are solitary, eccentric souls. As with Macon Leary in *The Accidental Tourist* by Anne Tyler,[1] compulsive and ritualistic behavior may be involved. Neatness and perfectionism manifested in elaborately ordered rows of spices, tools, and clothing dominate their personal style. While they are typically comfortable with solitude, sexual desire, vague loneliness, or social pressure may push them into intimacy when they are in their late thirties or forties.

However, once they are in a committed relationship, the emotional spark that ignited their moment of passion dies and they are back to their earlier dull and monotonous existence. Because emotional expression is synonymous with loss of control, they keep a tight rein on all feelings. Not only is anger kept under close surveillance, but emotional warmth and affection warrant equal supervision. With such rigid emotional control, moments of spontaneity and vitality are minimal or nonexistent. Governed by rules and logic, these overcontrolled individuals move like emotional zombies through their interpersonal world.

## Unbearable Loneliness for Partners

For their partners, life feels empty and devoid of human contact. Because the withdrawn person is difficult to reach in any emotionally meaningful way except for occasional sexual contact, the partner often experiences profound loneliness, depression, and self-doubt. The silence that hangs heavily over their conversational moments is often palpable and suffocating. Witness the many couples in restaurants who sit uncomfortably together in virtual silence, staring at their plates or looking out the window, unable or unwilling to communicate anything more than "Nice restaurant!" or "Isn't that steak tasty?" to each other. Even when intellectual discussions about history or politics fill a couple's dinner hours, the emotional vacuum can be deadly.

Joyce, a thirty-two-year-old interior designer, came into therapy ostensibly because of anxiety symptoms at work. As soon as these moments of panic abated, however, Joyce shifted the focus to her six-month-old marriage. She described the distance she felt in her relationship with her forty-year-old accountant husband, who preferred to spend time reading history texts or watching TV rather than interacting with her. While his sexual interest had always seemed minimal (in contrast to earlier partners), he had become apathetic about sex (in fact, he said that sex was "overrated") and routinely rejected her sexual advances. There had been satisfying sexual encounters during their two-year courtship, but starting with the honeymoon, his sexual desire seemed to vanish.

More important than the lack of sexual gratification, however, was the absence of verbal intimacy and physical manifestations of affection. Her husband seldom talked to her about personally meaningful issues and rarely hugged or touched her. Occasionally, he would engage in lengthy discussions about historical and political matters, topics in which he was well versed. An avid collector of expensive books and manuscripts dealing with the Napoleonic era, he was clearly more at home in the intellectual arena than in the emotional realm. While his emotional withdrawal seemed profound to most observers, he accused her of being demanding whenever she brought up the subject of his distance, and he would change the topic so that it was difficult for her to bridge the chasm by conversation.

Her husband's refusal to discuss their relationship, consider couples counseling, or change his interpersonal behavior toward her left Joyce with few options. While she did have emotional predictability and financial security in her marriage, the absence of sexual and verbal intimacy along with a dearth of mutual friends and interests left her feeling emotionally disconnected. In addition, she had become decidedly more self-doubting and self-blaming in her marriage than she had ever been previously. She tended to blame her husband's verbal withdrawal on her talkativeness and lack of intellectual sophistication; his sexual avoidance was attributed to her lack of "sexual appeal." While she could not specify what she lacked in the "sexual appeal" department, she reasoned circularly that if she had this quality, he would obviously be more interested. The fact that she had been generally regarded as an attractive woman, with her share of amorous male companions prior to her marriage, seemed to have little impact on her marital self-deprecating state. Her husband's failure to provide even minimal validation of her as a person by refusing to spend verbal, sexual, or affectionate time with her basically undermined her self-confidence.

When such profound erosion of self-esteem occurs in intimacy, the most likely outcomes are chronic depression, drug use, divorce, or an outside involvement (career, cause, or companion) to serve as a replacement for the lack of intimacy. Because ongoing withdrawal is often experienced as deliberate withholding of affection and as rejection, the partner has to seek emotional sustenance outside of the relationship or else deteriorate psychologically. Healthier individuals leave or find meaning in other activities, while the more vulnerable souls, who lack the strength to remove themselves from such psychologically toxic environments, wither away and eventually die. In Joyce's case, she began drinking heavily for a brief period before finally divorcing her husband. At the moment, she is rebuilding her damaged self-esteem in therapy and seeking to understand, and thereby change, her own motives for getting involved with psychologically withholding and abusive men.

## Chronic Avoiders

While we all tune out some of the time, emotional hermits regularly use withdrawal and avoidance as coping strategies to reduce conflict. Anytime their interpersonal world gets heated up by anger or disagreement, they emotionally retreat into the safety of the intellect, another scholarly pursuit, or a distraction, such as clubs or TV. Seldom having experienced an adaptive resolution to interpersonal conflict in their lives, they become frightened by intense emotionality and flee rather than fight such dangers. Unaware that their chronic withdrawal creates an emotional vacuum, a climate of neglect, and self-denigration in their partners, they tend to see themselves as peacekeepers rather than emotional misers. Unfortunately, their partners experience their withholding in a decidedly less benign manner. By withdrawing rather than facing conflict, emotional hermits inadvertently communicate disdain for their partners and an unwillingness to be involved, except under the best of circumstances.

## Passive-Aggressive Types

Similar to emotional hermits in their avoidance of overt conflict, passive-aggressive individuals are also abusive intimate partners. Because they rely on indirect methods of expressing anger, they are profoundly confusing to deal with. Rather than being openly argumentative, they appear agreeable but manifest their opposition in procrastination, forgetting, stubborn resistance, chronic tardiness, or hostile errors. While the underlying hostility is not always apparent, the entrenched nature of passive-aggressive behavior and its conflictual impact on intimacy partners betray its aggressive underpinnings. According to psychologist Scott Wetzler, who wrote *Living with the Passive-Aggressive Man*,[2] in addition to the above-mentioned trademarks, passive-aggressive men are characterized by ambiguity, lying, sulking, fostering chaos, and fears of intimacy.

Because a passive-aggressive style is deceptive, it is difficult to confront. If our partner regularly "forgets" to take out the garbage, for example, how can he be blamed for such a minor offense? Also, because he seems to have no control over his "forgetting," complaining about it seems demanding and inhuman. Saying nothing, however, results in a sense of helplessness and frustration, so we are left in a no-win situation. In fact, since passive-aggressive behavior is unconsciously designed to be frustrating, defeating, and blameless, there is no way of winning. Because blaming someone for benign mistakes feels cruel, we wind up blaming ourselves. "What makes his personality confusing is that he's passive, coaxing, elusive, but also aggressively resistant to you, to intimacy, to responsibility and reason," writes Wetzler.[3]

Jenny, a poised, vibrant woman, came into counseling with complaints of depression. She was convinced that there was something fundamentally wrong with her because she cried, felt sad, and was listless periodically for no apparent reason. An ex-dancer, she was currently in the advertising field where she had an opportunity to exercise her creative talents. Also, she was married to "a wonderful man who adores me" and whom she regarded as her best-friend. Because her life seemed to be going well, these unexplained periods of depression were baffling to her.

It was only after several months of therapy that the facade of an idyllic marriage began to fade. Gradually, it became clear that Jenny felt overburdened and resentful about her husband's difficulty in completing household chores. Mike would faithfully promise to do something and then promptly forget. For example, he regularly left his breakfast dishes on the table (rather than rinsing them off and putting them into the sink) and routinely threw his dirty clothes all over the bedroom floor. In response to Jenny's complaints, Mike would apologize and agree to mend his ways, but his behavior remained intractable. Kindly reminders were no more effective in changing his behavior than angry outbursts. In addition, he was quite careless about their finances and regularly overdrew on their accounts. Here again, no amount of logical persuasion on Jenny's part made a dent in Mike's resistance.

Mike's withdrawal from the power struggle around household chores left Jenny feeling confused and frustrated. Since Mike was such a loving husband in other ways (he was quite affectionate and verbally supportive), Jenny's anger toward him felt unreasonable. So, she attempted to bury the hatchet only to find herself bursting into tears on occasion with no apparent provocation.

## The Chinese Water Torture

Besides forgetting, other common passive-aggressive approaches are procrastinating until the partner is consumed with rage, habitual tardiness, and hostile errors. Procrastinating, or putting off chores for days, weeks, or even months, is the kind of torture that slowly drives intimate partners mad (both meanings of the word "mad" are appropriate here). Waiting for our partner to deliver on a commitment or promise erodes the fabric of trust and hope that a relationship ideally is constructed of. If our partners cannot be counted on for little things, how can we rely on them during the important crises that shake the very foundation of our relationship? The "I'll get to it, dear" uttered routinely and repeatedly can be frustrating and undermining.

Habitual tardiness is another passive-aggressive approach that is unnerving. Keeping one's partner waiting for hours on end is both a control issue and an expression of hostility. While tardiness may be a chronic problem that is difficult to change, failure to modify the behavior, especially when the waiting partner is upset by it, represents a cavalier disregard of the partner's needs. The offender stubbornly seems to be saying, "No one can make me do anything I don't want to do."

Often, the partner's helpless frustration smolders below the surface for days on end until an insignificant occurrence triggers a major eruption. However, regardless of whether the partner's anger ever gets expressed directly or not, chronic tardiness can create feelings of victimization and conflict in partners.

## Disguised Hostility

Hostile slips of the tongue and other unconsciously motivated errors also exact a psychological toll on intimacy partners. One man who angered his wife regularly by his blatant disregard of his mother-in-law during her visits could not understand why both his wife and mother-in-law got upset by his neglect. During her visits, he seldom directed his conversational attention to her and routinely "forgot" to offer her a drink while asking everyone else what their beverage preferences were. While it was understandable why he did not like his mother-in-law (she was opposed to their marriage), his indirect method of expressing hostility exacerbated the marital conflicts. After months of arguments about this issue, during which he vehemently denied any hostility toward his mother-in-law, his faux pas during a subsequent visit finally exposed his own motives to himself. In the midst of asking everyone what they wanted to drink, he skipped his mother-in-law once again and turned to the family dog, saying in a humorous manner, "Now Oliver, what do you want to drink?" His seeming preferential treatment of the dog over his mother-in-law loudly communicated his hostility in a manner that he could not ignore.

## Blamers

Blamers are particularly adept at self-esteem damage. Because they seldom take responsibility for any intimacy conflicts and routinely blame their partner, the partner feels under continuous attack. Every transgression or intimacy violation gets reframed so that the blamer is the "good guy" and the partner is the "bad guy." His temper outburst is due to her provocation; his withdrawal to her demandingness. Her complaints about the relationship are seen as manifestations of a neurosis or an insatiable need for love and, therefore, invalid. Like a good "spin doctor," who knows how to weave an acceptable slant or cover-up for every catastrophe, blamers are skilled excuse-makers. Seldom acknowledging their own mistakes, they rarely apologize.

Besides their externalizing style, blamers use emotional intensity to drive home their points. Their accusations are delivered not as factual presentations but as weighty, self-righteous judgments. The "How could you?" and "I can't believe you did that" uttered with appropriate indignation and shock magnify the indictment. Thus, we stand accused with the weight of morality, ethics, religion, and civilization compounding the gravity of our interpersonal crime.

## Charismatic Blamers

Blamers who are charismatic have even greater psychological power. Because their prominence, fame, or notoriety adds weight to their verbalizations, their comments are difficult to ignore. Their pronouncements delivered from a psychologically lofty pedestal reverberate with a godlike certitude. If we were to question their judgments, we would feel like insubordinate children challenging divine authority.

Ministers, CEOs, politicians, writers, and other creative talents are most likely to fall in this category. Because their accomplishments give them star billing and top decision-making authority within their circles, they often lack the self-awareness and humility to acknowledge their contributions to intimacy conflicts. Rather, they often utilize the full power of their positions to browbeat their partners into submission.

Kurt was a thirty-eight-year-old movie director whose wife was in treatment for depression. He was a good-looking, flamboyant, and successful man who had a large female following on the movie sets. Besides his charm and emotional power, he was a staunch believer in EST, a sociopsychological set of beliefs in which personal autonomy and willpower reign supreme. Given these characteristics, try to imagine what any confrontation between his mild-mannered wife and him would sound like when she tried to talk to him about her marital unhappiness! As we might suspect, he first leapt to his own defense in forceful and animated terms, tearing to shreds her complaints of insensitivity and inattentiveness, before attacking her for creating her own unhappiness. Since he firmly believed that no one can make another person feel anything and that we are all masters of our emotional fates, he had no empathy for her helpless rage and, in fact, blamed her for her depression. He was a master at disavowing himself of any responsibility before emphatically laying the blame at his partner's doorstep.

## Legacy of Guilt and Self-Doubt

As was the case with Kurt's wife, the expected result of excessive blaming is heavy-duty guilt. Because some of us are guilt-prone to start with and see ourselves as responsible for all the misfortunes that befall us, we readily accept the blame that gets tossed our way. Our partner's accusations, rather than being carefully examined or defended against, are absorbed as gospel truth.

Even if we are not guilt-prone, the constant barrage of criticism in intimacy destroys our self-confidence and leaves us questioning our motives and behavior. We wonder whether we had been as selfish or insensitive or manipulative as accused. Weighted down by the burden of too much blame and self-doubt, we move slowly and depressingly through our intimate world.

Jack's blaming style bordered on paranoia at times. He was an angry, insecure, and demanding man who flew off the handle with little provocation. Not only was he likely to go into a verbal tirade when he could not reach his partner by phone, but he screamed and swore at the dog, tradespeople, and colleagues whenever frustrated. In addition, he was highly manipulative, controlling, and guilt-inducing. For example, if he wanted Sylvia, his fiancee, to take care of his daughter from his first marriage while he worked late and Sylvia had other plans, he would rant and rave about how upset his daughter would be with a babysitter. His relentless pursuit of his desires frequently wore Sylvia down to the point where her planned engagement was ruined by her inner torment about whether she was doing "the right thing" or not. Or she simply changed her plans and acquiesced to his wishes in order to avoid conflict.

While Sylvia gained peace by accommodating Jack's wishes, the loss of autonomy was suffocating. After living together for a few months and experiencing his criticisms and demands on a daily basis, she began to feel trapped. The loss of personal freedom was oppressive. Unable to make decisions about meeting her own needs for fear of unleashing a torrent of guilt-inducing opposition, she became immobilized and depressed.

Jack's blaming and demanding interpersonal style would create havoc with any intimacy partner, but with a guilt-prone woman, the psychological damage is even more extensive. Women like Sylvia, who are unable to fight back, suffer endlessly. Because they cannot discern which criticisms are valid, they give each and every accusation equal credibility. In the process, their own perspectives get discarded as meaningless and they lose even greater self-respect. The erosion of trust in their own judgment and a helplessness borne of their failure to be heard by their partners lay the foundation for debilitating depression and/or drug use.

## Narcissists

Narcissists are so absorbed in their own grandiose thoughts, feelings, and beliefs that no one else really matters. Unable to shift gears and pay attention to another person for any length of time, narcissists seem to be intrigued by their own experiences and productions. Having fallen in love with their reflected image long ago, their conversations are designed to persuade their audience of their vast appeal. They want to convince the world that they have unusual intelligence, cunning, perspicacity, daring, or taste by relating endless tales of amazing accomplishments. While they are quite conversational and eager to talk about a broad range of topics, narcissists regularly return the discussion to their own achievements so that we get worn out by all the egotistical glitter and eventually withdraw.

While the grandiosity of narcissists is believed to be related to insecurity and low self-esteem, their self-absorption does not allow us ready access into their intimate zone. They keep intimate partners at a distance, ignoring them whenever possible, while pursuing their own ends. High-energy people with a propensity for making plans and keeping several balls in the air simultaneously, narcissists are admired from afar for their drive. However, their incapacity for intimacy tarnishes their appeal over the long haul.

Their difficulties in being attentive, empathic, and genuinely interested in their intimate partner leave the partner feeling unloved and lonely. He or she does not feel valued as a person, but rather toyed with—as if she were chosen only for her beauty or he for his money. In addition, because narcissists respond to most criticisms with rage, their partners wind up feeling helpless about how to voice their complaints about the relationship and connect with their narcissistic partner in a positive manner.

## Sex and Narcissism

While narcissistic characteristics appear to be shared equally by the sexes, men have tended to be grandiose about those characteristics associated with masculine achievement in our culture, such as job status, money, material possessions, and the conquest of women, whereas women have been somewhat more focused on those traits historically associated with feminine appeal, such as beauty and the admiration of men. Today with the blurring of traditional sex roles and the increased emphasis on professional attainment for women, the narcissistic differences between the sexes are less pronounced. For both sexes, admiration and attention are the sought-after interpersonal commodities that appear vital to their emotional survival.

Jane, an extremely attractive woman who was model-thin well into her fifties, drew attention to herself not only by her high-fashion clothing but by her constant references to herself in conversation. If a group of people were immersed in a discussion about existentialism, she would interrupt after a few moments with an oblique transitional comment, such as "Speaking of existentialism, my modeling career is filled with existential crises," before launching off into a monologue about the many facets of her work. Typically, her egotistical chattering was filled with exaggerations of all sorts: her earnings, the importance of the people she associated with, the scope of her travels, the price of the Oriental rug she purchased, and so forth. Her sense of entitlement, namely, the expectation that other people were interested in listening to her tales for hours on end, was profound.

Equally narcissistic, Paul was a psychiatrist whose megalomania centered around creating projects and programs for the treatment of alcoholism. Like inventors who spend time and energy trying to design perpetual motion machines, Paul was forever in pursuit of "the Great Idea" that would catapult him to fame. Constantly starting new projects, many of which would be dropped in midstream, he was a man of high energy who, like Jane, needed to dominate every conversation. The perceptions, opinions, and adventures of others appeared to have little significance when compared to his own.

The intimate partners of Jane and Paul, while seldom heard or attended to, derived some gratification from their partners' drive and star qualities. Jane's husband tended to walk in her regal shadow, looking a bit like a lost valet or man-in-waiting. Paul's wife, a shy but accomplished artist, seemed more self-contained and indifferent to his attention-seeking antics. In both cases, Jane and Paul were the kind of intimacy partners who provide excitement but little in the way of nurturance, empathy, and unconditional love.

## Peter Pan and Cinderella

Like their namesakes, Peter Pan and Cinderella are immature intimacy partners who never want to grow up.[4,5] Either they are having too much fun in same-sex, latency activities or they are passively waiting around for Prince Charming to rescue them from their drudgery.

Peter Pan, the eternal boy who loves adventure and play, often seeks out a maternal woman to take care of him. Preferring to spend time with "the guys" drinking, playing cards, gambling, or at sporting events, he often needs a woman to handle adult responsibilities. Because his occupational functioning is frequently impaired, his intimate partner needs to be the responsible adult in the partnership to earn money, pay bills, and take care of the family. Unless she derives a significant degree of gratification from this caretaking role, she will be depleted before long and either depressed or ready to leave.

Victor was a heavy-drinking gambler who attempted erratically to support his family by construction work. It was the lure of the big win at the horses or the card table, however, that frequently interfered with regular employment. Fortunately for him, his wife of thirty years was the dependable wage earner whose bookkeeping job in the parish rectory could be counted on to provide groceries. As long as she was available to take care of the family, Victor was free to enjoy the camaraderie of his male buddies and the pleasure of his hobbies. It was only after his wife became seriously ill with cancer that Victor, who was forced to take over child-care and financial responsibilities, finally grew up.

## Unresolved Oedipal Issues

Another version of the Peter Pan syndrome is the man who is a high achiever professionally but inordinately attached to his mother. Never having resolved Oedipal attachment in a healthy manner, he maintains an unusually close relationship with his mother throughout adulthood. While he may attempt intimate relationships with the opposite sex, they often fizzle out before long.

One youthful-appearing man of thirty "fell in love" with young women regularly but would bolt from these relationships suddenly after several months. All that he was aware of was that something was missing in his feelings toward them. The fact that he preferred to spend time with his mother, whom he described as his "best friend," did not strike him as unusual. His mother was his only confidante, the decorator of his apartments, and the consultant about all his decisions, including jobs, clothing, and friendships. Basically, the extent of his admiration for, involvement with, and enjoyment of his mother precluded another intimate relationship of much depth.

## Marital Triangles

In other instances, Peter Pans with strong attachments to their mothers get married. However, their relationships with their mothers serve as significant sources of conflict for their partners. The mothers, aware of their son's strong attachment, regularly lay claim to preferential treatment by loudly demanding time and attention. The partners, feeling left out and second best, also make demands. However, without the emotional clout of their mothers-in-law, they are frequently ineffective in getting their needs met and wind up feeling uncared about.

Frank, a thirty-eight-year-old man of Italian descent, left the priesthood after twenty years to marry a woman who was ten years his senior. Unfortunately, the newlyweds moved into the apartment building where Frank's widowed mother resided. As one might expect, this living arrangement turned out to be highly conflictual, with Frank caught in the middle. Frank's mother was regularly telling Frank what his wife should cook for dinner and how their holidays should be spent. In addition, she was demanding of Frank's time and attention with her many shopping and household repair requests.

While Frank's solicitousness toward his mother was commendable, his mother's dominating intrusiveness into their married life left his wife feeling powerless. As a result of daily criticism from her mother-in-law about her housekeeping shortcomings and a lack of support from her husband, Frank's wife gradually began to find the marital triangle intolerable. Feeling unloved and unsupported led to the erosion of her self-confidence and loss of affection toward Frank. After five years of marriage, she left the marriage one day and never returned. The burden of helping Peter Pan mature into an emotionally autonomous adult proved to be too overwhelming a task.

## Waiting for Prince Charming

Cinderella, Peter Pan's female counterpart, keeps hoping that the man of her dreams will one day stumble onto her doorstep and take her away. Then when she is safely removed from all independent decision-making and settled into her dream castle, Cinderella yearns to be pampered and protected for the rest of her days. In return for such an idyllic retreat from the world of adult reality, Cinderella typically promises to stay beautiful and shower gratitude on her powerful substitute daddy till death or divorce tears them apart.

Basically, Cinderellas yearn to be taken care of without expending much energy themselves. Often, in their families of origin, they were good girls who exercised little initiative because their needs were tended to by a doting parent. They may have had special status, such as "Daddy's little girl," and did not have to prove themselves to gain approval. Or they were overprotected as little girls so that whatever curiosity, spirit of adventure, and achievement motivation they possessed was snuffed out by their parents' anxieties. Whatever the cause, Cinderellas are left with a romanticized view of the world and strong, passive longings for nurturance and protection by a father figure.

Barbara's search for Prince Charming spanned forty years. A scholarly, religious woman with a doctorate in English, she left an unhappy twenty-five-year marriage when a charismatic preacher came into town. Because her husband was a mild-mannered, emotionally withdrawn computer programmer who had trouble taking care of himself psychologically, let alone his wife and five children, the appearance of his antithesis on the scene resulted in emotional sparks flying everywhere.

Barbara, the only daughter in a family of five children, had clearly been "Daddy's pretty little girl." However, he had also nurtured her scholarly activities, her writing, and the most adventuresome of her pursuits, a love of flying, which she briefly engaged in. In spite of these extraordinary accomplishments, however, she was basically a nonassertive and passive woman, always eager to please the father figures who came her way. And then when they were unable to provide for her, because of death (her father's), psychological limitations (her husband's), or choice (the preacher's), she became seriously depressed, functioning at marginal levels for several years subsequent to these losses.

After the ten-year spiritual and romantic attachment to the preacher finally ended (it consisted mainly of correspondence over long distances), Barbara moved to the town where her only son and his family resided. Her son, a handsome, dynamic, and successful banker, had become a powerful person in his local community. Once settled there, in exchange for food, rent, and a minimal allowance, Barbara began a five-year stint as daily caretaker for her young grandchildren, while her daughter-in-law worked. During this time while she was being taken care of financially by her son (he was also loaning her the mortgage payments on her unsold home out West), Barbara's scholarly pursuits suffered and her social/professional life declined.

While many grandmothers lovingly take care of their grandchildren during periods of crisis and gain self-esteem from the venture, Barbara's retreat from her intellectual world was humiliating and demeaning to her. In addition, her daughter-in-law, who resented the amount of money being loaned to her mother-in-law, treated her in a contemptuous manner, much the way some arrogant, upper-class women treat their household help. Thus, it appeared that in return for financial security and caretaking, Barbara had to give up self-respect and professional autonomy. Fortunately, but traumatically, the arrangement collapsed when her son, without any warning, told her to leave and repay some of the money he had loaned her. Apparently, the conflicts with his wife around her were exacting too steep a toll on his marriage. And so, once again, Barbara was deserted or disappointed by a father figure (in this instance, her son) and forced to rely on her own resources. Hopefully, with the assistance of therapy, she will be able to give up the wish for a Prince Charming this time around and develop her own power as a person.

While immature personalities are the most benign of the

"poor risk" intimacy candidates, their neediness is often overwhelming. Because of an inability to relate in an egalitarian manner to their intimate partners and a difficulty in being self-supporting, both financially and emotionally, they put a strain on the intimate system. Either the partner fills in the gaps, thus overtaxing his or her own personality resources, or else the system malfunctions, with both partners operating at lower psychological levels than they are capable of. While there are individuals who derive significant gratification from the nurturant role, the failure to get their own emotional needs met ordinarily stifles personal development.

*Chapter 11*

# Improving a Troubled Relationship

Intimate relationships flounder for a number of predictable reasons: too little responsivity, too many demands, abuse, lack of empathy, failure to take responsibility, or unequal distribution of power. Complaints of "too little responsivity" ordinarily revolve around lack of emotional, conversational, and/or sexual attention. "Too many demands" and "abuse" deal with verbal criticism, browbeating, domination, and/or physical battering. "Lack of empathy" is difficulty in understanding or in conveying appreciation of the other's point of view. With "failure to take responsibility," there is lack of initiative or poor management in tending to relationship needs, household chores, child-rearing, and/or financial demands. The "unequal distribution of power" factor centers around inequity in money-making or decision-making or popularity (love, affection, and respect from family members).

With all these factors, difficulties can occur along emotional, affectional, sexual, financial, and task dimensions (household responsibilities, child rearing). For example, we may feel emotionally alienated from our partners because they are insensitive to our emotional needs, verbally abusive, demanding of sexual performance, unwilling to spend time with the children, and con-

235

trolling about finances. In short, each of these factors may be separately but additively involved in our emotional alienation, or one particular cause, such as alcoholism, may be the underlying factor behind all these dissatisfactions. In other cases, one behavior, such as compulsive gambling with its impact on financial stability, may be the primary variable leading to relationship dysfunction. Ordinarily, however, several factors are involved before the level of dissatisfaction becomes critical to the survival of the relationship.

## Relationship versus Individual Needs

Another way of identifying problem areas is by looking at the system as a unit. In contrast to the needs of each member, the relationship as a whole has certain characteristics and requirements. The system has rules governing its operation, member roles, distance-closeness boundaries, degree of openness to the external environment, capacity to change, and ways of resolving conflict.

Among the questions that can be raised about the system are the following: Are the partners too enmeshed (entangled) or disengaged from one another? Is the relationship open or closed to outside influence? How does the system adapt to change and solve problems? Finally, does the relationship nurture or stifle the growth of each partner?

From the family systems perspective (theory derived from family therapy regarding the holistic function of the family),[1] it appears that an ideal intimacy unit or family has some rules but not too many, role flexibility, a moderate degree of closeness, openness to external influence, adaptability to change, effective conflict-resolution skills, and a maximum amount of growth enhancement. In short, the ideal is a relationship that provides high degrees of emotional support, flexibility, adaptability, and autonomy.

## Too Little or Too Much Space

In contrast, troubled relationships are dysfunctional in being too entangled or distant, rigid in structure, nonadaptable, conflict-ridden, and intent upon preserving the status quo rather than fostering growth. When a system is "too enmeshed," partners are overly involved in each other's business, privacy is not respected, and differences of opinion are abhorred. Michael Nichols, a psychiatrist with expertise in family therapy, writes: "Enmeshed subsystems offer a heightened sense of mutual support but at the expense of independence and autonomy."[2] The united-front couple is a prime example! Determined to agree at all costs, they appear to be an "ideal couple" until a child becomes symptomatic (e.g., anorexic) or one partner suddenly leaves. Because individual differences are swept under the rug, autonomy suffers. The stifling atmosphere of such a relationship is not conducive to emotional spontaneity and growth. Rather, the emphasis upon conformity frequently leads to personality constriction, somatic illness, and/or anxiety disorders.

By contrast, disengaged couples have so much individual freedom that needs for closeness and affection are seldom gratified. Each partner is so busy pursuing his or her own life that there is no quality time left for the relationship. Dual-career couples frequently fall in this category. In this situation, one or both partners may spin out of the relationship's orbit (e.g., "fall out of love" or meet someone else). Another possibility is that the emotional deprivation will result in drug or alcohol use, behavioral disorders, and/or the most likely syndrome when intimacy needs are ignored: depression.

## Rigid Rules and Roles

Another dysfunctional intimacy system is a rigid unit that has many rules governing its operation and fixed roles. The rules govern the nature of interactions between partners (e.g., don't speak about negatives, never point out Harry's failings because he'll explode, don't talk to Mary about problems in the family because she's too fragile, don't talk about the family to outsiders, etc.). The rules, which clearly inhibit spontaneous, direct communication, maintain the status quo.

Rigid roles also retard growth in one or both partners. One partner may be the strong, dominating person who cannot show weakness or vulnerability, while the other is the weak, submissive member who has to suppress initiative and organizational talent. Or one person may be the logical intellectual who cannot show emotion, while the other member is the histrionic partner who needs to keep intellectual talent under wraps for the sake of the system. Essentially, couples get locked into limited ways of interacting that constrict each individual's range of responses.

Rigid couples also lack resiliency in adapting to change. If one partner goes back to school to finish a degree or returns to work after a lengthy hiatus, the other is threatened. Any internal or external event that disturbs the stability of the system is viewed as dangerous. A child going off to school for the first time, an aging parent coming to stay, an unexpected pregnancy, sickness, and disability all represent crises to the rigid system.

## Warring Couples

Another kind of dysfunctional couple is the conflict-ridden pair locked in perpetual combat. Forever disagreeing about anything and everything, they may range from verbal snipers to physical abusers. Like George and Martha in Edward Albee's *Who's Afraid of Virginia Woolf?* or the Roses in the popular film *War of the Roses*, they are continually enraged with one another. Constantly correcting each other's commentary, they are engaged in an ongoing power struggle to determine who is right and, therefore, in control. Frequently unable to express positive feelings, which render them too vulnerable, their battles are often the only areas of contact. Because of this, their squabbling gets reinforced. The connectedness they experience in the midst of their shouting is often a brief respite from the distance and alienation they feel toward one another. While the partners might experience some momentary positive gain from the fighting, the children (when there are any) suffer. The constant exposure to warring parents—a situation more damaging than divorce—leaves them highly conflicted and emotionally torn.[3] The chronic discord in the family, with neither parent giving or gaining much emotional solace, results in unhappiness and low self-esteem for all.

## Where to Go Next?

Whatever the problem in a dysfunctional or troubled relationship, it is not always apparent what to do next. While some solutions are obvious because they stem from the diagnosis of the problem (e.g., "enmeshed" requires emphasis on individual autonomy; "conflict-ridden" suggests training in negotiation or problem-solving skills), we cannot see our own problems clearly when we are in the midst of them. For example, when our partner's behavior is a source of conflict, we often cannot decide how to deal with it. Should we confront it directly, drop hints, or bury our heads in the sand in the hope that the disturbing behavior will vanish overnight?

Similarly, when our own actions are being criticized, we feel confused. Often, we cannot understand why our partner is upset or critical with us when we are doing our best. We may find the objections to our behavior petty, demeaning, or demanding and so ignore them. Or we may take the criticism to heart and try valiantly to change ourselves to please our partner only to find that the hurt and resentment linger on.

If our partner told us that he could not stand listening to all our complaints, we would have a number of choices. While most of us would feel wounded by such a comment and respond defensively, saying something like, "I don't complain that much, and besides, you don't love me if you can't listen to what I have to say," we might decide thereafter to save our criticisms of the world for someone else. Or we might decide that our partner should listen to all our feelings, including the negative ones, and go on complaining as before. In addition, some of us would quietly wonder about our own need to complain so much or our partner's inability to tolerate the dark side of human nature.

## More of the Same

Unfortunately, when conflicts occur, most of us continue to repeat the troubling behaviors rather than shift gears. In fact, we do *more* of what we were doing; we dig in our heels and perform the annoying activity incessantly. If our partner is unable to listen to our complaints, for example, we complain more loudly about a broader range of topics, including his low tolerance for complaints. Even when it is clear that our partner has turned off emotionally, we turn up our vocal volume in hopes of somehow getting our message across.

Over time, these ineffective strategies wear out both partners, who wind up feeling frustrated, hopeless, misunderstood, uncared about, and resentful. Once this occurs, the choice is between expressing feelings openly in an attempt to bridge the chasm that has developed or withdrawing even further. While the first alternative is clearly preferred, the danger of voicing discontent repeatedly is that the complaints will be heard as "unreasonable demands" and dismissed. Since the chronic complainer, or nag, is regularly defended against by emotional retreat, the question becomes one of how to engage our intimate partners in dialogue about our mutual problems without turning them off. Besides improving communication and conflict resolution skills, limiting the number of complaints, learning to voice negative concerns in a less demanding manner, increasing space, utilizing conflict-free zones, and doubling positive reinforcements are important strategies.

## Reducing Demands

Too many demands or complaints transform an intimate relationship into a toxic situation that is difficult to tolerate. If in conversations with our partner, all we hear about are our short-comings and failings, our partner will become a source of strong aversive feelings for us. Similarly, if our unhappiness with the relationship is the primary focus of our interactions with our partner, we will become an unpleasant stimulus easy to avoid. All of us have difficulty tolerating criticism in heavy doses.

## One Complaint at a Time

Ordinarily, however, instead of limiting our conversational focus to one or two major sources of frustration during any one discussion, we throw in a backlog of resentment from bygone years: "Not only am I angry about the way you ignored me last night, but it's exactly the same thing you did twenty years ago at Emma and Charlie's house." With the opening of a Pandora's box of unresolved intimacy issues, we overwhelm our partner, who feels unfairly attacked and seeks any avenue of retreat. Unable to process all of the emotionally laden criticisms, our partner wants to crawl away and lick his or her wounds before venturing out again. With this kind of outpouring of complaints, nothing constructive gets accomplished. The intensity of emotional wounding typically leads to increased distance and alienation.

By contrast, when only one concern or complaint is discussed during a problem-solving session, there is greater opportunity for both sides to speak and be heard. Most of us can tolerate an occasional criticism and are able to process the emotional meanings of the behavior involved. For example, if our partner criticizes us solely for not spending enough time with him or her, we are able to examine our reasons for not being available and understand the impact on our partner of our limited attentiveness. Then we are in a better position to explain the pressing factors behind our unavailability, figure out constructive methods of dealing with our partner's feelings of abandonment, and/or increase time available for the relationship. By limiting the number of complaints to one or two major issues, the likelihood of us or our partner becoming overwhelmed and defensive is reduced. With diminished defensiveness, the chances of hearing and being heard are increased a hundredfold.

## Reducing the Intensity of Each Demand

Another means of improving our partner's receptivity to negative comments is by reducing the demanding quality of the message. If we are unhappy because our partner is seldom at home in the evenings, for example, insisting on his or her nightly presence is almost guaranteed to ensure the opposite. Because all of us (men, even more strongly) value autonomy and resent attempts at control, demands increase resistance. We prefer to exercise our own volition rather than comply because we feel backed into a corner. Besides, yielding to demands results in a sense of capitulation and childlike helplessness.

The psychological differences between requests, expressions of feelings, complaints, and demands are enormous with respect to the degree of hostility involved and the resulting resistance. In the example of the spouse who feels lonely and rejected because of her husband's absences, her responses could range from "Could you please spend more time at home?" (request), to "I miss you when you're not around" (expression of feeling), to "I resent it when you're gone all the time" (feeling and complaint), to "You had better be at home this evening or else I'm going to be enraged" (demand and threat). It is obvious that the first two are non-threatening expressions of desire and feeling, whereas the latter two examples are either blaming or demanding. As such, they are less likely to result in compliance.

## Chronic Complaints

If it is true that demands increase defensiveness, why do some of us chronically demand the same behavioral changes from our partners? There are several reasons. In some instances, we have been successful at getting what we have wanted from others by our angry insistence. Our temper tantrums may have been rewarded by intimidated parents who yielded out of desperation. If our intimate partners are guilt-prone and helpless, they, too, will give in because acquiescence seems to be the course of least resistance. Unfortunately, when their compliant behavior is motivated by guilt coupled with a sense of unfair coercion, the accompanying resentment will create distance and/or fuel passive-aggressive behavior.

In other instances, demands continue at high levels of angry intensity even when they are ineffective in altering a particular situation. The "nag" or "hysterical" partner may continue to vocalize the same complaints for years, usually at a frenzied pitch, in spite of their futility. These demanding partners cannot accept the reality of limited control, namely, the idea that we cannot force, under normal conditions, another adult human being to do anything. All we can do is create facilitating or interfering conditions that increase or decrease the odds of getting our own way.

## Futile Demands

Sarah, an attractive and successful saleswoman, kept calling her rejecting former boyfriend every few weeks with the same demands. At the end of every telephone conversation, she would sob, plead, scream, and angrily insist that he take her back. In spite of his consistently negative responses, the telephone calls persisted for several years. What she could not accept was her lack of control in influencing him. Somehow, she believed that if she persisted long enough, he would come around. She had a hard time accepting the reality that a badgering, demanding stance, which can be effective in sales, was counterproductive, if not destructive, in intimacy.

Sarah's difficulty in coming to terms with her own helplessness in the face of certain life circumstances appeared to stem from her mother's abrupt departure from her life when she was ten. After an unusually warm and loving relationship with her mother during her early years, her mother's sudden abandonment of her and her sister was particularly jarring. Not only did Sarah have to face the reality of loss at an early age but her sense of helplessness in preventing such loss was especially traumatic. From that time on, it appeared that the issue of control became paramount in her life. Whenever she felt she was being rejected in intimacy through no fault of her own, her insecurity generated desperate attempts to recoup her losses. By sheer persistence, she seemed determined to regain what she had lost. Paradoxically, however, while Sarah's desperate behavior was intended to reestablish an intimate connection, her angry demands served to distance her boyfriends and cement the dissolution of her relationships. All that she gained to some degree was a measure of control. For if she could point to her own behavior as the cause of rejection, she felt more like the master of her fate than its victim.

## Need for Space

Whenever a relationship becomes chronically aversive to one or both partners, retreat from the battle zone needs to be considered. The retreat can be momentary, regular (e.g., an hour each evening, one evening a week), or occasional (a weekend now and then). Just as reducing demands is a way of reducing the toxicity of the intimate environment, so withdrawal from unrelenting conflict can be restorative. We replenish our emotional resources and gain a more objective perspective on the relationship when we are away from the heat of the battle, even temporarily.

Our space away from the relationship can be utilized to think through the problems, gain insights from friends, savor leisure-time pleasures, or simply take a breather from the ongoing harassment. Because ongoing intimacy conflict is both draining and depressing, we need respite along with sustenance from other sources. For some of us, solitude provides peace and new perspectives; for others, conversations with friends bring stimulation and insights. Still others prefer reading or working with their hands to achieve the quiet gratification and sense of accomplishment necessary for psychological survival. No matter the form, adaptive withdrawal from conflict has recuperative powers similar to the functions of sleep. "Sleep that knits up the ravelled sleeve of care"[4] and temporary withdrawal from a difficult situation enable us to generate healthy solutions to our interpersonal problems.

## The Value of Separation

Time away from the relationship also allows us to reexperience the positive feelings we may have about our intimate partners. When we are caught up in chronic conflict, the positive aspects of the relationship get buried under an avalanche of resentment. Frequently, all we are aware of is the frustration and distance we feel. When we are away from the pitch of battle, we are freer to remember the desires for closeness we have felt in the past and the moments of happiness. "Absence makes the heart grow fonder" by enabling us to go beyond the present reality of anger and boredom to a prior romantic time of closeness.

Sometimes, however, absences work in reverse and harden the heart. When there were few positive moments in the past, when the reality of daily living destroyed the earlier fantasies, or when the interpersonal conflict was so severe that it eroded all desire, absence will be experienced as a relief and little else. The partner will not be especially missed or longed for. Rather, the freedom from constraint will be experienced as exhilarating when contrasted with the sense of caution in the relationship. In such instances, liberation from bondage is the dominant motif overshadowing all other themes. While this kind of separation outcome is typically the beginning of the end, a joyful separation is a signal to committed partners that the relationship is floundering and in need of improvement. Frequently, the restrictions on spontaneity need to be reduced so that each partner can experience intimacy as a fulfilling rather than confining experience.

## Counting to Ten

Temporary retreat is also a way of reducing emotional overload and preventing an angry interchange from escalating into a destructive confrontation. Because the intensity of verbal attack and counterattack can easily lead to out-of-control exchanges where physical violence is likely, withdrawal serves to defuse anger. A "time-out" cools down the intensity of angry emotion and thereby may limit the extent of relationship damage.

One couple whose verbal battles led to physical blows on several occasions found a "time-out" signal an effective tool for halting the emotional escalation. Whenever either partner made the time-out hand sign, they agreed to stop the conversation in midsentence, leave the room, and separate until the heat of angry passion died down. Usually, the topic of conflict would be put on the back burner for a day or two. In that way, this couple controlled the severity of their violent confrontations and subsequent emotional or physical pain.

"Counting to ten" and other time-honored techniques have been used for decades to gain control of overwhelming emotion. By counting while breathing deeply and slowly, the intensity of feeling can be reduced and rationality introduced into the affect-laden area, making us less likely to utter those vitriolic and cruel words that are not easily forgotten. In addition, we can think more clearly, deeply, and broadly about the problem at hand when intense emotion is not obfuscating the issues. By introducing a pause or delay into the midst of heated, unproductive exchanges, we regain control, resume a respectful attitude toward our partner, and table the problem temporarily so that we can problem-solve constructively at a later time.

## Conflict-Free Zones

When a relationship is overloaded with conflict, interactions around neutral or positive topics are needed to balance the pleasure-pain equation. Any relationship that is filled with nothing but hostile exchanges will sink under the weight of such baggage. Daily doses of enjoyment and/or companionship prevent a wounded partnership from becoming permanently maimed.

Conflict-free zones can be any topic, area, or activity that has been either a source of pleasure for both partners or an area devoid of past conflict. Usually, these zones represent the best times in a couple's life together and, as such, are jointly protected as "off limits" for serious battling. These conflict-free areas can be leisure activities, such as movies, concerts, bowling, dancing, or long walks together. Or they can be long conversations about art, music, history, gift choices for relatives, favorite holidays, vacations, or restaurants.

## Ordinary or Exotic Spots?

Conflict-free zones can be ordinary places, such as parts of the house, in addition to romantic retreats. Since most battles occur in the kitchen and bedroom, areas symbolic of the frustration of the most basic of intimacy's needs (food, love, and sex), other parts of the house and outside surroundings may have a more neutral or positive valence. Typically, our associations to the living room, porch, and garden, for example, are filled with memories of company, relaxation, leisure, and pleasure rather than conflict. Spending some mutual time in these settings can partially offset the unpleasant interactions that take place in other parts of the house. One conflictual couple, for example, loved to spend leisure hours sipping coffee and reading newspapers peacefully on their porch, which overlooked an attractively landscaped backyard filled with large shade trees and flowering shrubs.

Another battling couple found their sailboat to be an ideal conflict-free zone. Since both of them enjoyed the outdoors and water activities, their sailboat provided not only hours of pleasure and relaxation but a mutual purpose. In contrast to their argumentative style with each other on land, they would spend many hours together cleaning and polishing the boat without a word of friction. United in their love of the sea and sailing, their mutual goal of keeping their boat in tip-top shape for their sailing adventures overrode their value differences in other areas.

While most couples cannot afford a weekend retreat on a boat or in a summer house, most of us have favorite spots replete with warm memories. Sharing these positive associations—these secret gardens—with one another in conversation or in actuality can revitalize a relationship drained of emotional resources by conflict. Relating positive experiences (e.g., "I saw Mary downstairs today and we had a good laugh over her dog's antics") also serves the same replenishing function. If we are able to switch to the positive or neutral some of the time rather than fill all of our conversational moments with acrimony, we can save a relationship from destruction. By varying the nature of our interactions with our intimate partners, we keep the relationship balanced and afloat.

Unfortunately, when we are hurt and angry with our intimate partners, we tend to restrict both the range and number of interactions. The cold shoulder and silent treatment tend to prevail, interrupted only by sarcastic comments. Needless to say, the continued distance and hostility compound the initial hurt and render it difficult to reach compromise. While it is difficult to put our upset aside until we can resolve troubling feelings, maintaining civility and courtesy with one another keeps communication lines open and improves the likelihood of reaching mutually agreeable resolutions to conflict.

## Heavy Doses of Pleasure and Other Positive Reinforcements

None of us ever outgrow our needs for validation, approval, warmth, and affection. Psychologically, they rank right up there with physical needs for food, drink, and shelter. While these psychological needs may diminish in intensity with increased self-confidence and maturity, their gratification seldom fails to provide us with deep pleasure. We profoundly enjoy being told that we did a good job, that we are good persons, or that we are admired.

If compliments and appreciation are so gratifying, why do we give and get so little of them in intimacy? Basically, we are determined to punish our intimate partners by withholding these psychological "goodies" because we believe they have been stingy in gratifying our needs. And so, we treat them with surliness and disdain while reserving our charm for neighbors and near strangers. The best of us tends to be saved for the least important of our relationships.

## A Dearth of Pleasure

Dysfunctional intimate relationships have been described as pleasure-deprived. Either the high rate of hostile, negative interactions outweighs any positives, or the frequency of pleasing responses is so low as to be insignificant.[5] Ordinarily, whatever pleasure existed in the relationship at its outset has been eroded by conflict over time. Gone for the most part are the sexual, sensual joys, along with laughter, peaceful companionship, and mutual enjoyment of hobbies, vacations, and leisure pursuits. Even civility vanishes by the time a relationship arrives at the dysfunctional stage.

To infuse an impoverished relationship with vitality, pleasure and other positive reinforcements need to be reintroduced gradually. Starting with courteous responses, such as "please" and "thank you," which are harmless and yet kind, the improvement protocol can be expanded to include praise and idiosyncratic pleasures, such as back rubs or breakfast in bed. Lists of individually meaningful, positive experiences or objects can be prepared and shared with one another, with an agreement to take turns providing a specific number of pleasures to each other on certain days. For example, these "pleasing days" could consist of five specific tasks chosen by the performing partner from the list and might include such diverse activities as taking out the garbage, feeding the children, doing the shopping, going out to dinner, doing the dishes, and listening to music together. On certain days, called "love days," the number of pleasures might be doubled to enhance the mutual enjoyment that couples derive from each other.[6] By an increase in pleasurable exchanges, we can become more positive figures for our partners and they likewise for us.

## Communication Skills

According to Patricia Noller and Mary Ann Fitzpatrick, authors of an article on marital communication, dysfunctional couples use more destructive communication patterns than happy couples.[7] They criticize, deprecate, and belittle their partners while disguising their motives and feelings by indirect, obscure, sarcastic, or distracting maneuvers. Adept at paradoxical communication with hidden agendas, dysfunctional couples, especially men, typically avoid conflict until it is intense and overwhelming. Then, when they reach the overt conflict stage, they engage in lengthy, unproductive, escalating exchanges, wherein the negative behavior of one partner is reciprocated by the negative communication of the other.[8] This negative escalation consists of an unbroken sequence of attacking and counterattacking comments. These poor communication skills, which include inaccuracy in interpreting the partner's nonverbal cues, actually precede the onset of marital distress.[9,10]

Underlying most of the communication difficulties is lack of empathy. The complaint "He doesn't understand me" is so widespread as to be universal, especially between the sexes. Deborah Tannen's best-selling book, entitled *You Just Don't Understand,*[11] deals with gender differences in communication, primarily those dealing with power, control, and related issues, which render mutual understanding difficult, if not impossible, at times. And yet, unless we feel understood some of the time, we wind up feeling invalidated. Being told repeatedly that our point of view is flawed leads to self-doubt and lowered self-confidence.

One thirty-five-year-old woman who, as a child model, had performed with her mother in fashion shows felt that she had been treated as a nonperson—a baby doll all dressed up to parade before the public. In treatment for depression and severe marital conflict, Rosemary (see "Fear of Losing Autonomy" section in Chapter 2 for more detail) did not feel understood by either parent but rather manipulated into meeting her mother's needs. When she married a critical, domineering man who was adamant about the correctness of his views, the experience of being invalidated by an intimate figure continued. What was different this time, however, was the rage she experienced whenever she was told by her husband that she was wrong. This resentment from a lifetime of unmet needs would erupt whenever she felt misunderstood and criticized. No matter how many different ways she tried to explain her point of view, she was inevitably judged in error and dismissed. The resentment and sense of hopelessness about ever being able to communicate with her husband created so much distance in her relationship that she eventually divorced him. Happily for her, her current fiancé appears to be an empathic, patient person who believes that differences of opinion can be resolved through open communication.

## Empathy: The Key to Understanding

The most important communication tool in intimacy is empathic listening. Developed originally for the counseling domain, empathic or active listening involves suspending our own perspective to understand the complexities and richness of the other's phenomenological world. It entails tuning into the content and feelings of another to appreciate the depth of meaning that frequently accompanies verbalizations. Essentially nonjudgmental, empathic responding is altruistic and other-focused.

The empathic person in the act of listening tries to figure out what need the other is experiencing, what danger he or she might be in, and what is being asked for. For example, in response to a husband's complaint about the kids' toys being strewn all over the house, the empathic spouse might say, "You sound frustrated. What happened?" or "It really gets to you when the kids do that after you've told them so many times to put away their toys," or "Sounds like you're in the mood for a quiet evening." All of the above responses are understanding, validating, and basically fostering of continued communication.

The more typical spousal comments, which are defensive, critical, or minimizing, are as follows: "They're just kids" (minimizing), "You're so crabby—you never have a good thing to say" (critical), or "Don't blame me! I've worked hard all day, too" (personalizing and defensive). Following these remarks, the conversation would either come to a screeching halt or become acrimonious shortly thereafter.

Empathic listening is not only a means of validating the experiences of the other through understanding, but it leads to greater self-acceptance on the part of the recipient and reduced depression, anxiety, and defensiveness. It also keeps a conversation flowing in a nondefensive, mutual, give-and-take manner.

## Empathy and Intimacy: A Difficult Merger

If empathic responding is such a potent cure for what ails intimate relationships, why is its value not shouted from the rooftops? Even though there are individual differences in empathic ability, empathic responding can be taught and in fact is an essential part of most counseling, couple enhancement, and marital therapy programs. However, the reason why empathy is not more widely touted as a magical elixir in intimacy has less to do with the efficacy of the technique than with the nature of intimacy itself. In close relationships where we feel exposed, vulnerable, and likely to be overwhelmed by our own feelings, it is difficult to keep our own issues in abeyance while we attempt to understand the other. Then, too, with control and power issues coming into play, we tend to hang on to our own perspectives with the tenacity of moral righteousness. John Gottman and others, authors of *A Couples Guide to Communication*, have documented lengthy conversations between embattled spouses, in which each person simply restates his or her position over and over again after the other has spoken without acknowledging the other's perspective (the Summarizing Self Syndrome).[12] The difficulties in being open to another's point of view are dramatically illustrated by these authors.

In spite of the problems in being empathic with our intimate partners, the skill of empathic listening is worth developing. While intense feelings frequently override this complex cognitive and intuitive skill, empathic listening has clear-cut benefits at lower levels of arousal. The empathic attitude or a sincere attempt to understand the other's frame of reference enhances emotional intimacy. Basically, we feel connected when we feel understood! Also, the empathic attitude, when it permeates a conversation, leads to greater depths of self-disclosure.

Very often, relationship impasses occur because we do not understand what a particular position or behavior means to the other. With one couple who could not reach agreement about whether their children should be "forced" to clean up their rooms or not, a breakthrough of understanding for the wife came years after their children had grown up and left the family home. The husband finally acknowledged, in the midst of a quiet conversation about child-rearing practices in general, how much he hated to insist upon neatness. The chronic conflict between his parents and older sisters, to which the demand for cleanliness had led, was so traumatic as to be avoided at all costs. The husband's self-disclosure radically altered his wife's perception of his unwillingness to follow through on the "room cleaning" issue. Instead of seeing him as stubborn and uncooperative, his wife understood the depth of anxiety behind his reluctance.

Similarly, a young wife was baffled by her husband's refusal to deal openly with her about anger rather than in a passive-aggressive fashion (e.g., he kept forgetting chores). Only when her husband was able to tell her how frightening his father's overt violence had been did it become clear that his avoidance of direct confrontation resulted not from deviousness but from discomfort about expressing anger. With increased understanding of a particular behavior, an alternate framework for viewing that behavior leads to changes in perception and feeling. In addition, when we are able to grasp the historical roots of current behavior, we are more likely to be in an accepting, tolerant mode than in an angry, blaming one. Thus, empathy in fostering understanding leads to alternate perceptions and greater acceptance.

## Self-Disclosure: The "Me" Side of the Coin

While an empathic stance is the most important attitude to be donned in interactions focused upon the other, our own needs, wishes, and feelings represent the other half of the equation. In the ideal "I and Thou" relationship, a balance between the I and Thou components is exquisitely achieved. Like the ebbing and flowing of tides, so the energy in ideal intimacy shifts from one person to the other.

For some people, usually shy, introverted types, self-disclosure is considerably more difficult than an other-focused orientation. The risks of self-disclosure, normally fears of rejection, ridicule, disappointment, or criticism, are greater than the risks involved in a listening stance, where energy and attention are the basic requirements. Because acknowledging our needs for love, attention, and reassurance exposes us to possible attack, we prefer to remain guarded. However, in doing so, we limit the degree of emotional connectedness we feel and the likelihood of getting our needs met. While self-disclosure is not the only means of achieving emotional intimacy, revealing ourselves is one of the most reliable means of doing so.

### Why Self-Disclosure?

What needs to be shared? Our deepest fears, hopes, and wishes along with more mundane concerns and aspirations. Our feelings about the world in which we live, jobs, kids, parents, friends, and church or synagogue are all grist for the intimacy mill. The more that can be talked about openly with our intimate partners, the greater the degree of closeness and trust that will ensue. And the better we are known, the greater the degree of self-acceptance we feel.

Besides fear, the problem with self-disclosure of inner states for some people is lack of awareness. Some of us (men more than women) are not particularly tuned in to the subjective world of perceptions, images, and feelings because our perceptual orientation is geared to the external world of objects and people. However, as with a foreign language, we can learn. For example, we can learn to keep daily "feeling logs," in which we track shifts in feelings, and practice "I" messages, in which we assertively ver-. balize our wants, fears, hopes, and needs. By becoming more adept at expressing inner states and sharing our ideas about a broader range of topics, our intimate world can be enriched.

## Parts of Messages

Direct and open communication is also enhanced by learning how to discriminate between the different components of messages (observations, conclusions, inferences, feelings, and needs) and utilizing these distinctions clearly. When these distinctions are not specified, communication is often garbled, condensed, and confusing to the listener. For example, if we notice that our spouse is wearing a wrinkled shirt, we may make only the pejorative comment, "This isn't a pig pen." This condensed message, which communicates little information except for contempt, is provocative and inflammatory. Instead, a more explicit message is richer in information and potential for dialogue: "I noticed that your shirt is wrinkled (observation) and wondered whether you don't care how you look at home (conclusion or inference). This upsets me a lot (feeling) because I need to feel that you respect me" (need). With all this information, the spouse is able to understand his or her partner's feelings and correct any or all message parts. The spouse might say, "I hadn't noticed that my shirt was wrinkled," or "It doesn't bother me because I like to feel relaxed at home," or "This has nothing to do with respect at all." Whatever the response, there is opportunity for continued communication to correct distortions on both sides.

## Calling a Spade a Spade

Another kind of verbal sharing that is important to the enhancement of intimacy is communication about relational problems and negative feelings. A direct feedback technique called "leveling" attempts to put parameters around the negative message and thereby reduce its harmful impact.[13] The structure for feedback entails specifying the disturbing behavior in question and the resultant emotional impact without name-calling, character assassination, absolutes, and/or generalizations. Instead of shouting "You never pay attention to me!" the leveler calmly says "When I'm talking to you and you turn away to look at the TV, I don't feel listened to." The speaker attempts to describe what has transpired (both factually and emotionally) without the assaultive attack that usually accompanies hurt feelings.

The DESC Structure (Describe the behavior, Explain your feelings, Specify what you would like, and elaborate on the Consequences of the change)[14] fosters open communication in a non-threatening way. In the prior example about not being listened to, the speaker could add the S and C components as follows: "If you would look at me when I am trying to explain something, I would feel valued by you." With all this explicit information, the listener is in a better position to understand, make changes accordingly, or explain why change is not possible at this time.

## Conflict Resolution Skills

Even when communication is clear and direct, intimacy impasses develop that require resolution. If one of us wants to go out this evening and the other wants to stay home, we have three clear-cut choices: both of us go out, both of us stay home, or one stays home while the other goes out. In arriving at a decision, both partners typically spend some time talking about what their initial positions mean to them and how important they are. Henry might talk about how tired he is, while Mary would elaborate on how she has been at home all week and is sick of the house. Eventually, Henry or Mary would decide that the other person's position has more value, meaning, or significance than his or her own and would yield. While "giving in" feels charitable and generous, we (as givers) expect to have our wish or preference granted the next time. We hope for mutual give-and-take over time. Otherwise, we wind up feeling resentful at doing the preponderance of the giving and not having our needs met in any substantial way.

## Stages of Resolution

In resolving conflict, the first stage usually entails an airing of complaints or stating of initial positions: "I don't like it when you promise to take out the garbage and then don't," or "I really want to see my parents for the holidays." In the second, or elaboration, phase, the underlying concerns are specified in greater detail and the reasons for the preference or complaint are spelled out. Because not all wishes, preferences, or complaints have the same weight, the emotional or motivational significance of an issue needs to be elucidated so that its degree of importance can be assessed. If it is extremely important to one partner that the couple be involved in a specific activity, and the other person has only mild investment in another mutually exclusive function, the decision is easier for both partners to make. Unfortunately, the importance of an issue may be colored more by power and control concerns, such as how much one partner wants his or her own way, rather than by the content of the issue itself. However, when both partners are operating without hidden power agendas, the significance of a preference or complaint provides important decision-making information about whose needs are more important at a given moment in time.

The last stage of problem-solving—the determination of mutual solutions phase—typically requires both creativity and objectivity. While common solutions such as giving in, compromising ("We'll do your thing today, provided we do mine next week"), or letting fate decide (toss of a coin, highest card) are straightforward, more complex solutions necessitate a degree of ingenuity. For example, if Henry wants to stay at home to relax this evening and Mary wants to go out for excitement and a change of pace, staying at home with an interesting video or going out to a low-key, classical concert might combine the opposing relaxation-stimulation needs of both partners in a satisfactory manner. Or if Jack wants a strict bedtime schedule for the children and Janet prefers more laxity, they might agree on a rigid schedule for weekdays and greater flexibility on weekends.

Sometimes, moving the discussion to a higher level of abstraction, at which opposing positions can fit together, yields new mutual goals (e.g., two different vacation preferences could be understood as a mutual need for adventure, relaxation, sightseeing, or simply an opportunity to spend time together). The quarrels about chores might relate to unequal division of labor or insufficient positive contact with one another. Similarly, disagreements about child-rearing or leisure activities can be translated into feeling unloved and unattended to, which can be altered by greater appreciation and attention. Whatever the solution, trying to work out differences demonstrates a level of cooperation and flexibility that bodes well for the relationship.

## When All Other Strategies Fail

Sometimes, however, no matter which strategy is utilized, both partners are so locked in to a competitive power struggle that efforts to resolve conflict fail. Because compromise or "giving in" signifies a loss of status to the embattled, hanging on stubbornly to the original demand is viewed as a mark of strength and self-preservation. Also, each partner may be convinced that the relationship can be improved only if the other partner changes, so each repeatedly tosses the ball of responsibility into the other's lap, resulting in a chronic stalemate.

To act cooperatively, partners need to feel that they are able to compromise and resolve conflict and that their partner is able to do likewise. Prior success at negotiating differences is a decided asset in reinforcing this sort of cooperation. Unfortunately, the partners in most troubled relationships are adept at sweeping problems under the rug between eruptions and so have had little experience with successful conflict resolution.

## Initiating Change

When an intimate relationship gets bogged down by unresolved conflict, one partner needs to start the ball of change rolling even though the other resists. Because change requires adaptation and counterchange, one partner's new behavior tends to reverberate throughout the system. Changes made by a nondrinking spouse, for example, will affect the drinker's complacency even though the drinking itself is primarily under the drinker's control. Changes made by any member of the family system will have repercussions on everyone else, thus creating a spiraling effect. Going back to school, changing jobs, joining a support group, or pursuing individual counseling (if our partner is resistant to joint therapy) all have the potential of disturbing the maladaptive equilibrium and setting the wheels of change in motion.

New information, novel insights into our own behavior, or a different perspective on our partner can lead to attitudinal or behavioral change. Similarly, new or deeper friendships provide the emotional support that leads to greater self-acceptance and an increase in motivation for change.

Each member is responsible for altering those unhealthy aspects of the system that he or she has control over. Even when the primary intimacy problem is the partner's responsibility, the asymptomatic member can initiate the change process. In the case of a drinking partner, for example, joining Al-Anon is often the catalyst for self-discovery on the part of the nondrinker and the impetus for the drinker's changes. Seeking spiritual or psychological counseling can also serve the same change-initiation function. Just as there are many roads to Rome, so there are many pathways to the transformation of a conflict-ridden couple into a reasonably contented pair.

## A Joint Approach

Couples counseling is one particularly useful avenue for change. Because both members are participants in the change process, the emphasis is on relationship-fixing rather than partner-blaming. Also, participation of both members is a good-faith demonstration of commitment to the relationship that is apparent to both of them. Since both members are present at every session for the most part, the availability of session information to both of them gives neither partner a psychological advantage. Thus, the process of couples counseling, apart from its content, is egalitarian, nonblaming, and optimistic.

The focus in couples therapy may be on the system as a whole (rules, roles, alliances, distance-closeness boundaries) or on specific communication patterns, such as lack of directness, avoidance of certain topics, or garbled messages. The "presenting problem," whatever is creating the most distress in the relationship system, is usually selected as the initial focus. Even though the couple may have been distressed for years, the presenting problem is typically the last straw, the one that pushed them over their tolerance limits. It may be the discovery of one partner's infidelity, an escalation in drinking or drug use, increased depression, heightened anxiety, or disturbed behavior in a child that propels a couple to seek assistance. The presenting problem is ordinarily the pivotal construct around which the therapeutic interventions are organized.

## Focus on the Present versus the Past

At times, the therapeutic emphasis is on the here-and-now, while in other instances, forays into the past are necessary to understand the historical roots of a given feeling or behavior. With added insight into the origins of our needs, beliefs, and motives, we develop better control and more awareness of how realistic they are. This perspective also enables us to separate the historical components from the current determinants to establish where our needs, motives, feelings, and behaviors are coming from. For example, is our unhappiness about being unloved entirely a function of our partner's difficulty in being affectionate, or did it arise during earlier years of neglect? Similarly, is our sensitivity to criticism a function of childhood experiences with a demanding, critical parent or our current partner's excessively high standards? As Maggie Scarf, author of *Intimate Partners*, wrote, "It is in marriage that we resurrect not only the intensity of our first attachment feelings, but the miseries of old frustrations and repressed hatreds as well."[15] Understanding the impact of the past tends to free us from its tyranny. In addition, by distinguishing past from present causality, we are better able to discern what needs changing: ourselves, the current interaction patterns, and/or our partners.

Improving a troubled relationship often requires an overarching perspective that goes beyond the needs and expectations of each member. Because it is difficult for each of us to step outside the boundaries of our skin to achieve an overview of our relationships, a third person can provide this sort of objectivity. Allied with the relationship system as a whole rather than with the partners individually, the couples counselor can address the system's requirements. Like a mechanic, he or she can fine-tune the communication patterns, readjust closeness-distance boundaries, roles, and rules, lubricate the system with more pleasurable activity, and help to reduce conflict. When the system is running more efficiently with less strain to any part, the counselor's job is done for the most part. However, whether his or her recalibrations last or the relationship reverts to its former chaotic state will depend on the motivations and mutual reinforcements provided by the two people involved. All the counselor can do is point out what kind of readjustment and fine-tuning are needed and hope they will take hold.

# Chapter 12

# Happy and Healthy Relationships

## Common Ingredients

The phrase "happy and healthy" refers to mutually enhancing and satisfying partnerships devoid of psychological symptoms, such as excessive drinking, drug use, gambling, depression, chronic anxiety, and/or eating disorders. While these unusual unions may have been "made in heaven," what sustains the partners over time? What keeps the sparkle in their eyes, the enthusiasm in their voices, and the vitality in their interactions? Are they best friends, great lovers, good companions, or substitute mommies or daddies for one another? In other words, what are the factors that differentiate happy relationships from the distressed unions that abound in today's society?

When we think of the exceptional couples of stage, screen, or literature, we see that they tend to have an intense, shared passion for something. They may be outstanding actors (Woodward and Newman; Tandy and Cronyn), comedians (Burns and Allen), scientists (the Curies), or poets (the Brownings). Their common passion is not only central in importance to their lives but it serves as the chief organizing principle for their day and evening hours.

263

Besides being good friends with similar values, they are frequently united in their mutual love for an activity, goal, or purpose that transcends other mundane considerations.

## A Shared Vision

Having shared significant goals appears to be one of the major characteristics of satisfied couples. Whether they are pursuing church activity, music, literature, art, or politics, building a new country, or traveling around the world, their mutual goal cements their togetherness and fuels their passion for one another. An important, joint goal keeps them on a single track in spite of the differences that may divide them.

### Typical Adhesive Factors

While a shared love for a club, cause, interest, or activity unites the outstanding couples we read about, the more common unifying goals are religion, ethnicity, and family. A mutual commitment to any of these three factors adds stability and cohesiveness to a relationship. In addition, because all three areas can have deep and central emotional connections for us, sharing these important dimensions with our partners intensifies the emotional bond.

However, it is apparent that simply being a member of the same religion or ethnic group is not enough to guarantee intimacy happiness. It is only when these conjoint values are of central importance to both partners that the relationship is enhanced. Likewise, family and love of children have to be of main significance to both partners for this value to be unifying. It is when our mutual goals or values have the status of a "philosophy of life," "a vision," or "a passion" that they operate to solidify the relationship. The early immigrants traveling the storm-tossed Atlantic Ocean together, the pioneers trekking to the West in covered wagons, or Jewish families trudging to Israel from all over the world illustrate how unifying and motivating shared central values can be. While lesser mutual interests and goals typically have less of a unifying property, they create a common ground of reciprocally enjoyable experiences, which is positive for any relationship.

## A Deep Religious Bond

Pat (age fifty-five) and Bob (age fifty-seven) do not have an "ideal" relationship, but they illustrate the staying power of a shared religious commitment. It is not ideal because Bob had a drinking problem early in their marriage, and they have had several rocky periods necessitating counseling. Currently, they would rate their relationship as a "seven or eight" on a scale of ten, with both feeling that the present time is one of their best. Life is easier now because their children are grown and there is less financial pressure.

Married for thirty-four years, their mutual religious convictions (they are both dedicated Catholics) formed the basis of their attraction and have continued to be the primary glue for their connection to one another. Bob feels that their religious conception of marriage as a permanent union ("till death us do part") has kept him from committing "the dastardly deed that would have dissolved our relationship" and has forced them to work out their problems. Because they never entertained the possibility of breaking up, they did all they could "to make it work."

Describing himself as a "workaholic and poor communicator," Bob needed to learn that feelings were "neither right nor wrong but simply there." He used to say, "You ought not to feel that way," and bury his head in a book when Pat blew up; he had a hard time accepting Pat's point of view as legitimate. She, on the other hand, used to wait "too long" before bringing up a conflictual issue; that is, she would let feelings build to the point of explosion. Today, they are able to "get mad at each other and yell without taking it too personally." Several stints of marriage counseling and involvement in marriage encounter programs helped them learn how to deal more openly with one another.

When Bob met Pat at the Christian Center in college, he was looking for a Catholic girl to marry. She was "a nice-looking girl, easy to talk to, with a deep faith that was important to her." For Pat, Bob's upperclassman status was impressive (she was a lowly, brand-new freshman on campus for two weeks), but she, too, was drawn to the depth of his religious conviction. Pat describes her faith as "my life" and said that it has always been the one over-riding factor in all her decisions. While Pat maintained a strong interest in Bob from the beginning, his attraction to her waned for six months or so while he "comparison-shopped." When he re-sumed contact, Pat was still annoyed about his wandering, cau-tious but yet delighted to reconnect. After that, their three-year progression from courtship to marriage was steadier and more even.

In their traditional marriage where Bob is the breadwinner and Pat the homemaker, they have had to struggle with family responsibilities, financial hardship, and personality differences. He was the extrovert and she the introvert, almost at opposite ends of the continuum. However, over time, they have moved closer to the middle. At one point in their marriage when Pat was over-whelmed with child care (they have six children), she stopped entertaining, much to Bob's chagrin. He had loved the parties and household gatherings but currently enjoys quieter times together.

Pat and Bob's relationship is characterized by hard work, determination, and very little play (they have not had a real vaca-tion in over ten years; Bob works two jobs). They live on a farm in the suburb of a large metropolitan center where Bob works. Their social life consists of family- and church-related activities and they go out to dinner occasionally. According to Bob, who has always felt that "life is responsibility," he has no regrets because he de-rives pleasure and enjoyment from his work. Pat, however, is less contented and yearns to travel all over the world just as her friends and relatives have. Both feel that she has been patient, giving, and accommodating, and yet is ready to "cash in her chips." With decreased financial and child-care responsibility, they can see their way to more leisure activity in the future.

In some fundamental ways, their relationship, based as it is on salt-of-the-earth, rural, turn-of-the-century values, is an anachronism. Emphasizing mutual respect, self-sacrifice, hard work, and a clear-cut division of labor, they seem to be marching to the beat of an older drummer. More modern relationship concepts, such as social exchange (quid pro quo), equity (rewards versus costs), role flexibility, and egalitarianism, seem less relevant to their life than religious and marital commitment. While an infusion of pleasure-filled activity would undoubtedly add to their enjoyment, theirs is a solid, Rock of Gibraltar relationship that will endure for as long as they live.

## Similar Souls or Opposite Types?

The literature is fairly clear. There are more similarities than differences among satisfied couples. Happy couples tend to be more similar than dissimilar in personality,[1,2] attitudes,[3] and physical attractiveness.[4,5] They also tend to agree more with each other and have similar interests. Similar demographics and proximity (living and working near each other) are also related to interpersonal attraction, suggesting that happiness is more likely if we pair off with a kindred soul.[6] Like Narcissus, we are better off falling in love with our reflections.

### Some Unrealistic Underpinnings

What about the attraction of opposites? Clearly, opposites do attract and marry, but their relative absence from "happy couple" rosters suggests that more neurotic or conflictual motivation often underlies this phenomenon. For example, attraction based on the longing for our ideal self or the desire to connect with someone whose characteristics will compensate for our deficits is unrealistic. The sociability of an extrovert seldom changes the shy, introverted soul; the emotional expressiveness of the hysteric fails to rub off on the inhibited intellectual. In fact, these opposite qualities frequently become a "bone of contention" for the partner. Somehow, these admired qualities become tarnished because they were not delivered up and failed to transform the partner. Thus, sociability becomes irritating garrulousness and spontaneity is seen as wanton lack of control.

Another common, maladaptive, underlying motivation for the attraction to opposites is the desire for mastery of a past conflictual relationship. We seek out a distant, brooding man like our father or an intrusive, dominating woman like our mother in hopes of rewriting the old story. Unfortunately, the new disappointments open the old wounds, intensifying the pain and frustrated longings, and we are left with another unhappy relationship.

With partners who are similar in attitudes, personality, values, and interests, there is less conflict. Having a subjective appreciation of the other's experience becausᵉ it is similar to our own, we can more easily identify with, understand, and feel empathic toward our partner. Similarities provide the common ground or base of understanding upon which the differences can be appreciated. Similarity provides the solid foundation for the relationship, while differences add color, sparkle, and vitality.

## The Chemistry of Differences

If there were no differences between ourselves and our intimate partners, the relationship would be relatively static and boring. The impetus for growth and change comes from differences that need to be resolved. However, the degree of difference needs to be small enough so as not to be immobilizing. Slight differences add spice and spark change, while greater degrees of dissimilarity provide fertile ground for ongoing conflict.

While Betty (age fifty-five) and Bill (age sixty) have similar family values, friends, and backgrounds, their differences provide and maintain the chemistry between them. Bill is an outgoing and rugged salesman who enjoys hunting, fishing, boating, and politics (among other activities). Betty is a quiet churchgoer (an elder, choir member, and Sunday school teacher) who has devoted her extrafamily life to charity projects. Incidentally, religion is not a bonding source for them (he seldom attends church), but neither is it a source of conflict.

Besides their varying interests, their temperamental styles also differ. Betty, an even-tempered Libra, is more likely to retreat into silence when wounded, while Bill, a mercurial Gemini, will bellow in outrage when upset. He is clearly the expressive, lively one while she is the stable, sensitive partner. These complementary characteristics were sources of attraction from the beginning. At the time when they met, Betty, who was recovering from the death of her father, was drawn to Bill's personality ("he was great fun to be with") and Bill, who mentioned Betty's "knock-out looks" as the initial basis of attraction, also commented that she was "a solid citizen," referring to her church work and the fact that she dropped out of college to take care of her ailing father. Thus, they saw in each other opposite traits that have continued to be appealing.

In spite of their differences, Bill and Betty consider each other "best friends," talk to each other about everything, and are "utterly frank" with one another. The only limitation on honesty for both of them is a cardinal rule they have lived by. Bill said emphatically, "Never, never have we called each other a name," believing, as his mother did, "in sugarcoating your words because you never know when you'll have to eat them." For Bill and Betty, honesty has been tempered by restraint.

Married for thirty-three years with three grown, married children, Bill and Betty live in the same suburban area they grew up in and maintain many of the friendships they developed in high school. They enjoy sailing, partying, dancing, dining, and conversing with one another. For both of them, family commitment, both to their extended and immediate families, has been a dominant value. With their children, who were the central focus of their lives during the child-rearing years, both of them maintained a high degree of involvement, such as Cub Scout den mother, PTA president, and basketball coach. In addition, yearly family vacations to exotic and faraway places were an eagerly anticipated source of pleasure and family cohesion. Regular extended family get-togethers (Sundays and holidays) have been the norm throughout their married lives. Further illustrating their family commitment and pride is the Scottish flag flying alongside Old Glory at the front of their house for patriotic holidays.

Bill and Betty's traditional marriage with clear-cut division of labor (she is in charge of the inside; he the outside) was aided by Bill's travels (one three-to-four-day period per month). His absence provided a safety valve in allowing tensions to dissipate and in helping to keep conflicts in perspective. When he arrived back in town, they were usually very happy to see one another, no matter what their status was when he left. These monthly absences clearly helped to "make the heart grow fonder" and rendered conflicts pale in significance.

While Bill and Betty's siblings have not fared well in their attempts at intimacy (his brother and sister are divorced; her brother is married for the third time), Bill and Betty have achieved a solid, happy union that has withstood Betty's recent heart transplant. In fact, the stresses surrounding her illness have strengthened their commitment to one another. Their combination of similarities (goals, values, and background) and differences (interests, degree of religious commitment, and personalities) plus their friendship and respect for one another have resulted in a viable partnership that shows no signs of strain.

## Different Highlights

A similar marriage with different details and emphases is Sarah (age forty-eight) and Alan's (age fifty-three) twenty-six-year union. While Sarah and Alan appear on the surface to be more similar in personality and interests than Betty and Bill are, they have the same high level of family commitment and mutual communication. Child-rearing is an important shared involvement (they have two sons, ages twenty-two and seventeen), and talking to each other is as natural and valued as breathing.

In fact, Sarah and Alan talk a lot to each other about a broad range of topics, including their relationship, and are able to "go beneath the surface" to resolve conflicts. Incidentally, they never scream or yell at one another; "snarling" is as far as they go. By deepening the level of their discussions, they sort through the personal meanings of any impasse to reach new levels of understanding. For example, when their eldest son went off to plant trees in Louisiana after college graduation, their initial reactions (he was positive and she negative) led to hours of meaningful discussion about Sarah's regrets at the roads not taken, e.g., not pursuing a Ph.D. (Alan has a Ph.D. in English and teaches at a university; Sarah has a master's degree and works as a training coordinator in a hospital.) Thus, they serve supportive and therapeutic functions for each other.

Both from Jewish backgrounds with strong interests in art, music, literature, movies, theatre, political philosophy, and ethnic restaurants, they have similar tastes. In fact, when watching a movie or a play, they know how the other is reacting because of their own responses. They agree on child-rearing practices (although Sarah acknowledges a tendency to be overcontrolling and worry too much like her mother), vacations, leisure activities, and politics. Neither watches TV much and they both love to cook.

While all their friends regard theirs as a perfect marriage because of their mutual respect and admiration, shared interests, and easy communication, Sarah and Alan began to outgrow their initial quid pro quo contract after fifteen to twenty years of marriage. For years, he was the strong, dependable, wise father figure, while she was the emotionally intense, witty, lively, and dependent girl. He had been attracted to her vitality—he remembers her standing in the library, talking to someone with arms gesturing enthusiastically in the air—and what appeared to be her independence. She had been drawn to his being "an older man, so grown up, a graduate student with his own car—a man of the world."

With her parents' divorce when she was three and a half and subsequent loss of her father (he moved to a geographically distant city), Sarah needed a man to rely on. So for fifteen years, she got what she wanted from Alan, who was accustomed to being everyone's daddy, including his mother's and sister's. Since his father's death in high school, Alan was the substitute head of the family for his mother and sister, a role that sometimes "got on his nerves." In their quid pro quo contract, Alan got part of what he wanted—the vitality—but not the independence he thought he was looking for. Sarah's quick wit has always been a source of admiration and enjoyment for Alan (he calls her "a wisecrack artist"), and in fact, Sarah's mother attributes their marital longevity to Alan's "laughing at all her jokes."

Over time, however, Alan got tired of always being "the helper" and Sarah began to question her overdependence (looking to Alan repeatedly for direction and reassurance). In the course of their many discussions, they renegotiated their contract. He began to ask for more of what he needed (comfort, reassurance) and she became more autonomous through psychotherapy, the focus of which had been her professional frustrations and lack of clear direction.

Throughout their marriage, Sarah and Alan have learned from each other, adopting each other's strengths to become more rounded persons. She has picked up patience from him; he has learned to tell jokes. While their admiration of one another's talents borders on envy at times (e.g., Sarah's positive feelings about how Alan's career is moving in contrast to her own "stuck" position), they are not in begrudging competition with one another. Rather, they admire, cherish, and observe each other to see how they might further develop their own untapped potential.

## Separate Selves

The paradox of intimacy is that separateness enhances healthy closeness. By maintaining our own individuality, we are in a better position to come together without loss of identity. When two separate selves are united, fears of merging or suffocating are less likely to occur and the relationship can flourish without sacrificing individual autonomy.

In unhealthy relationships, the self tends to be submerged for the sake of the other. We lose our individual voices whenever we fear that self-expression is likely to result in abandonment, rejection, criticism, or ridicule. Speaking with the other's tongue, we become echoes of the other, mouthing "company policy" rather than our own formulations. Not knowing where we begin and the other ends, we finish each other's sentences and nod in agreement at every word. While this sort of merged twinship may be envied by a casual onlooker, the blurred ego boundaries stifle individual growth.

## The Retiree Twinship

A common, widespread example of the phenomenon of loss of individual identity in intimacy is the older, retired couple. With the loss of vocational pursuits and physical vitality, the departure of children from the home, and the death of close friends and relatives, sources of independent gratification dry up and older couples are left with little besides one another. With such dwindling extramarital resources, the other becomes more valuable, resulting in a vicious cycle of dependency and environmental constriction. As they become more dependent, they narrow their worlds even more, thus rendering each other even more important.

Fred's retirement at age sixty-two began a twenty-year period of increasing isolation from others with concomitant merging between himself and Mae. While his wife of forty-two years (at the time of retirement) had never worked outside of the home and had always been a private, inhibited person, Fred had been a sociable, outgoing man with many interests: church committees, bowling, golf, and cards. However, almost as soon as he retired, his outside life began to wither away and die.

Like many other retired couples, Fred and Mae moved away

from the familiar, urban environment in which they lived all of their lives to a strange, rural retirement community in the South. With their departure and uprooting, they left children, siblings, and friends behind. While many retirees make this arduous transition more easily because of the social, leisure, and climatic advantages of the new location, Fred and Mae had difficulty in establishing themselves on this new soil. With Mae in particular, who had few interests outside of homemaking, her shy, somewhat suspicious, and critical nature was a barrier to the formation of new friendships. Fred tried initially to be as active as he had been earlier by joining church and civic organizations, but Mae's isolation and criticism of these new groups put pressure on him to resign. And so, within five years of their retirement, they were left in a new world solely with each other.

"What is wrong with that?" a romantic soul might query. The basic answer is that they have become caricatures of each other. After fifteen years of doing practically everything together (shopping, speaking on the phone simultaneously, watching TV, exercising in the living room), they speak with one voice, completing each other's thoughts. Because Mae is deteriorating intellectually at a noticeably more rapid rate than Fred, he regularly acts as her alter ego, filling in the gaps in her memory and grasp of reality, but Mae also interrupts to embellish Fred's words. They imitate each other's gestures, facial expressions, and speech characteristics and regularly look at the other for validation. Except for a rare visit from their children and other relatives, their lives revolve around meals, TV, their physical health, doctor's visits, and each other. Their narrow, constricted world has given them both a two-dimensional, dull demeanor lacking in vitality and spontaneity; they seem to be existing rather than living life to the fullest.

## Separate but Together Unions

In contrast to Fred and Mae's merged union is Donna and Steve's separate but together relationship. According to Donna, who feels that her marriage is "unusually good," and her husband agrees, the key is "letting each other be their own person. We love each other but we're not so tied into one another!" By "not so tied into one another," she was referring to their separate activities. However, at a deeper level, she seemed to be alluding to sources of gratification and self-esteem that are independent of one another. Each of them is able to enjoy life apart from the other without any threat to the relationship. And yet together they seem even happier, enriched by the mutual enjoyment they derive from one another.

What stands out about Donna and Steve's relationship is the amount of quality time spent together *and* apart. Married for nineteen years with four children (ages twelve, ten, six, and two), they have planned their lives so as to be able to spend at least one special, long vacation together each year (e.g., biking in Spain and Portugal) and several smaller trips apart (e.g., skiing with same-sex friends). Fortunately, her mother is a willing and available babysitter. In addition, they have a multitude of mutual interests, such as cooking, landscaping, camping, tennis, canoeing, biking, softball, skiing, theatre, and the symphony, some of which they pursue together and some individually. While Steve's separate time is often work-related (he travels widely as part of his job), Donna is on a women's softball team, plays tennis regularly, and has acted in five or six local theatre productions over the last ten years.

Although they spend time in separate activities, Donna and Steve (both of whom are forty) are clearly similar souls rather than opposite types. Besides their common interests, they have strong commitments to their children, extended families, church, and friends. They grew up in the same suburban town and went all through grade school, junior high, and high school together before really noticing each other in a senior chemistry class. However, they are not carbon copies of one another and, in fact, their differences provide the spark for the chemistry between them. She is Mediterranean in temperament and ethnic background, while he is the steady, calm, more reserved WASP. As a result, she's more likely "to point out the Emperor isn't wearing any clothes," while he is prone to logical analysis and "peacekeeping at all costs." "He doesn't like to rock the boat," Donna commented, "while I'm always confronting things head on." These common male-female differences along the emotional-rational dimension and the approach-avoidance of conflict continuum provide some tension between them.

However, they are able to talk through conflictual areas and reach agreement. Relying on consensus before implementing important decisions, both of them feel that their differences are few and far between. In fact, the biggest crisis in their marriage was not related to their relationship per se, but to extended family fallout from the discovery of Steve's father's long-standing affair with another woman. Steve, who admired and worked with his father, was devastated by the news and torn by conflicting loyalties for his parents. However, in spite of being demoralized, he and Donna drew closer together as a result. The long hours spent talking together about painful feelings and Donna's support served to heal the trauma and cement their connectedness.

Besides the exquisite balancing of separateness and togetherness, their relationship is characterized by extreme role flexibility and egalitarianism. Since they both love to cook, entertain small groups, perform child-rearing tasks, and do garden work, they take turns performing these activities, depending on each other's schedule and outside commitments. With practically all household tasks they can easily substitute for one another when the other is away from the home. While their own families of origin had traditional divisions of labor, their coming of age in the late sixties when Women's Liberation was on every college student's lips and their own personality flexibility enabled them to establish different roles for themselves.

Steve and Donna were initially attracted to each other's physical characteristics: "her big eyes, good looks, and popularity" (she was a cheerleader) and "his looks, athletic, and theatre ability—he reminded me of Michael Landon as Little Joe Cartwright in *Bonanza*." However, they allowed their infatuation years to develop into more mature love. During most of college, they dated others in addition to one another before finally making the commitment that led to their marriage. Theirs was not a desperate passion intent upon merging but rather a slow-developing ardor sparked by temperamental differences and forged by common interests. .

## Emotional Responsiveness

We all yearn to be acknowledged, understood, appreciated, and cared about by our intimate partner. Emotional responsiveness connotes all of these loving attitudes and actions but especially positive attentiveness, which is the most basic form of love. We want to be looked at in a warm and loving fashion when we walk into a room and listened to when we talk about anything, even the most superficial of topics. We learned that love and attention go together at about six weeks of age when we smiled back with pleasure at the sight of our parents' beaming faces and their cooing sounds. So we have come to expect attention, warmth, and empathy from the people we have allowed into our intimate zone. And happy couples meet that expectation for each other.[7,8]

### Sensitivity to the Other's Moods

Besides behaving in generally affectionate ways, happy couples tend to be tuned into one another's feelings and not easily threatened by the messages they read. They are generally able to read each other's nonverbal cues accurately and respond accordingly.[9] For example, if Henry looks tired, Mary will readjust her expectations and behavior in the light of this information. She might postpone her desire to go out to dinner, play some calming music, and/or inquire gently about his fatigue. In addition, she might offer a back rub or a glass of wine or put his favorite food in the oven. The specific words and activity are selected with Henry's exhaustion in mind.

In contrast, with unhappy couples, trouble begins the moment a distressed wife lays eyes on her husband's face. Instead of interpreting the frowns and downturned lip lines as fatigue, she views them as anger, not just generalized frustration, but as resentment at herself. Not only does she misinterpret the emotion, but she personalizes the feeling and becomes defensive and critical as a result. Her comment, "Now, what did I do?" delivered sarcastically the moment he walks in the door, sets the negative tone for the remainder of the evening. The unhappy wife and husband have difficulty in being responsive without feeling threatened and being threatening.

## Providing What Is Needed

While accurate reading of the other's nonverbal cues is the first part of positive emotional responsiveness, the second phase entails a willingness to accommodate. Rather than being critical of the other's emotional need, the emotionally responsive partner tries to provide the missing ingredient and deliver the reassurance, nonjudgmental ear, or acknowledgment called for. Whether the giving partner is secretly entertaining the hope of reciprocity at a later time or believes, along with Shakespeare and Buscaglia,[10] that unconditional love is the pathway to relationship heaven, positive emotional responsiveness is a powerful validation tool.

From the beginning, Kate (age forty-five) and Marty's (age forty-eight) relationship was characterized by mutual need gratification. Starting off as good friends who could talk to each other about anything, they found in one another most of what they longed for emotionally. He was "kind, gentle, and liked me." She was "a good listener who cared about what I had to say." As colleagues in graduate school working on computer projects together, they spent long hours in each other's company in a natural, nondating manner before noticing each other romantically and sexually. Their beginning was clearly not "love at first sight" but friendship and emotional intimacy that gradually developed into romance.

Their positive emotional experiences with one another—feeling cared about and attended to—were in sharp contrast to their earlier familial relationships, which were cold, critical, competitive, and repressive in orientation. In fact, their entire twenty-five-year marriage (they have a twenty-one-year-old daughter) seems to be the antithesis of their prior experiences. It seems they were determined to create something entirely new and positive out of the twisted wreckage of their pasts. They knew what *not* to do, namely, what they had been exposed to, and relied on their professional training (they are both psychologists) to provide direction as to where to go next. They wanted to be whole people "practicing personally what we preach professionally" and have been able to do so with each other's support.

Kate's mother died when she was six—a traumatic loss that was never talked about in her family. When her father married her aunt (her mother's sister) shortly thereafter, a conspiracy of silence about emotional issues developed in her family. Because she kept pointing out painful issues to family members who wanted to see, hear, and speak no evil, she became the family scapegoat, blamed for all sorts of family ills. All in all, her childhood was painful.

While Marty was not the focus of anger in his family, he, too, was unhappy. As the sickly, second son, he never felt "as good as" an athletic older brother who was the apple of his father's eye. Not able to compete with him and his younger brother, who was the charming "baby of the family," Marty was the lost middle child without a place in the sun. A dominating, intrusive mother who ran the family like a tyrant and a passive father unable to defend himself and his sons from his wife's wrath added to the cold, tension-filled climate that characterized his childhood.

When Kate and Marty announced their engagement, they set off a storm of protest that rivaled Romeo and Juliet's family feuding. Marty's Orthodox Jewish family was appalled that he would consider marrying a non-Jew, while Kate's German Lutheran family was equally aghast at her choosing a non-Christian. Kate's family eventually calmed down and came to her wedding. Unfortunately, Marty was disowned by his family, none of whom showed up for the nuptials. Their blissful union that began so promisingly had to weather intense family conflicts created by their interfaith liaison.

However, rather than destroying their union, their extended families' ostracism served to cement it. Because it was literally "the two of them against the world," they turned to each other more than they would have under normal circumstances. Also, since they had to learn how to solve serious problems from the beginning, they developed confidence in their problem-solving ability. Nothing has since arrived on their doorstep as threatening to their survival as those early days of family rejection and financial hardship. "It was an uphill struggle back then, but it's been easy coasting since," Marty said.

Twenty-five years later, they are still remarkably devoted to each other and companionable. They talk to one another openly about anything and everything, including the laundry. Every day they speak to one another on the phone two to three times and spend hours in the evening relating the day's events or letting off steam about daily frustrations. Whether they are working on computers, chatting about psychology, hiking in the woods, swimming, or spending time at Disneyworld, they love to be together. When they see each other at the airport after brief absences, their fast-beating hearts remind them that the excitement about their relationship is alive and well.

While Kate and Marty's relationship appears idyllic and "too good to be true," it is worth noting that they do fight occasionally. They scream and yell at each other when frustrated because they do not want emotional issues to build up, but, most importantly, they do not feel threatened by these outbursts. They know that momentary conflicts are situation- or content-specific and not likely to destroy the relationship. Their differences about neatness (she) and messiness (he) and extroversion (he) and introversion (she) seem minor to both of them, given the emotional gratification they derive from one another.

Their basic values are very similar. Both secular humanists, liberals, and environmentalists (formal religion has never been important to either of them), they believe in a nontraditional and nonsexist marriage with role flexibility. For example, their basic criteria for division of household labor has been "who likes it most?" and "who likes it least?" As a result, Marty does more of the cooking and laundry, while Kate handles repair work, the social calendar, and their finances. As to child-rearing tasks, they have been more traditional in their emphasis with the lion's share of the responsibility going to Kate by choice.

The most salient aspects of Kate and Marty's nontraditional marriage is their solid friendship, high degree of communication with one another, egalitarian division of labor, and reciprocal emotional responsiveness. They are good friends first and foremost. Their unhappy childhoods and the family injunctions against their union threw them together with such intensity that they appear permanently bonded. Having survived cataclysmic upheavals early on, they both believe that their union will last forever.

## Equity and Social Exchange

Besides shared values, similarity, autonomy, and emotional responsiveness, justice or fairness is associated with relationship satisfaction. For example, dual-career couples who perceive their spouses as doing their share of the housework experience greater marital satisfaction than those who have the opposite perception.[11] In addition, married women in general report greater happiness when they are involved with a cooperative and caring husband, who shares in child care and housework, than when they are not.[12]

When what we give (inputs) relative to what we get (outputs) is proportional to our partner's gain, we tend to have an equitable relationship. Equity theory assumes that justice affects our contentment. Both equally benefited couples and overbenefited individuals tend to be happier than the underbenefited, who not only feel they put in more than they get but believe their partner is getting more out of the relationship than is deserved. Underbenefited partners express more sexual dissatisfaction and report more extramarital affairs than equitable or overbenefited partners. The underbenefited person is often angry and depressed, while the overbenefited may feel guilty at receiving more than his or her due.[13] To balance this sort of inequity, the underbenefited partner needs to give less or get more of the psychological benefits available in intimacy, such as more comfort, affection, sex, companionship, and/or free time.

Evelyn, an energetic, married professional with three children and a demanding career, took care of the shopping, cooking, laundry, child care, and social life arrangements, while Tom, who also held a time-consuming, professional position, paid bills, performed household repairs, and handled outside chores. While this traditional division of labor was similar to the arrangements that existed in their families of origin, Evelyn had to work from dawn till bedtime to keep up with her responsibilities. Tom, on the other hand, managed to watch TV most evenings after dinner. Because she was working longer hours than Tom, Evelyn began to resent his greater leisure and feel taken advantage of as a result. The traditional division of labor, which fit their nonworking mothers' and wage-earning fathers' lives, was inequitable for this dual-career couple. When Evelyn became depressed and distant in her interactions with Tom, a fairer division of labor, with Tom taking on some laundry and child-care chores, was worked out.

### Quid Pro Quo

Social exchange theory, while similar to the concept of equity, asserts that relationships are satisfying when they are more rewarding than costly (or at least equivalent), regardless of our partner's benefits. Contrary to prevailing religious and romantic beliefs, which emphasize unconditional love and giving more than we receive, we feel more satisfied when we are receiving at a rate that may be greater than (or at least equal to) our expenditures. However, while there is research support for this social exchange conception of intimacy,[14] there are contradictions in the literature. For example, an exchange orientation may be associated with happy friendships but unhappy romances.[15]

The exchange orientation emphasizes strict reciprocity in a relationship; the nonexchange orientation, by contrast, endorses unconditional love and sensitivity to the other's needs. In our love lives, we clearly favor the nonexchange orientation, wanting to believe that unselfish love is the primary motivation in ourselves and in our partners rather than economic or cost-accounting considerations. The person who keeps a credit-debit ledger in the love department is viewed as crass and as miserly as Scrooge before his nighttime encounter with the Christmas ghosts. Essentially, we want to be loved unconditionally and without limits ("to the depth and breadth and height my soul can reach": Browning),[16] and any suggestion that love is tainted by self-centered interest is rejected outright. Thus, while fairness and justice do play a role in our relationship satisfaction, we wish they did not.

## Trust—The Bottom Line

When we are assured that our partner has our best interests at heart and will not hurt us intentionally, we are free to be the most authentic self we can be. Letting down the myriad defenses we erect to protect our vulnerabilities, we can speak spontaneously whenever we trust. Not fearing criticism, ridicule, rejection, attack, disappointment, or abandonment at every step of the way, we can walk lightly. With happily connected couples, trust is at the foundation of their relationship.[17]

Ordinarily, trust develops slowly in adult intimacy. By the time we have lived twenty to thirty years, we may have been hurt many times. In order to trust, we repeatedly have to experience reliability, caring, and trustworthiness in a prospective partner. Only then, with diminished fear of attack, can we risk exposing our weaknesses. Because of trust's slow development, "love at first sight" is reckless, occurring as it does before trust has an opportunity to flourish.

However, no matter how much strength trust garners over time, trust is forever fragile, destroyed easily by a single staggering blow. A serious act of betrayal, infidelity, or devastating criticism can reduce trust to a whisper in the cacophony of the relationship, which is why a union crushed by extreme insensitivity or cruelty will take months to rebuild. An apology is not sufficient for near-mortal blows. We need to be shown that the assaultive or damaging behavior will not reoccur. We need the kind of proof that time alone can provide.

The year following a near-fatal blow to an intimate union is often critical in determining its survival. After years of infidelity or other intimacy-destroying behavior, the guilty partner may amend his or her ways and stand ready to resume the kind of closeness that existed before the damage. Unfortunately, the betrayed partner may still be nursing wounds and be unable to trust. One woman, whose husband's drinking and abusive behavior had stopped six months earlier when he was treated for his alcoholism, had flashbacks of his aggressive behavior whenever he tried to get close to her. As a result, she would recoil whenever he touched her, much to his upset and disappointment. He was clearly hurt by her rebuffs, especially since he had been making a concerted effort to turn his life around and make amends for his past transgressions. They were in two different spots: he was trying to regain her love and approval, while she was still healing. Time does not "heal all wounds," but the passage of months can demonstrate whether significant changes have occurred that render it safe for trust to flower anew.

## Other Factors

Communication, flexibility, honesty, joint leisure activity involvement, physical affection, sex, and shared spirituality are other variables related to couple satisfaction. Of these factors, communication is clearly at the top of the list, demonstrating, in fact, the strongest relationship to marital happiness.[18] Sex, while important, has a less significant impact upon contentment than other factors, such as emotional and verbal intimacy.

## Frequent and Positive Communication

Happy couples, who are generally satisfied with the social and emotional aspects of their relationship, talk a lot to each other.[19] They talk more frequently, directly, and positively than distressed couples. It is not that happy couples refuse to see the negatives (they do talk over conflictual matters openly) but rather that they are not in conflict frequently and do share positive feelings and ideas with one another. Talking about a broad range of topics, such as work, school, home maintenance, other family members, other relationships, conversations with others, and food, they are more likely to agree, approve, and laugh together so that talking itself is a pleasurable activity. Even their enjoyment of mutual leisure-time pursuits is enhanced by communication during the activity.[20]

In addition, happy couples are able to talk about their important feelings, experiences, and values with one another. Depth of self-disclosure is clearly related to emotional intimacy and couple satisfaction.[21,22] In fact, the degree of emotional involvement evident in premarital communication is a good predictor of marital satisfaction years later, with greater emotional expressiveness being associated with more satisfaction.[23] Interestingly, our own level of self-disclosure is the most important consideration (rather than our partner's) in determining our happiness. We feel satisfied as long as we are free to talk about what is important to us.[24]

Happy couples resolve conflict more quickly and with less emotion than distressed couples. Rather than engaging in negative behavior reciprocity or "tit for tat" arguing, they are less emotionally reactive and are able to end negative interchanges rapidly. In addition, they are less prone to see disagreements as win-or-lose struggles and are more likely to compromise. In general, they appear less threatened by differences and have better problem-solving skills.

## Sex and Satisfaction

The relationship between frequency of sexual contact and happiness is not straightforward and linear. While there is a positive correlation between frequency and marital contentment,[25] what is more important is how closely actual frequency of sex approximates what is desired.[26] When we have sex as often as we wish, we are happy. Also, when we are in agreement about which sexual behaviors are pleasing, we are likely to be contented.[27] Sexual and relationship satisfaction also increases the more we communicate about our sexual feelings and preferences. However, while positive sexual communication is related to satisfaction, negative communication, or arguing (if frequent), is not. Specifically, frequency of sex minus arguments is the measure that bears a striking association to satisfaction.[28] Too many negative interchanges, no matter how frequently sexual behavior occurs, reduce the positive valence of the relationship.

# In Conclusion

Happy couples have similar values, attitudes, interests, and to some degree, personality traits. They also share a philosophy of life, religion, vision, or passion that keeps them marching together in spite of minor differences. In addition, they are autonomous, fair-minded, emotionally responsive individuals who trust one another and love spending time together, especially in communication with one another. Because they are separate selves, they also enjoy spending time apart to solidify their own individuality without feeling threatened by potential loss or abandonment. Moments of separateness and union are balanced, one following the other as naturally as night follows day.

To some degree, the coming together of two separate persons to form a joyous partnership seems determined by luck or fate rather than foresight or planning. Their initial meeting, for example, is clearly one of chance in most cases. They seem to have stumbled onto each other's path and, once there, had the good sense to take advantage of their good fortune by recognizing the appropriateness of the match and making a commitment. While they are not home free from that point on, a wise initial choice prevents needless conflict. People are able to learn adaptive ways of dealing with one another (as the success of couples therapy and marital enrichment programs attests),[29] but the struggles are easier if there is a good fit to start with.

Psychiatrist Harvey L. Ruben, who wrote *Super Marriage*, estimates that only about 10 percent of all marriages are super marriages, with 40 percent falling "somewhere in the range between mediocre and pretty good" and 50 percent ending in divorce or disaster.[30] Given that highly successful intimate unions are few and far between, why do we keep trying? Tennyson gives us one answer: "'Tis better to have loved and lost than never to have loved at all."[31] Most of us are willing to suffer the slings and arrows of togetherness rather than suffer life alone. Besides, with the potential rewards of intimacy being so great, we would rather gamble at love, hoping to grab the brass ring and achieve a happy relationship, than have no one at all.

# Notes

---

## Introduction

1. Eric Berne, *Games People Play* (New York: Grove Press, 1964).
2. Philip E. Slater, "Some Social Consequences of Temporary Systems," in *The Temporary Society*, ed. Warren G. Bennis and Philip E. Slater (New York: Harper & Row, 1968), p. 99.
3. Clifford J. Sager and Bernice Hunt, *Intimate Partners: Hidden Patterns in Love Relationships* (New York: McGraw-Hill, 1979), pp. 6–7.
4. Joan Shapiro, *Men: A Translation for Women* (New York: Dutton, 1992).
5. Federal Bureau of Investigation, cited in Richard J. Gelles and Murray Straus, *Intimate Violence* (New York: Simon & Schuster, 1988), p. 99.
6. Nancy Loving, "Spouse Abuse: The Hidden Crime," *Engage/Social Action*, March 1982. Published by the Board of Church and Society, the United Methodist Church, 100 Maryland Ave. N.E., Washington, DC 20002.
7. Cheryl Lavin and Laura Kavesh, "Many Singles Joining the 'I Quit' Brigade." Tales from the Front. *Chicago Tribune*, January 8, 1986, sec. 5, p. 1f. © Copyrighted January 8, 1986, Chicago Tribune Company. All rights reserved. Used with permission.
8. Ibid.

## Chapter 1

1. "Alfie," song copyrighted by Famous Music Corporation, New York, 1966. Used with permission.

2. Charles Dickens, *A Tale of Two Cities* (New York: Dodd, Mead, 1942), p. 3.
3. Steven Prasinos and Bennett I. Tittler, "The Existential Context of Lifestyles: An Empirical Study," *Journal of Humanistic Psychology* 24 (Winter 1984), pp. 95–112.
4. Dorothy Tennov, *Love and Limerence: The Experience of Being in Love* (New York: Stein & Day, 1979).
5. Robert J. Sternberg, *The Triangle of Love* (New York: Basic Books, 1988).
6. Douglas H. Ingram, "Remarks on Intimacy and the Fear of Commitment," *American Journal of Psychoanalysis* 46 (1986), pp. 76–79.
7. I. Altman and D. A. Taylor, *Social Penetration: The Development of Interpersonal Relationships* (New York: Holt, Rinehart & Winston, 1973).
8. Sharon S. Brehm, *Intimate Relationships* (New York: Random House, 1985).
9. Stephanie Covington and Liann Beckett, *Leaving the Enchanted Forest: The Path from Relationship Addiction to Intimacy* (San Francisco: Harper & Row, 1988), p. 139.
10. Harriet G. Lerner, *The Dance of Intimacy* (New York: Harper & Row, 1989), p. 3.
11. Betty E. Tolstedt and Joseph P. Stokes, "Relation of Verbal, Affective, and Physical Intimacy to Marital Satisfaction," *Journal of Counseling Psychology* 30 (1983), pp. 573–580.
12. Sigmund Freud, *Introductory Lectures in Psychoanalysis*.
13. Berne, *Games People Play*.
14. Freud, *Introductory Lectures in Psychoanalysis*.
15. Judith Rossner, *Looking for Mr. Goodbar* (New York: Simon & Schuster, 1975).
16. Erik H. Erikson, *Childhood and Society* (New York: Norton, 1950).
17. Gregory Bateson, *Naven* (2nd ed.) (Stanford, CA: Stanford University Press, 1958).
18. Edward Albee, *Who's Afraid of Virginia Woolf?* (New York: Atheneum, 1962).

## Chapter 2

1. "You Always Hurt the One You Love," music and lyrics by Allan Roberts and Doris Fisher, Copyright © 1944 (renewed), 1972 Allan

Roberts Music & Doris Fisher Music. Allan Roberts Music (ASCAP). administered by Music Sales Corporation for the World. International copyright secured. All rights reserved. Used by permission.

2. Erich Segal, *The Class* (New York: Bantam Books, 1985), p. 360.
3. Larry B. Feldman, "Marital Conflict and Marital Intimacy: An Integrative Psychodynamic-Behavioral-Systemic Model," *Family Process* 18 (March 1979), pp. 69–78.
4. Erikson, *Childhood and Society*, p. 252.
5. Annie Gottlieb, "The Emotionally Draining Man," *McCalls* 112 (March 1985), pp. 50–54.
6. Harriet G. Lerner, *The Dance of Intimacy: A Woman's Guide to Courageous Acts of Change in Key Relationships* (New York: Harper & Row), p. 21.
7. Megan Marshall, *The Cost of Loving* (New York: Putnam, 1984), p. 31.
8. Ibid.

# Chapter 3

1. Claudia Black, *It Will Never Happen to Me* (Denver: MAC, 1981).
2. Christine A. Courtois, *Healing the Incest Wound: Adult Survivors in Therapy* (New York: Norton, 1988).
3. Black, *It Will Never Happen to Me.*

# Chapter 4

1. Milan Kundera, *The Unbearable Lightness of Being* (New York: Harper & Row, 1984), pp. 297–298.
2. Carl Rogers, *Client-Centered Therapy* (Boston: Houghton Mifflin, 1951).
3. John Welwood, "On Love: Conditional and Unconditional," *Journal of Transpersonal Psychology* 17 (1985), pp. 33–40.
4. Harry F. Harlow, "The Nature of Love," *American Psychologist* 13 (1958), pp. 673–685.
5. Naomi Breslau and Kenneth Prabucki, "Siblings of Disabled Children: Effects of Chronic Stress in the Family," *Archives of General Psychiatry* 44 (December 1987), pp. 1040–1046.

## Chapter 5

1. Cheryl Lavin and Laura Kavesh, "When Love Gets Too Good—Well, That's Too Bad." Tales from the Front. *Chicago Tribune.* March 5, 1986, sec. 5, p. 5. © Copyrighted March 5, 1986, Chicago Tribune Company. All rights reserved. Used with permission.
2. Eric Berne, *Games People Play* (New York: Ballantine, 1978), p. 60.
3. Harville Hendrix, *Getting the Love You Want: A Guide for Couples* (New York: Holt, Rinehart & Winston, 1988), p. 92.

## Chapter 6

1. Eleanor Maccoby and Carol Jacklin, *The Psychology of Sex Differences* (Stanford, CA: Stanford University Press, 1974).
2. Shapiro, *Men: A Translation for Women*, p. 160.
3. William Fezler and Eleanor S. Field, *The Good Girl Syndrome: How Women Are Programmed to Fail in a Man's World—And How to Stop It* (New York: Macmillan, 1985), p. xii.
4. Dan McAdams, *Intimacy: The Need to Be Close* (New York: Doubleday, 1989).
5. Ibid.
6. Robert J. Sternberg, *The Triangle of Love: Intimacy, Passion, and Commitment* (New York: Basic Books, 1988).
7. Dorothy Tennov, *Love and Limerence: The Experience of Being in Love* (New York: Scarborough House, 1978).
8. Donald G. Dutton and Arthur P. Aron, "Some Evidence for Heightened Sexual Attraction under Conditions of High Anxiety," *Journal of Personality and Social Psychology* 30 (1974), pp. 510–517.
9. Gregory L. White, Sandford Fishbein, and Jeffrey Rulstein, "Passionate Love: The Misattribution of Arousal," *Journal of Personality and Social Psychology* 41 (1981), pp. 56–62.

## Chapter 7

1. Ogden Nash, "Reflections on Ice Breaking," *Ogden Nash: Verses from 1928 On* (Boston: Little, Brown, 1952).
2. William Shakespeare, *Macbeth*, act II, scene 3.

3. David C. McClelland, William N. Davis, Rudolf Kalin, and Eric Wanner, *The Drinking Man: Alcohol and Human Motivation* (New York: Free Press, 1972).
4. Marian Sandmaier, *The Invisible Alcoholics: Women and Alcohol Abuse in America* (New York: McGraw-Hill, 1980), p. 100.
5. Claude M. Steiner, *Healing Alcoholism* (New York: Grove Press, 1979).
6. Sandmaier, *The Invisible Alcoholics*, p. 9.
7. George E. Vaillant, *The Natural History of Alcoholism: Causes, Patterns, and Paths to Recovery* (Cambridge, MA: Harvard University Press, 1983).
8. Black, *It Will Never Happen to Me.*
9. Sharon Wegscheider, *The Family Trap: No One Escapes from a Chemically Dependent Family* (St. Paul, MN: Nurturing Networks, 1976).
10. James R. Milam and Katherine Ketcham, *Under the Influence*, cited in C. D. Weddle and P. M. Wishon, "Children of Alcoholics: What We Should Know; How We Can Help," *Children Today* 15 (January-February 1986), p. 8.
11. Black, *It Will Never Happen to Me.*
12. *Alcoholism: A Family Illness* (New York: Christopher D. Smithers Foundation, 1974), p. 12.

# Chapter 8

1. Federal Bureau of Investigation, cited in Richard J. Gelles and Murray Straus, *Intimate Violence* (New York: Simon & Schuster, 1988), p. 99.
2. Suzanne K. Steinmetz, "Violence between Family Members," *Marriage and Family Review* 1 (1978), pp. 1–16.
3. National Committee for Prevention of Child Abuse, print and television public service announcements, cited in Gelles and Straus, *Intimate Violence*, p. 99.
4. Lenore E. Walker, *Terrifying Love: Why Battered Women Kill and How Society Responds* (New York: Harper & Row, 1989), pp. 114–123.
5. Joan Kaufman and Edward Zigler, "Do Abused Children Become Abusive Parents?" cited in Gelles and Straus, *Intimate Violence*, pp. 121–122.
6. Gelles and Straus, *Intimate Violence*, p. 89.
7. Ibid., p. 88.

## Chapter 9

1. Eugene O'Neill, *The Iceman Cometh* (New York: Random House, 1946).
2. William Shakespeare, *Sonnets*, 116.
3. Donald W. Winnicott, *Collected Papers: Through Pediatrics to Psycho-analysis* (London: Tavistock, 1958).
4. Frederick S. Perls, *Gestalt Therapy Verbatim* (Lafayette, CA: Real People Press, 1969), p. 4.
5. David A. Smith, Dina Vivian, and K. Daniel O'Leary, "Longitudinal Prediction of Marital Discord from Premarital Expressions of Affect," *Journal of Consulting and Clinical Psychology* 5 (1990), pp. 790–798.
6. G. Alan Marlatt and Judith R. Gordon (eds.), *Relapse Prevention: Maintenance Strategies in the Treatment of Addictive Behaviors* (New York: Guilford Press, 1985).

## Chapter 10

1. Anne Tyler, *The Accidental Tourist* (New York: Knopf, 1985).
2. Scott Wetzler, *Living with the Passive-Aggressive Man* (New York: Simon & Schuster, 1992), pp. 35–37.
3. Ibid., p. 18.
4. Dan Kiley, *The Peter Pan Syndrome: Men Who Have Never Grown Up* (New York: Dodd, Mead, 1983).
5. Colette Dowling, *The Cinderella Complex: Women's Hidden Fear of Independence* (New York: Summit Books, 1981).

## Chapter 11

1. Irene Goldenberg and Herbert Goldenberg, *Family Therapy: An Overview* (Pacific Grove, CA: Brooks/Cole, 1985), pp. 28–54.
2. Michael P. Nichols, *The Power of the Family* (New York: Simon & Schuster, 1988), p. 191.
3. H. Raschke and V. Raschke, "Family Conflict and Children's Self-Concepts: A Comparison of Intact and Single-Parent Families," *Journal of Marriage and the Family* 41 (1979), pp. 367–374.
4. William Shakespeare, *Macbeth*, act II, scene 2.

5. Neil S. Jacobson and Gayla Margolin, *Marital Therapy: Strategies Based on Social Learning and Behavior Exchange Principles* (New York: Brunner/Mazel, 1979).
6. Richard Stuart, "An Operant Interpersonal Program for Couples," in *Treating Relationships*, ed. D. H. L. Olson (Lake Mills, IA: Graphic, 1976).
7. Patricia Noller and Mary Ann Fitzpatrick, "Marital Communication in the Eighties," *Journal of Marriage and the Family* 52 (November 1990), pp. 832–843.
8. K. Hahlweg, L. Reisner, G. Kohli, M. Vollmer, L. Schindler, and D. Revenstorf, "Development and Validity of a New System to Analyze Interpersonal Communication," in *Marital Interaction: Analysis and Modification*, ed. Kurt Hahlweg and Neil S. Jacobson (New York: Guilford Press, 1984), pp. 182–198.
9. Howard J. Markman, "Prediction of Marital Distress: A Five-Year Follow-up," *Journal of Consulting and Clinical Psychology* 49 (1981), pp. 760–762.
10. Howard J. Markman, S. W. Duncan, R. D. Storaasli, and P. W. Howes, "The Prediction and Prevention of Marital Distress: A Longitudinal Investigation," in *Understanding Major Mental Disorder: The Contributions of Family Interaction Research*, ed. Kurt Hahlweg and Michael J. Goldstein (New York: Family Process Press, 1987), pp. 266–289.
11. Deborah Tannen, *You Just Don't Understand: Women and Men in Conversation* (New York: Ballantine, 1990).
12. John Gottman, Cliff Notarius, Jonni Gonso, and Howard Markman, *A Couples Guide to Communication* (Champaign, IL: Research Press, 1976), pp. 6–7.
13. Ibid., pp. 27–43.
14. Sharon A. Bower and Gordon H. Bower, *Asserting Yourself* (Menlo Park, CA: Addison-Wesley, 1976).
15. Maggie Scarf, *Intimate Partners: Patterns in Love and Marriage* (New York: Random House, 1987), p. 80.

## Chapter 12

1. Andrew Kim, Don Martin, and Maggie Martin, "Effects of Personality on Marital Satisfaction: Identification of Source Traits and Their Role in Marital Stability," *Family Therapy* 16(3) (1989), pp. 243–248.

2. London S. Richard, James A. Wakefield, and Richard Lewak, "Similarity of Personality Variables on Predictors of Marital Satisfaction: A Minnesota Multiphasic Personality Inventory (MMPI) Item Analysis," *Personality and Individual Differences* 11(1) (1990), pp. 39–43.
3. Donn Byrne, *The Attraction Paradigm* (New York: Academic Press, 1971).
4. Bernard I. Murstein and Patricia Christy, "Physical Attractiveness and Marital Adjustment in Middle-Aged Couples," *Journal of Personality and Social Psychology* 34 (1976), pp. 537–542.
5. Richard A. Price and Steven G. Vandenberg, "Matching for Physical Attractiveness," *Personality and Social Psychology Bulletin* 5 (1979), pp. 398–400.
6. Clyde Hendrick and S. Hendrick, *Liking, Loving, and Relating* (Monterey, CA: Brooks/Cole, 1983).
7. Robert A. Bell, John A. Daly, and Christine M. Gonzalez, "Affinity-Maintenance in Marriage and Its Relationship to Women's Marital Satisfaction," *Journal of Marriage and the Family* 49(2) (May 1987), pp. 445–454.
8. Cas Schaap, Bram Buunk, and Ada Kerkstra, "Marital Conflict Resolution," in *Perspectives on Marital Interaction*, eds. Patricia Noller and Mary Ann Fitzpatrick (Philadelphia: Multilingual Matters, 1988), pp. 203–244.
9. Noller and Fitzpatrick, "Marital Communication in the Eighties," pp. 832–843.
10. Leo F. Buscaglia, *Loving Each Other: The Challenge of Human Relationships* (New York: Holt, Rinehart & Winston, 1984).
11. Sara Yogev, "Relationship between Stress and Marital Satisfaction among Dual Career Couples," *Women and Therapy* 5 (Summer/Fall 1986), pp. 313–329.
12. Grace Baruch, Rosalind Barnett, and Caryl Rivers, *Life-prints: New Patterns of Love and Work for Today's Women* (New York: New American Library, 1983).
13. Brehm, *Intimate Relationships*, pp. 174–181.
14. Ibid., pp. 146–159.
15. Bernard I. Murstein, Mary Cerreto, and Marcia G. MacDonald, "A Theory and Investigation of the Effect of Exchange Orientation on Marriage and Friendship," *Journal of Marriage and the Family* 39 (1977), pp. 543–548.

16. Elizabeth Barrett Browning, "Sonnets from the Portuguese," in *Norton Anthology of English Literature*, vol. 2 (New York: Norton, 1962).
17. Kim et al., "Effects of Personality on Marital Satisfaction," pp. 243–248.
18. Howard J. Markman, "Prediction of Marital Distress: A Five-Year Follow-up," *Journal of Consulting and Clinical Psychology* 49 (1981), pp. 760–762.
19. Schaap et al., "Marital Conflict Resolution," pp. 203–244.
20. Noller and Fitzpatrick, "Marital Communication in the Eighties," pp. 832–843.
21. John K. Antill and Sandra Cotton, "Self-Disclosure between Husbands and Wives: Its Relationship to Sex Roles and Marital Happiness," *Australian Journal of Psychology* 39 (April 1987), pp. 11–24.
22. Noller and Fitzpatrick, "Marital Communication in the Eighties," pp. 832–843.
23. Smith et al., "Longitudinal Prediction of Marital Discord from Premarital Expressions of Affect," pp. 790–798.
24. Lawrence B. Rosenfeld and Gary L. Bowen, "Marital Disclosure and Marital Satisfaction: Direct-Effect versus Interaction-Effect Models," *Western Journal of Speech Communications* 55(1) (Winter 1991), pp. 69–84.
25. Gary R. Birchler and Linda J. Webb, "Discriminating Interaction Behavior in Happy and Unhappy Marriages," *Journal of Consulting and Clinical Psychology* 45 (1977), pp. 494–495.
26. Lewis M. Terman, Paul Buttenweiser, Leonard W. Ferguson, Winifred B. Johnson, and Donald P. Wilson, *Psychological Factors in Marital Happiness*, cited in Brehm, *Intimate Relationships*, p. 123.
27. Joellyn L. Ross, Ruth E. Clifford, and Russell Eisenman, "Communication of Sexual Preferences in Married Couples," *Bulletin of the Psychonomic Society* 25(1) (January 1987), pp. 58–60.
28. J. W. Howard and R. M. Dawes, "Linear Prediction of Marital Happiness," *Personality and Social Psychology Bulletin* 2 (1976), pp. 478–480.
29. Howard J. Markman, Frank J. Floyd, and Scott M. Stanley, "Prevention of Marital Distress: A Longitudinal Investigation," *Journal of Consulting and Clinical Psychology* 56(2) (April 1988), pp. 210–217.
30. Harvey L. Ruben, *Super Marriage: Overcoming the Predictable Crises of Married Life* (New York: Bantam Books, 1986), p. 12.
31. Alfred Lord Tennyson, *In Memoriam* (1850), canto 27, stanza 4.

# Index